DOCUMENTS COLLECTION-UWGB

Sources of Conflict
in the
21ˢᵗ Century

Regional Futures and U.S. Strategy

AF207773

Edited by
Zalmay Khalilzad
Ian O. Lesser

Prepared for the
United States Air Force

Project AIR FORCE

RAND

Approved for public release; distribution unlimited

DOCUMENTS COLLECTION UWGB

This book brings together three regional security assessments, along with an overview of global trends in the strategic environment. Each of the regional assessments—covering Asia, the greater Middle East, and Europe and the former Soviet Union—examines key trends and potential sources of conflict through the year 2025, and identifies the implications for the U.S. Air Force and for U.S. national security policy more broadly.

The chapters in this volume reflect research undertaken in 1996 for a study on "Sources of Conflict and Their Implications for Air Force Operations," conducted within the Strategy and Doctrine Program of RAND's Project AIR FORCE. The study, sponsored by the Deputy Chief of Staff, Plans and Operations, was intended to serve Air Force long-range planning needs. The findings are also relevant to broader ongoing debates within the Department of Defense and elsewhere, especially in the context of the Quadrennial Defense Review. Our analyses and conclusions should be of interest to a wide foreign and security policy audience.

PROJECT AIR FORCE

Project AIR FORCE, a division of RAND, is the Air Force federally funded research and development center (FFRDC) for studies and analyses. It provides the Air Force with independent analyses of policy alternatives affecting the development, employment, combat readiness, and support of current and future aerospace forces.

Research is performed in three programs: Strategy and Doctrine, Force Modernization and Employment, and Resource Management and System Acquisition.

CONTENTS

ACKNOWLEDGMENTS

The analyses collected in this volume benefited greatly from discussions with official and unofficial observers in the United States and abroad. The authors wish to thank all those who contributed their views and expertise. We are particularly grateful to the sponsors of this research in the Air Staff, the late Major General Robert Linhard, and Major General Donald Peterson, as well as Lieutenant Colonel Jim McBride and his staff in the Office of Regional Plans and Issues (DCS, Air and Space Operations). The chapters also benefited greatly from the comments of RAND colleagues Robert Levine and John Godges, Philip Gordon at the International Institute for Strategic Studies, and the editorial assistance of Jeanne Heller and Rosalie Heacock. Luetta Pope assisted with the administrative details and in the coordination of the manuscript.

Chapter One

INTRODUCTION

Ian O. Lesser

NATURE OF THE PROBLEM

Global, long-range defense planning has changed enormously since the end of the Cold War. The task has become more difficult in several respects.

First, the sources and types of conflict for which military establishments must plan have become more diverse and less predictable, even if less dangerous in the worst case. For the United States in particular, the end of the Cold War has opened up new debates about how, where, and why the employment of military forces should be considered. The range of potential adversaries is larger, despite the likelihood that the United States will have no true military peers through the year 2000 and beyond.

Second, the range of missions for military forces now gives considerable weight to low-intensity and nonconflict capabilities often considered marginal during the Cold War.

Third, and perhaps most important with regard to future demands and constraints on military forces, the nature of security itself is changing on a global basis. The security agenda has expanded in functional terms. Formerly peripheral challenges such as migration and economic competition, together with more obvious risks from the spread of weapons of mass destruction, now compete with conventional military rivalries as factors affecting the use of force.

Functional changes in the nature of security "problems," together with post–Cold War political transformations, are also changing the geographical terms in which policymakers, military leaders, and analysts must think about long-range planning. Simply put, many of the traditional distinctions between theaters are eroding under the pressure of cross-regional challenges—from migration and terrorism to the steadily increasing range of weapons systems available worldwide. The latter phenomenon is especially striking in its potential effects on U.S. freedom of action, and may ultimately reintroduce the issue of "homeland defense" as a leading element in strategic planning. The increasingly interdependent character of security across key regions—a reality noted at many points in this book—poses new intellectual and practical challenges for a defense community whose thinking and organization are still necessarily influenced by planning for *regional* security: in "Europe," the "Middle East," "Asia" and elsewhere. That said, it remains true that key regions of concern to the United States continue to exhibit characteristic trends, with significant implications for how and where conflicts might arise.

Looking beyond the next five to ten years poses formidable challenges for the imagination. How many of today's leading adversaries, from Iran to North Korea, will remain adversaries long after the end of the century? Leaderships will change, perhaps many times. Longstanding allies may change their orientation. New opponents, whether state or nonstate actors, might arise as a result of ideological, latent economic, or geopolitical cleavages. Systemic changes in the global economy, communications, and, not least, military technology might alter strategic stakes and capabilities. There is a need to consider alternative strategic "worlds," including those that might flow from dramatic shifts in power and security perceptions.

THE STUDY APPROACH

The chapters in this volume were originally prepared as contributions to a project on "Sources of Conflict and Their Implications for Air Force Operations." The Strategy and Doctrine Program of RAND's Project AIR FORCE undertook this work to bring regional security expertise to bear on Air Force planning concerns. With the Air

Staff devoting considerable effort to long-range planning throughout 1996, the timing seemed especially useful.

The study objective was to provide a systematic description of the range of future demands and constraints likely to be imposed on the U.S. Air Force as a result of developments in critical regions. Our description took two forms: (1) analysis of key trends affecting the strategic environment, roughly through 2025, including a discussion of "alternative strategic worlds"; and (2) development of regional scenarios offering varying demands and constraints on the use of air power. Overall, we have sought to characterize the kind of environment the United States will face in employing military power over the next three decades. What will our forces be called upon to do? What sort of opponents will we face? Who will help? What specific opportunities and constraints will arise as a result of the likely location and nature of conflict or nonconflict scenarios?

In consultation with our research sponsors, we focused on three regions critical—and, in our judgment, likely to remain critical—to U.S. defense planning throughout the period under consideration: Asia, the greater Middle East, and Europe and the former Soviet Union. We have not treated Latin America or sub-Saharan Africa, although these regions—especially Latin America—could have considerable importance as sources of conflict and demands on military forces. Both regions are certainly worthy of assessment, especially in the context of military operations other than war (MOOTW). Only constraints on time, and a desire to concentrate our efforts on regions central to current planning debates, prevented our doing so. However, Chapter Two, an overview of the future security environment, offers a number of conclusions relevant to the evolution of the strategic environment beyond the three regions under discussion.

We have also gone beyond regional dynamics and strategic futures to offer insights about the kind of Air Force the nation will need to protect and advance its interests through the first 25 years of the next millennium. We focus the discussion on four qualities we believe will be critical to that Air Force:

- *Global awareness.* The future U.S. Air Force will increasingly find itself in the information business.

- *Global reach.* The conflicts of the early 21st century will break out all over the world.

- *Rapid reaction.* Clear and direct warning will remain a rare and elusive commodity.

- *Appropriate force.* The Gulf War showed that air forces no longer need to deliver immense explosive power to have strategic impact on a war's outcome.

Many features of the world painted by our analysis remain dangerous and challenging, but are very different from those the United States is used to facing. Technological diffusion means that adversaries might field weapons, sensors, and systems that are roughly comparable in quality to those used by U.S. forces. Furthermore, enemies might have access to information of a quality and a quantity that have hitherto been available only to U.S. commanders. While fundamental U.S. interests—the survival of the nation, for example—do not face the kind of threat they did during the Cold War, lesser objectives seem likely to be under almost constant challenge. In particular, an increasing burden of humanitarian and peacekeeping functions and other MOOTW will likely be levied on the U.S. military.

As the only superpower, the United States will to some extent enjoy the luxury of picking and choosing if and when to get involved in combating these less salient and more ambiguous threats. If history is any guide, however, the United States certainly *will* get involved here and there, time and again. In doing so, it will want to conduct these optional military expeditions with expectations of "zero defects": few casualties, limited material losses, and rapid success. At the same time, the nation will want to maintain the capability to respond powerfully to any threat to its core interests. Such a capability presupposes both shaping the security environment in ways that preclude or make difficult the rise of a global adversary and reconstituting or reinforcing U.S. military strength in time to counter any emerging competitor.

The U.S. Air Force that will operate successfully in this world, in defense of the United States, will face real challenges and difficult tradeoffs. At first blush, it appears to us that this U.S. Air Force will emphasize quality and agility over quantity and mass. Quick, decisive responses to rapidly changing demands will be the hallmark of this Air Force, and flexible adaptive planning and execution will be its keystones.

STRUCTURE OF THE BOOK

In Chapter Two, "Overview of the Future Security Environment," David Shlapak and Zalmay Khalilzad (with Ann Flanagan) offer a series of propositions about the future world in security terms, including the character and scope of U.S. engagement. The authors put forth three alternative "worlds"—from the evolutionary to the benign to the malignant—and identify important "wild cards" capable of upsetting straight-line analyses. This overview summarizes the implications of the three regional analyses to follow.

The subsequent chapters provide a detailed discussion of regional trends and their meaning for strategy and planning. In Chapter Three, Ashley Tellis, Chung Min Lee, James Mulvenon, Courtney Purrington, and Michael Swaine examine changing trends and sources of conflict in Asia. Their discussion pays particular attention to the evolution of economic and military power relationships in the Asia-Pacific region, and the consequences for stability and U.S. freedom of action. In Chapter Four, Bruce Nardulli and Lory Arghavan join me in exploring trends shaping the future of the greater Middle East, from North Africa to the Persian Gulf, with emphasis on the security links to adjacent regions and the implications of the spread of weapons of mass destruction and longer-range delivery systems. In Chapter Five, John Van Oudenaren examines likely developments in Europe and the former Soviet Union, with a strong emphasis on the social, political, and economic trends shaping European and Eurasian futures.

In a final chapter, Zalmay Khalilzad and David Shlapak offer "Conclusions and Implications for the U.S. Air Force of 2025," emphasizing strategic-level observations, their meaning for air and space power and for national security policy more broadly.

The appendix brings together a selection of the regional scenarios developed over the course of the study and written by various authors. David Shlapak's introduction offers some thoughts on what we can and cannot expect of scenario building as a planning tool.

Chapter Two

OVERVIEW OF THE FUTURE SECURITY ENVIRONMENT

Zalmay Khalilzad and David Shlapak, with Ann Flanagan

INTRODUCTION

This overview attempts to weave highlights of the three regional analyses together with independent judgment to present an overall picture of possible alternative geostrategic worlds and what they might mean for the United States and U.S. Air Force planners.

We begin this overview with nine tenets about global trends in the next 25 years. We offer these propositions in great measure because of their power to shape the security environment as we enter the next century. The nine propositions are as follows:

1. The United States will remain a globally engaged actor.

2. The global distribution of power will change.

3. Great-power relationships will be in flux.

4. Regional divisions will be increasingly blurred.

5. The U.S. homeland will be more exposed to attack.

6. The rise of a "global competitor" is uncertain.

7. Technology, including military technology, will spread rapidly.

8. The spread of nuclear, chemical, and biological (NBC) weapons will remain a major problem.

9. The U.S. military will be called upon to respond not only to major regional warfare but also to other crises, and to play a key role in shaping the future security environment.

We then describe three alternative future worlds, as shown in Table 1. The first represents a base case of what 2025 might look like. In many ways, it is a linear projection of today's world. While not based upon dramatic fundamental departures from the world as we know it, this base case does present some new and intriguing challenges to the planner.

Our second alternative is a more benign world than the first one. The second world might be characterized as a world of convergence and cooperation rather than conflict. While not completely devoid of strife, the great powers are at peace and actively cooperate in preventing or terminating such clashes as do arise among or within lesser actors.

Table 1

Three Alternative Worlds

Element	Base Case	Benign	Malign
Europe	Muddling along	EuroFederalism	EU fragmentation
Russia/FSU	Russian confederation	Dynamic Russia	Sick man of Eurasia
Middle East	Regional competition	Stable prosperity	Anarchy
China	Assertive	Liberalizing	Hegemonic
Japan	Continuity	Proactive partner	Regional competitor
Asia	U.S. preponderance	Pax Americana—plus	Regional dominance
NBC proliferation	Modest	Low	High
Power relations	Evolving	Stable	Unstable
Global competitor	Uncertain	No	Yes

SOURCES: Internal RAND 1996 area papers—Ian O. Lesser, Bruce R. Nardulli, and Lori Arghavan on the Middle East; John Van Oudenaren on Europe and the FSU; and Ashley Tellis, Chung Min Lee, Courtney Purrington, and Michael D. Swaine on Asia.
NOTE: FSU = Former Soviet Union; EU = European Union.

The third world we describe is one in which things have, quite simply, gone bad. Beset with economic, demographic, and political turmoil, it is a world of instability, weapons proliferation, and tenuous peace. This world is also the only one of our three worlds that features a global rival to the United States.

These future worlds are described according to analyses based in large measure on trends that are observable in the mid-1990s. In addition to these trends, there are a number of potential "wild cards"—unforeseen events that could cause a major discontinuity or fundamental change in U.S. national security objectives and/or the role of the U.S. military in pursuing them. We suggest that there are three broad classes of such wild cards: environmental, politico-cultural, and techno-scientific.

Any of a baker's dozen of potential wild cards may come into play:

- A highly lethal airborne virus emerges and kills millions.

- Astronomers identify an asteroid or comet on a collision course with earth.

- A powerful earthquake devastates highly populated areas of coastal California.

- Unchecked global temperature increases cause massive crop failure and large-scale coastal flooding around the world.

- An economic depression grips the United States.

- A major regional ally suffers revolutionary collapse and disorder.

- Congress repeals or dramatically revises the restrictions on U.S. military involvement in domestic law enforcement.

- Neofascists or extreme fundamentalists come to power in a nuclear-armed country.

- A new cold war arises along "civilizational" cleavages (i.e., Islam versus the West).

- An energy source is developed that provides clean, inexpensive, and virtually limitless power.

- A new technology promises to revolutionize daily life—and war-fare—as dramatically as aviation and computers did in the 20th century.

- New technologies cut the cost of launching payloads into earth orbit by an order of magnitude.

- Sensor technologies render the oceans transparent.

Clearly, we are not suggesting that the United States revamp its whole defense-planning infrastructure to cope with such possibilities. We wish only to call attention to a class of factors that is often overlooked as we lay out future military requirements and to suggest that U.S. interests will be served best by a strategy with built-in flexibility to hedge against the unexpected—prepared both to absorb unanticipated shocks and to exploit new opportunities.

NINE PROPOSITIONS ABOUT THE FUTURE WORLD

1. The U.S. Will Remain a Globally Engaged Actor

We are convinced that the United States will remain engaged as a major player on the global scene through the first years of the 21st century. Indeed, despite the occasional eruption of isolationist sentiments, we believe that the nation simply has little choice in the matter. The sheer magnitude of the U.S. economy; the country's dense and increasing web of commercial, cultural, political, and security ties to other nations and actors; and its sheer pervasiveness and prominence make the United States the globe's "500-pound gorilla" whether we like it or not.[1]

---

[1]We would do well not to underestimate the degree to which the United States remains culturally dominant even when its economic and political preeminence is seen by some to be fading. Wander the streets of Paris, Tel Aviv, or Tokyo and note the number of Michael Jordan jerseys being worn by teenagers, the number of U.S. films being shown in cinemas, and the explosion of Pizza Huts and McDonald's. In how many languages do people wonder, "Who shot J.R.?"

These linkages are *not* trivial; in some ways they may be deeper and more lasting than political ties (recall that Levis blue jeans were a status symbol in the pre-*perestroika* USSR). And this enmeshing—which seems likely to endure so long as kids worship sports stars and Hollywood remains synonymous with "entertainment"—makes the United States a threat and a target for regimes and creeds that wish to resist our influ-

With the end of the global East-West competition, the United States can be more selective in its military involvement around the world than was the case during the Cold War. However, as a powerful actor with global interests, the United States will remain likely to become involved in a variety of foreign contingencies, ranging from forward defense of a threatened ally to disaster relief and other varieties of humanitarian assistance. The U.S. military will be called upon to play a major role in some such undertakings. As such, it seems desirable that the armed forces, including the Air Force, remain "full-service" providers. It is difficult to identify what existing *deployable* capabilities the military can afford to divest itself of in the face of the possible menu of challenges confronting the United States over the next quarter century.

Should the United States somehow manage to withdraw from the world stage, the implications would be staggering. Globally, the competition to fill the vacuum left behind by the retreat of American power could lead to widespread instability and conflict, endangering former friends and emboldening former adversaries. Within the United States, the military establishment would undoubtedly shrink dramatically as budgets declined.[2]

This withdrawal would be an unlikely turn of events. U.S. involvement in the world—in Latin America and Asia particularly—long predates the Cold War and will likely long survive it. Commercial ties and humanitarian concerns will continue to link the United States to the world at large. The role the United States chooses—or is, by the weight of historical circumstances, compelled—to play in the world will itself be a primary determinant of the kind of world the United States confronts.[3]

---

ence, either out of insular motives or a desire to supplant our message with their own. Thus do security implications grow from seemingly frivolous cultural connections.

[2]See Zalmay Khalilzad, "Losing the Moment? The United States and the World After the Cold War," *The Washington Quarterly*, Spring 1995, pp. 87–107.

[3]For a discussion of the options possibly available to the United States, see Zalmay Khalilzad and David Ochmanek (eds.), *Strategic Appraisal 1997*, Santa Monica, CA: RAND, MR-826-AF, 1997.

2. The Global Distribution of Power Will Continue to Change

For several hundred years, Europe and North America have been the world's centers of wealth and power. Just as this millennium fades into the new, so, too, will Western dominance decline. The world's liveliest economies are in Asia. Led by China and the four "tigers"—Hong Kong, Singapore, South Korea, and Taiwan—the region has experienced some of the highest rates of sustained economic growth in recent history, rates that are likely to remain relatively high for at least another two decades (Tellis et al., 1996). China today is widely regarded as having the world's second largest economy, after gross domestic product estimates are adjusted to reflect parity in purchasing power. The World Bank expects that, by 2020, China will have the world's largest economy. It would not be surprising if political influence and ambition grow in Asia to accompany this phenomenal expansion of wealth; indeed, in historical terms, it would be more surprising if they did not.

From a U.S. perspective, Asia's growing importance as a trading partner accentuates the importance of the region's economic growth. Today, Asia consumes roughly 30 percent of all U.S. merchandise exports and supplies over 40 percent of American merchandise imports; in contrast, the rest of North and South America combine to provide 31 percent of U.S. imports and buy 37 percent of her exports. And, as Figure 1 shows, Asia's role in U.S. trade patterns displays an inexorable rise over the last 20 years.

In contrast to Asia's dynamism, Europe finds itself in a period of relative stasis, meaning, in this context, relative decline. While seven of today's 10 largest economies are in Europe, only two are projected to be by 2020.[4] Further, while a truly unified Europe would be a powerful counterweight to the United States and Asia, there are many obstacles to be overcome before a Europe "whole and free" can be realized. Uncertainties abound concerning the future course of Russia, Ukraine, and other former Soviet states, and there are many questions regarding how to integrate the ex-Communist states and statelets of Eastern Europe into the continent's political, economic, and security institutions.

____

[4]R. Halloran, "The Rising East," *Foreign Policy*, No. 102, Spring 1996, p. 11.

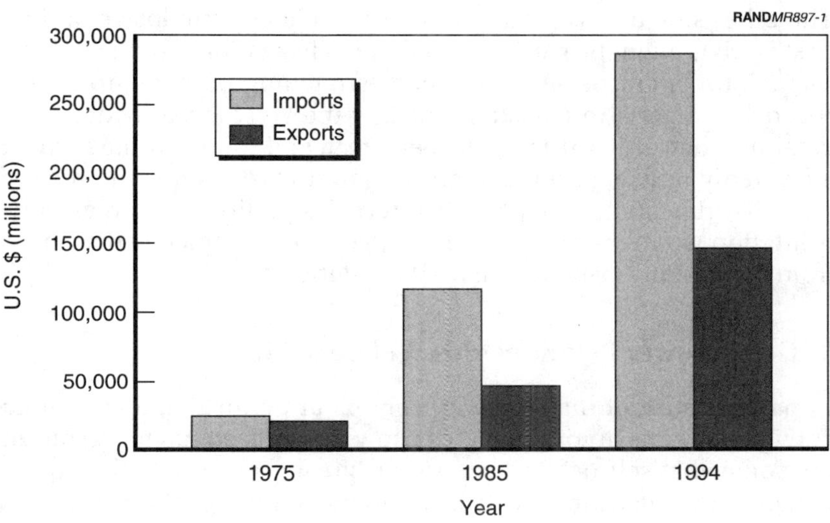

Figure 1—U.S. Trade with Asia: 1975, 1985, and 1994

The greater Middle East will remain a flashpoint demanding constant U.S. attention.[5] Beset by powerful systemic stresses arising from demographics, failed governments, dysfunctional economies, growing resource scarcity (especially water), major ideological cleavages within and between various countries, and ethnic problems, the states of the region face an array of challenges that could explode into widespread inter- or intrastate conflict at virtually any moment. These pressures will only grow over the coming years, meaning that the region—whose oil reserves supply an increasing proportion of the world's energy demands—will remain as important as ever to the global economic well-being. The future Middle East could well be characterized by events pulling people along in many cases with no one in control, leading to serious prospects of overall breakdowns.

---

[5]A key failing of many Persian Gulf states may be their failure to use their oil income to develop economies that are less reliant on the export of petroleum products. Virtually every Gulf country—Bahrain excepted—garners over 80 percent of its export earnings from oil sales. While the nature of the demand for oil may make these states less vulnerable to disruption than might otherwise be the case, such reliance on a single export product typically characterizes a weak and fragile economy.

The other side of this picture of an unstable and implosive Middle East is what might be called the "clash of civilizations" model, which pits a loosely knit Islamic crescent—stretching perhaps from Morocco and Algeria to Pakistan—against the West (broadly defined), creating a new Iron Curtain between north and south. While such an admittedly unlikely arrangement might at least offer some respite from worries about, say, Saudi internal stability, the larger confrontation would have worrisome aspects not completely dissimilar from those of the 1945–1990 East-West standoff.[6]

3. Great-Power Relationships Will Be in Flux

In part because of the changing centers of political and economic gravity, relations among the great powers—indeed, membership in the somewhat self-defined coterie *of* "great powers"—will be quite dynamic through the next two decades. Simply put, great uncertainty prevails.

The single largest variable might be China. How will China carry her rapidly growing weight on the global scene? Will economic security make Beijing a status quo power or whet her appetite for power and influence?

A second key actor is Russia. Russia's location, its vastness, and its potential economic and military prowess mean that Moscow's eventual destiny is tightly intertwined with the fates of her neighbors in Europe, Asia, and the Middle East. Whether Russia emerges from her present painful transition as a stable, democratic, and economically strong power—a "Russian miracle" analogous to those seen in postwar West Germany and Japan—or as a new "sick man of Eurasia," the impact will be felt globally.[7]

Other questions abound as well. For example,

* Will Germany and/or Japan conclude that the time is right to emerge from their postwar places in the wings of the global stage

---

[6]Interestingly, Lesser, Nardulli, and Arghavan (1996) note that the term "cold war," or *guerra fria*, was first used by Spanish commentators to describe the competition between Spain and the Ottoman Empire.

[7]Van Oudenaren (1996) discusses these and other possible Russian futures.

and take on the geopolitical stature to which their economic weight would seem to entitle them? The implications could be significant: For example, one alternative in the event of a failure of European integration could be a German-dominated central-European political-economic bloc that could find itself in competition with Russia to the east (Van Oudenaren, 1996).

- Germany's role in the future world will be strongly conditioned, of course, by the outcome of the ongoing process of European unification. A strong, federated Europe, as noted earlier, could help offset Asia's steadily growing stature. Failed integration, on the other hand, could accelerate Europe's relative decline in influence, making it neither a strong rival from a U.S. viewpoint nor a strong partner on global or regional issues. (Van Oudenaren, 1996).

- Finally, we are likely to be approaching the conclusion of the 50-year conflict between North and South Korea,[8] which does not strictly fit the category of "great-power relationships." The nature of the endgame, however, will have a tremendous impact on Asia's evolution. A major war—one perhaps involving the use of NBC weapons and attacks on territory outside the Korean peninsula—remains a possibility; the negative consequences of such a conflict would reverberate throughout Asia and the world.[9] Even should unification proceed peacefully, the transformations it could spark in Asia's internal dynamics—involving China, Japan, and Korea itself—could be profound.

It is important to recognize that increasing dynamism does not necessarily imply escalating friction. In what we will later call a *convergent world*—one in which there is broad adherence to what might be called "Western" standards of pluralistic political and market-oriented economic intercourse—the emergence of new power constellations need not imply increased competition. At the same time, however, significant divergences—on cultural, ethnic, political, historical, or economic grounds—will increase the likelihood of clashes arising from shifting power balances. Regions replete with

---

[8]See, for example, A. N. Shulsky, "Korea," in Z. Khalilzad (ed.), *Strategic Appraisal, 1996*, Santa Monica, CA: RAND, MR-543, 1996.

[9]The future of Korea is discussed in depth in Tellis et al. (1996).

such cleavages—the Middle East almost certainly, and Asia quite probably—will be more likely to suffer from profound transitional anxieties and the possible eruption of conflict as status shifts among actors.

Interregional power relations will also be in flux. Changes in relations will not be as consequential for global stability as those among great powers, but these interregional trends will have significant implications for cooperation, conflict, and access for U.S. forces in U.S. dealings with specific regions.

4. Regional Boundaries Will Be Increasingly Blurred

It is by now a truism that the world is growing increasingly interconnected and interdependent. From the standpoint of U.S. national security strategy, there is a growing likelihood that tensions and conflicts in one area will spill over into neighboring regions.

Any division of the globe into distinct regions has always been artificial; one need only recall the 14th-century spread of the black plague from Asia to Europe. However, as the century turns over, technology has not only netted the four corners of the earth more closely together, it has also made possible an increase in the strategic reach of nations and groups. A hacker sitting at a personal computer in Finland can be simultaneously everywhere and nowhere; he can wreak havoc on the unsuspecting or the unprotected. On a more physical plane, Figure 2 shows the areas threatened by a ballistic missile with a 3000-kilometer range based near Algiers, Tehran, or Beijing. Note that every major European, Asian, and Middle Eastern capital city falls into one or another range ring.[10]

The end of the Cold War has also unleashed religious, ethnic, and nationalistic aspirations that had previously been long suppressed or lost in the noise generated by the superpower confrontation. The Kurdish dilemma, for example, bridges Central Asia, the Middle East, and Europe. Similarly, Islam as a unifying identity has little regard

____

[10]The most notable exception being Helsinki.

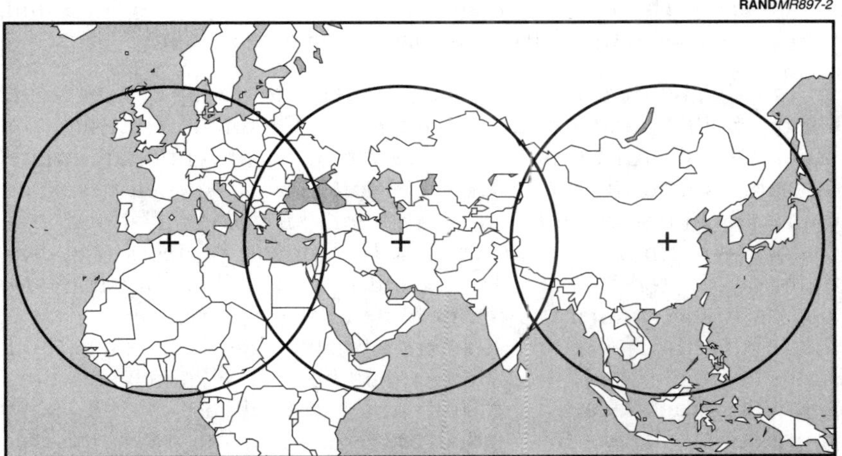

Figure 2—Areas That Would Be Threatened by 3000-km–Range Missiles in
Algeria, Iran, and China

for traditional regional boundaries, and events on one edge of the
Islamic world—the acquisition of nuclear weapons by Algeria, for
example—would have repercussions not only in North Africa but
halfway around the globe and beyond.

The world has been growing steadily smaller for hundreds of years; in
the next century, it will no longer be possible for any country, including the United States, to rely on physical distance to separate it from
the dangers of the world. And the U.S. military command structure,
organized around tidy divisions of the globe into well-defined geographic entities, may find itself under considerable stress as more
and more crises arise that straddle those neat demarcations.

5. The U.S. Homeland Will Be More Exposed to Attack

A second consequence of the shrinking world is that the United
States homeland—for almost two hundred years a sanctuary from
foreign hostile action—will be in increasing jeopardy of coming un-

der attack.[11] These attacks could go well beyond the run-of-the-mill terrorist acts with which we have become all too familiar.[12]

Porous U.S. borders and the sheer number of tempting targets in the United States point toward an increasing likelihood of strikes on American soil. An adversary might attempt unconventional warfare operations against militarily significant targets—airfields, space-control facilities, seaports, command-and-control installations, and so forth—in an attempt to disrupt U.S. power-projection operations.[13] Countervalue attacks directed against civilian targets might also occur as opponents attempt to deter U.S. involvement or raise the costs of intervention. It seems possible that, by 2025, several states hostile to the United States might be able to launch very limited NBC attacks against the United States; a suitcase or a shipping container might be as likely a delivery vehicle as a long-range missile, and the perpetrator could even be a nonstate actor rather than a country.[14]

During the Cold War, Americans faced the prospect of instantaneous annihilation at the hands of the Soviet Union. While Russia and perhaps one or two other countries will retain into the next century the ability to devastate the United States, Moscow's behavior will be conditioned by the same cold calculus of deterrence that kept the peace during the years of East-West confrontation. The emerging and more immediate threat is not one of societal destruction but of smaller, damaging attacks, some of which could originate from states

---

[11]Obviously, Soviet nuclear forces aimed at the United States constituted a very real and compelling threat; however, the fact remains that no foreign power has conducted organized military operations on U.S. soil since the War of 1812. Some die-hard adherents to the Confederate cause might argue that Union "aggression" against the South constituted "foreign hostile action" as recently as 1865. The authors, however, stand as Lincoln stood: that the Confederacy consisted of states in rebellion and not a sovereign power and that therefore the Civil War was just that—an internal conflict.

[12]For a seminal discussion of how terrorism might develop, see Brian M. Jenkins, *New Modes of Conflict*, Santa Monica, CA: RAND, R-3009-DNA, 1983.

[13]For a discussion of how small teams of ground forces could disrupt U.S. Air Force air base operations, see David A. Shlapak and Alan J. Vick, *"Check six begins on the ground": Responding to the Evolving Ground Threat to U.S. Air Force Bases*, Santa Monica, CA: RAND, MR-606-AF, 1995.

[14]At least four countries—Russia, Great Britain, France, and China—are capable today of striking the United States with nuclear weapons. We are here referring to a future threat emanating from other, smaller powers.

or groups less susceptible to the "logical" cost-benefit accounting of "rational" deterrence theory. Defending the nation against these sorts of adversaries will be a significant new challenge for the U.S. armed forces over the coming years.

6. The Rise of a "Global Competitor" Is Uncertain

Our analyses suggest that a number of countries—China in particular—could dramatically increase their strategic weight and military reach over the next 25 years. China might even attempt to challenge the United States and its interests worldwide.[15]

Many other countries could also increase their military capabilities to achieve some degree of parity with the United States in one or more arenas of military competition, and we can identify powers whose ambitions may exceed those normally attributed to "regional" opponents. So the United States will probably encounter challengers who have some *peer* capabilities—what might be called "niche competitors"—and *supraregional* appetites. From the perspective of 1997, however, it seems unlikely that any power has, or will in the near term have, *both* the ambitions and the resources necessary to mount a global challenge to the United States.

In saying this, however, we must bear in mind that history is notoriously unpredictable and that 30 years can be quite a long time. In 1945, the Soviet Union had the largest army and air force in the world and, despite the immense losses it had suffered in four years of combat with Nazi Germany, it stood astride Eurasia as a colossus. Twenty-five years earlier—roughly the same temporal distance as that between now and 2020—the USSR was in turmoil, possessor of a collapsing, largely agrarian economy and engaged in the last stages of a bloody civil war. Five years before that (1915, 30 years before the Red Army raised the hammer and sickle over the ruins of the Reichstag), the Soviet Union did not even exist, and its predecessor state—imperial Russia—was embarked on an ill-advised war that would end in catastrophic military defeat and revolution. Even without war,

------

[15]"Global competitor" means precisely that—an adversarial power that would attempt to challenge the United States and its interests worldwide. The Soviet Union was a true global competitor to the United States during the Cold War; Napoleonic France and Britain are another, more historically distant, example of global competitors.

dramatic and unanticipated changes can occur in the balance of power, as was the case with the rise of Germany and the United States between 1870 and 1910.

Because things can change radically over a period of even a few decades or even years, and because we are uncertain about the emergence of a global challenger in the next two decades, U.S. policy must remain cognizant of the possibility of new competition. Precluding such an eventuality should be the most important U.S. objective into the 21st century.[16]

7. Technology Will Spread Rapidly

In March 1977, a small company called Apple Computer filed articles of incorporation with the state of California. About a month later, the company's eight employees rolled out their first product—the Apple II home computer—at the West Coast Computer Faire in San Francisco.[17] Today, barely 20 years later, there are approximately 16 million desktop computers in homes across America—not including the countless other computers that run our automobiles and home appliances.

Ten years ago, cellular telephones were an expensive rarity. Today, they are an order of magnitude cheaper, much smaller, more capable, and ubiquitous. In the next 10 years, direct-satellite service and high-speed wireless data transmission promise to revolutionize communications as completely and surely as the first cell phones did.

---

[16]Our colleague Robert Levine made the excellent observation that, while it may be unlikely that China will develop either the appetite or the capabilities to constitute itself a true "global" challenger to the United States, Beijing could marshal sufficient resources to create a strategic nuclear threat to the U.S. homeland—comparable, in terms of retaliatory capability, to that fielded by the former Soviet Union. Such a development would at the least necessitate a revival of some aspects of a classical deterrence posture by the United States. Moreover, such a development could create a trilateral U.S.-Russian-Chinese strategic equation, the balancing of which could prove challenging. In either event, the implications for U.S. Air Force force structure and planning could be significant. We are indebted to him for this point.

[17]Stephen Levy, *Hackers*, New York: Dell Publishing, 1984, pp. 263–264.

These are just two of the most striking examples of the pace of contemporary technological change. Computers and computer components—processing units, memory, storage devices—continue to climb in performance while dropping in price; as they do so, they are driving a revolution in how people worldwide live, work—and make war. For cellular communications and powerful laptop computers are not just a convenience for fast-moving business people—they can also form the backbone of, for example, a highly redundant and robust mobile military command-and-control system.

Technologically, the watchword for the coming years is "diffusion." As commercial needs and standards increasingly dominate, dual-use technology—technology with both civilian and military applications—will proliferate widely, with important security implications. This will be true on the large scale—where pharmaceutical knowhow can be equally applicable to chemical weapons or aspirin, to biowarfare toxins or antibiotics—and the small—where the realtor's cellular modem becomes the terrorist's remote detonator.

The next 20 years will also witness a revolution in the nature and extent of access to space-based capabilities. High-resolution multispectral imagery from space, once the province of superpowers alone, will be widely available at low cost.[18] The pictures thus acquired will speed around the globe on a world-girdling information network of which today's World Wide Web is just a precursor.[19] The Global Positioning System (GPS)—or a successor family of satellite navigation aids—and satellite communications are just two hightech common-user utilities available to one and all.[20]

---

[18]See, for example, "Public Eye," *Scientific American*, August 1996, p. 18; and Charles Lane, "The Satellite Revolution," *The New Republic*, Vol. 215, No. 7, August 12, 1996, p. 22.

[19]In 1986, the National Science Foundation's (NSF's) NSFNet "backbone," then the heart of the Internet, ran at 56 kilobits per second (KBPS). By 1992, it was up to 45,000 KBPS, or 45 megabits per second (MBPS)—an 800-fold increase in six years. This year, MCI (one of the commercial carriers who took over Internet management from the NSF in 1995) set up a 122-MBPS backbone. Cable modems, meanwhile, promise user-to-host connectivity at up to 10 MBPS, over 350 times faster than today's 28.8 KBPS modems. (Glen Banta, "Internet Pipe Schemes," *Internet World*, Vol. 8, No. 10, October 1996, pp. 62–70.)

[20]Commercial GPS receivers, for example, first came on the market carrying price tags in the thousands of dollars. By 1994, they had dropped to the mid-hundreds. In the

Military-specific technology will also spread quickly and widely. As the global arms market becomes ever more competitive, profit-making pressures will likely allow advanced weapons and weapon technologies to get into more and more hands. The future U.S. Air Force could encounter NBC weapons, ballistic and cruise missile systems, advanced sensor capabilities, and sophisticated air-defense weapons at almost any turn. Highly lethal "fire-and-forget" beyond-visual-range air-to-air missiles could turn even a poorly trained enemy pilot into a deadly opponent for U.S. air crews. To visualize the implications, imagine Somali "technicals" with SA-18s and laser-guided mortar shells in addition to AK-47s, or Bosnian Serbs with stealthy ground-launched cruise missiles having GPS guidance and chemical warheads, or Saddam Hussein with functioning nuclear warheads tipping advanced medium-range ballistic missiles (MRBMs).[21]

8. The Spread of NBC Weapons Will Remain a Problem

As the preceding paragraph suggests, the proliferation of NBC weapons will be a continuing problem through 2025. By then, several dozen countries will almost certainly have the capability to build and deliver NBC weapons, although the number with known arsenals may be considerably smaller. As relations among powers shift in perhaps-unpredictable ways (see assertion 3, above), more countries may perceive it to be in their interests to have NBC weapons as a sort of "security blanket" against the unexpected. Further, as the expertise to build these devices becomes more widespread, reasonably well-heeled nonstate groups—terrorist organizations, insurgencies, criminal rings—may find themselves able to acquire small numbers of them.

As the number of actors possessing nuclear arms and other weapons of mass destruction increases, so, seemingly, does the likelihood of their falling into the hands of individuals or groups who may see

---

fall of 1996, a local Washington, D.C., sporting-goods retailer advertised three-dimensional GPS receivers for $289.

[21] However, there may well be some countries in which a variety of factors—cultural, economic, and educational—may impede the integration of advanced technology into the military or may reduce the military's ability to employ advanced weapons effectively.

them as usable instruments; the 1995 nerve-gas attack on the Tokyo subway is a disturbing precedent. Although the United States can employ a range of strategies against such actors, some may prove frustratingly hard to deter.[22] It may be the case that most future overseas military operations will be undertaken in the shadow of NBC weapon use. This would represent a radical break with the past, and it would have major implications for U.S. forces and operations, including the possibility that a future president would be deterred from intervention, even in a situation in which U.S. interests were clearly at stake.

9. The U.S. Military Will Be Called Upon to Respond to Crises Other Than "Traditional" Warfare

In the wake of the Cold War, the U.S. armed forces have increasingly turned their attention to so-called "military operations other than war" (MOOTW). These kinds of activities—lesser conflicts, punitive raids and expeditions, peacekeeping, humanitarian operations, and so forth—seem likely to remain a frequent feature of the world scene through the first part of the 21st century.

To term such undertakings "other than war" risks understating the level of violence that may be involved in such operations. For example, counterproliferation operations—whether conducted via air strikes, special operations forces, or insertion of software "agents" that "soft kill" the weapons—could prompt the targeted group or country to use their NBC weapons before they lose them. Whether the target of such strikes was U.S. forces, an ally's capital, or the American homeland, the results would certainly feel a great deal like "war" to those unfortunate enough to be in the way. Similarly, it seems possible that a future president could be confronted with a situation in which American citizens must be evacuated from a country whose regime would forcibly oppose any effort to extract them. Although not "war," successfully carrying out the mission would likely require the judicious and effective use of force.

---

[22]For an evaluation of alternative deterrence strategies against opponents having small nuclear arsenals, see Dean Wilkening and Kenneth Watman, *Nuclear Deterrence in a Regional Context*, Santa Monica, CA: MR-500-A/AF, 1995.

Humanitarian assistance will remain a U.S. vocation, as well. For decades, the U.S. military has been dispatched to assist victims of flood and famine. civil war, and technology run amok. We do not see the demand for such aid decreasing over the years to come. Indeed, it seems to us likely that the number and severity of humanitarian crises will increase over the next 30 years. Continuing urbanization will stress already-limited resources in the less-developed world.[23] Disease pandemics, spreading quickly through impoverished and squalid cities, will exact an enormous toll.[24] Economic failures, political chaos, and ethno-religious strife will create prodigious refugee flows.[25] Meanwhile, the U.S. military will remain the organization best equipped to respond to this menu of challenges.

If responding to, say, a typhoon striking an overcrowded, brutally impoverished, AIDS-ravaged coastal African city seems insufficiently challenging, more-desperate scenarios can be created by overlaying the humanitarian mission with one or more of the other factors discussed in the preceding pages. For example, imagine a situation in which several densely populated South Asian cities have been struck with nuclear weapons by India and Pakistan in an ongoing regional conflict. The United States would surely be called upon to lead relief efforts, and the U.S. military would be at the leading edge of any response.[26] Likewise, internal conflicts in countries important to U.S. interests, such as Saudi Arabia, Mexico, Egypt, and Cuba, might produce irresistible demands for U.S. military involvement—directly or indirectly in support of allies and friends. In short, while U.S. forces must continue to be able to deter and, if necessary, defeat large-scale military aggression, they must also expect to be called upon to engage in many kinds of difficult smaller-scale operations as well.

---

[23]According to the United Nations, the urban population will grow from 21.9 to 43.5 percent of total population in the least-developed countries between 1995 and 2025. (United Nations Population Division, Department for Economic and Social Information and Policy Analysis, *World Urbanization Prospects: The 1994 Revision,* 1994.)

[24]In parts of sub-Saharan Africa, for example, nearly *25 percent* of the population is HIV-positive.

[25]In January 1995, the United Nations High Commissioner for Refugees reported that more than 27 million people fit the UN's definition of "refugee." The number of refugees has increased dramatically over the past 20 years or so.

[26]We thank colleague Bruce Nardulli for this example.

ALTERNATIVE FUTURE WORLDS: THREE EXAMPLES

We next describe three alternative future worlds. They are not intended to represent the full range of possibilities, but are snapshots of three kinds of security environments, with some discussion of what each might imply for the United States and its military.

The first represents a base case of what 2025 might look like. In many ways, it is a linear projection of today's world. While not based upon dramatic fundamental departures from the world as we know it, this first world does present some new and intriguing challenges to the planner.

Our second alternative is a more benign world than the first one. It might be characterized as a world of convergence and cooperation rather than conflict. While not completely devoid of strife, the great powers are at peace and actively cooperate in preventing or terminating such clashes as do arise among or within lesser actors.

The third world we describe is one in which things have, quite simply, gone bad. Beset with economic, demographic, and political turmoil, it is a world of instability, proliferation, and tenuous peace.

We recognize that it is highly unlikely that *any* of these three worlds will come to pass as we describe them. We are not trying to predict how the world *will* change, but how it *might* change and what those changes might mean to U.S. national security planning.

World I: Evolutionary

Description. Table 2 lays out our base-case world, which is an evolutionary descendent of 1996.

In this world, Europe has not moved decisively toward either federalism or renationalization, but continues to operate with a complex mix of intergovernmental and supranational mechanisms. Shifting subgroups of countries work together in particular areas without decisive leadership from any quarter. (Van Oudenaren, 1996.)

Russia, meanwhile, has become the center of a revitalized confederation of the Slavic components of the former Soviet Union. Be-

Table 2

Three Alternative Worlds—World I

Component	Base Case
Europe	Muddling along
Russia/FSU	Russian confederation
Middle East	Regional competition
China	Assertive
Japan	Continuity
Asia	U.S. preponderance
NBC proliferation	Modest
Power relations	Evolving
Global competitor?	Uncertain

SOURCES: Internal RAND 1996 area papers—Ian O. Lesser, Bruce R. Nardulli, and Lori Arghavan on the Middle East; John Van Oudenaren on Europe and the FSU; and Ashley Tellis, Chung Min Lee, Courtney Purrington, and Michael D. Swaine on Asia.

NOTE: FSU = Former Soviet Union; EU = European Unicn.

larus, Ukraine, and the Russian-populated parts of Moldova and Kazakhstan are reunited with Russia proper in a confederation (in Ukraine's case, perhaps loosely so), while the Central Asian and Transcaucasus countries drift away from Russia and toward Asian and Middle Eastern powers. (Van Oudenaren, 1996.)

In this world, the greater Middle East is dominated by an essentially secular competition among regional rivals. In addition to the United States, the countries of China, Russia, and Pakistan are important extraregional actors in a geopolitical free-for-all in which stability depends on either an external power's influence or the emergence of a regional hegemon. (Lesser, Nardulli, and Arghavan, 1996.)

In Asia, China develops into a great power, one that is considerably more assertive about its role and perquisites in Asia, albeit without active aspirations for regional military dominance. For this peaceful development to happen, Beijing's desire for a placid regional environment and its growing linkages with foreign economies must outweigh its (potentially destabilizing) nationalistic impulses (Tellis et al., 1996). Japan also embraces continuity, focusing on managing its economic development and relying on its partnership with the United States to maintain its security. Elsewhere in Asia, American preponderance holds in the context of new, multiple, rising regional power centers (Tellis et al., 1996).

This is a world of modest NBC proliferation. While efforts to curb the spread of these weapons have not been universally successful, the number of actors with access to NBC means has not exploded. Power relations among the major actors are changing gradually; the new centers that are arising are by and large integrated into a fairly stable global order. The mischief that arises—and it could be considerable—originates with those who are not so well plugged into this order.

Finally, in this world, no global competitor to the United States is likely to emerge.

Implications. In world I, defense of territory remains an important driver of U.S. force structure and planning. The United States needs to retain the ability to confront and defeat an aggressor rapidly and decisively in a large-scale regional conflict. The context of such operations is somewhat different in that (1) operations in urban environments have become increasingly important, and (2) the United States is likely facing an adversary with at least some NBC weapons and delivery capabilities.

In this world, the United States remains the preeminent power, sitting in the center of a web of security treaties and arrangements. As has been the case in the past, these relationships will be a mixed blessing to the United States, as its friends and allies act sometimes as partners in advancing collective security (as they were in the Gulf in 1990 and 1991) and other times as brakes on U.S. policy desires and initiatives (as they frequently did with regard to Bosnia from 1992 to 1995).

Key unknowns in this world are

- What form, exactly, would the projected "Russian union" take? Would any adventuristic impulses inform Moscow's behavior, either toward the "near abroad" or Russia's more-distant neighbors?

- How stable are the gray areas and buffers within and between the key regions (e.g., the Balkans, Central Asia, the Mediterranean)?

- How rapidly would NBC weapons spread? In particular, how many new members of the nuclear club will there be in 2025? How effective will U.S. forces be in defeating these weapons?

World II: Benign

Description. Table 3 incorporates our second world, which is a relatively peaceful and prosperous variant. It might be called a *convergent* world—one in which democratic institutions and market mechanisms are the norm.[27]

In this case, Europe has succeeded in achieving federalist unification. In so doing, it constitutes a power with half again as large a population as the United States and a gross domestic product (GDP) some 40 percent greater. Importantly, this new superpower would field a European army and develop both a common defense and security policy and the institutions and capabilities to carry it out. (Van Oudenaren, 1996.)

Table 3

Three Alternative Worlds—World II

Component	Base Case	Benign
Europe	Muddling along	EuroFederalism
Russia/FSU	Russian confederation	Dynamic Russia
Middle East	Regional competition	Stable prosperity
China	Assertive	Liberalizing
Japan	Continuity	Proactive partner
Asia	U.S. preponderance	Pax Americana–plus
NBC proliferation	Modest	Low
Power relations	Evolving	Stable
Global competitor?	Uncertain	No

SOURCES: Internal RAND 1996 area papers—Ian O. Lesser, Bruce R. Nardulli, and Lori Arghavan on the Middle East; John Van Oudenaren on Europe and the FSU; and Ashley Tellis, Chung Min Lee, Courtney Purrington, and Michael D. Swaine on Asia.

NOTE: FSU = Former Soviet Union; EU = European Union.

---

[27]It is the sort of world Francis Fukuyama speculated about in *The End of History and the Last Man*, New York: The Free Press, 1992.

Russia in this world is a strong, dynamic actor whose internal structure has evolved in a truly democratic and market-oriented fashion. Externally, Moscow is a status quo power that inevitably exercises a high degree of influence on its neighbors through trade and investment but not through military coercion.

The Middle East in world II enjoys a comprehensive and durable settlement of the Arab-Israeli dispute, successful political and economic reforms and peaceful transitions from authoritarian rule, and movement toward regional integration and effective security architectures. Secularism, democracy, and free-market economies flourish. (Lesser, Nardulli, and Arghavan, 1996.)

The China of this world is similar to that portrayed in world I. In this case, however, the transition to a new leadership generation combined with ever-increasing trade and investment linkages to the outside world have led to a gradual liberalization of the regime and slow movement toward democratization and a full market economy.

This Japan, too, is broadly comparable to that of the baseline world. In the benign world, Tokyo's economic strength and growing self-confidence make Japan a strong but cooperative partner to both the United States and China, for whom she serves as something of a model. Indeed, the maturation of the U.S.-Japan partnership creates conditions that allow all of Asia to experience a period of stability and economic prosperity.

In this world, NBC proliferation is low. Indeed, some nuclear powers, including Israel, have followed South Africa's lead and dismantled their nuclear arsenals. Power relations among the major actors are stable, with enduring U.S.-European and U.S.-Japanese ties forming the bedrock of the global order. Obviously, in this world no global competitor to the United States will emerge.

Implications. In world II, very different—and very much reduced—demands are levied on the U.S. military. The flash points for large-scale conflict are many fewer than in world I, and the other great powers—federal Europe, Russia, China, and Japan—are able to deal much more effectively with such outbursts as do threaten to erupt. The Middle East, in particular, is radically transformed from what we know today; the stability that prevails there is, in many ways, the hallmark of this peaceful world. While U.S. defense planning still needs to hedge against the breakdown of the placid global order, missions such as disaster relief, humanitarian assistance, counterterrorism, and suppression of international criminal activities—mostly undertaken in concert with other powers—constitute the main activities of the U.S. armed forces. We might therefore expect the forces to be much smaller and very different in composition from those that exist today.

Important variables shaping world II include the depth and durability of amity between the great power dyads in Europe and Asia.

- Can a dynamic and self-confident Russia and a strong European Union coexist without friction along their peripheries?

- Can Japan and China overcome decades of distrust to cooperate politically and economically and in security matters?

- Can China liberalize itself without unleashing the kind of centrifugal forces that tore apart the Soviet Union in the wake of *glasnost* and *perestroika*?

- Will political and economic reform in the Middle East be deep and pervasive enough to eliminate inter- and intrastate strife in the long term?

World III: Malign

Description. Our final planning case is illustrated in Table 4; it is a world of violent competition and frequent conflict.

In Europe, the failure of integration efforts create a vacuum of power and influence. Western Europe is unable to project stability and prosperity into Eastern Europe and the Balkans, a void that could be filled by a powerful Germany or by renationalization and possible conflict recurring along national and ethnic lines. The NATO alliance has either become irrelevant or has disintegrated because of disagreements among member states. Although the Russia of world III is "authoritarian but weak" in the wake of failed political and economic reform, the overall depressed state of Europe could allow Moscow to reemerge as a potential hegemon, at least over the eastern part of the continent (Lesser, Nardulli, and Arghavan, 1996). China tugs on Russia from the east, and Iran and Pakistan from the

Table 4

Three Alternative Worlds—World III

Component	Base Case	Benign	Malign
Europe	Muddling along	EuroFederalism	EU fragmentation
Russia/FSU	Russian confederation	Dynamic Russia	Sick man of Eurasia
Middle East	Regional competition	Stable prosperity	Anarchy
China	Assertive	Liberalizing	Hegemonic
Japan	Continuity	Proactive partner	Regional competitor
Asia	U.S. preponderance	Pax Americana-plus	Regional dominance
NBC proliferation	Modest	Low	High
Power relations	Evolving	Stable	Unstable
Global competitor?	Uncertain	No	Yes

SOURCES: Internal RAND 1996 area papers—Ian O. Lesser, Bruce R. Nardulli, and Lori Arghavan on the Middle East; John Van Oudenaren on Europe and the FSU; and Ashley Tellis, Chung Min Lee, Courtney Purrington, and Michael D. Swaine on Asia.
NOTE: FSU = Former Soviet Union; EU = European Union.

south. Amidst these tensions, a catastrophic breakdown of a country that still possesses thousands of nuclear weapons is a never-too-distant possibility.

In the Middle East of world III, we find anarchy and chaos. The region is home to any number of "failed states" in which the economic, political, and social order has broken down (Lesser, Nardulli, and Arghavan, 1996). In this world, the global thirst for oil has presumably not abated; the internal weakness of the Gulf states, in particular, invites both external predatory attack and frequent internal struggles for control of resources.

China in world III eschews democratization and normalization for an accelerated program of military modernization, especially air and naval power-projection capabilities (Tellis et al., 1996). Japan might choose to go in one of several directions in the face of China's drive for regional superiority. Tokyo might decide to ally itself with Beijing; it might seek U.S. support in balancing China; or it might compete with China for Asian leadership. In the worst case—our world

III—Japan loses faith in U.S. security guarantees and chooses the latter path. Tokyo begins converting its economic power into military strength and deploys a small nuclear arsenal to defend itself and its interests against what it perceives as malign Chinese designs. In the rest of Asia, the second-tier powers jockey for position alongside one or another of the competitors within a complex context of border and resource disputes.

In this world, NBC proliferation proceeds at a rapid clip, as actors see nuclear weapons in particular as insurance policies against the dangers around them. Power relations are fluid to the point of instability as small countries seek protectors and larger powers recruit clients. And in this world, it seems likely that a global competitor to the United States could emerge, perhaps as a result of an alliance of convenience between one of the Asian competitors and Russia.

Implications. This world is the polar opposite of world II—where in that world we found stability, here there is anarchy and conflict.

The United States in world III confronts multiple dangers without strong, reliable partners. Tensions run high in Europe, Asia, and the Middle East. In particular, a weak Russia relying on its nuclear arsenal to protect itself could pose a constant danger to important U.S. interests worldwide.

The lack of dependable allies forces the United States to field a military capable of waging a major conflict with limited forward basing and minimal support from friendly forces. The need to operate "from arm's length" is reinforced by the widespread proliferation of NBC weapons, which endanger any large-scale forward deployment of U.S. forces.

Despite world III's potential for massive human suffering—especially among the "failed states" of the greater Middle East—the United States may ironically find itself involved in less humanitarian relief than in either of the other two futures. Again, the dangers of projecting large numbers of people into an NBC-rich world and the absence of international support could limit American willingness to undertake MOOTW-like operations overseas.

This is a nasty and brutish world; just how unpleasant it is would be significantly affected by the following:

- Is Moscow weak enough to feel under siege but sufficiently strong to lash out against those it sees as threatening her?

- How extensive and intensive are the military aspects of the Sino-Japanese competition for Asian dominance? A contest that is primarily political and economic will obviously be much easier to manage and have much less dangerous implications.

- Can Western Europe get out of great-power competition and set itself off from the chaos in the east and south, or will it increasingly be forced to organize itself as a major power, perhaps under German dominance, that might then come into conflict with Russia?

- Will a global competitor emerge to challenge Washington's necessarily piecemeal efforts to sustain and advance U.S. interests in this fragmented world?

Overall Implications

While these three worlds do not exhaust the possible, let alone probable, arrangements of the global environment in the early years of the next century, they might shed light on some drivers of the form that environment will take. These include

- the fate of democratization and market reform in Russia and China,

- the manner in which the countries of central and eastern Europe are reintegrated into the continent's political-economic structure, and how Russia responds to that process,

- the pace and extent of European unification,

- the internal dynamics of the greater Middle East, especially the outcome of the Arab-Israeli peace process,

- the evolution of Sino-American relations and Beijing's choices about its role in Asia and the world, and

- the rate and extent of the spread of NBC weapons.

WILD CARDS

Introduction

We have described the future world—or future worlds—according to analyses based in large measure on trends that are observable in the mid-1990s. In addition to these trends, there are a number of potential "wild cards"—unforeseen events that could cause a major discontinuity or fundamental change in U.S. national security objectives and/or the role of the U.S. military in pursuing them.

History features many examples of wild cards shaping the course of events. While the rise of National Socialism in intrawar Germany was perhaps a predictable outgrowth of the social and economic problems of the Weimar Republic, for example, the charismatic and messianic Adolf Hitler was not. Without Hitler's leadership, the Nazi Party would likely have remained a fringe right-wing group. And had the *führer*less National Socialists somehow attained power, Germany's course in the 1930s and 1940s would almost certainly have been vastly different from the tragic trajectory it in fact followed with Hitler at the helm.

One might speak of three broad classes of wild cards:

- *Environmental* wild cards, such as the devastation of Europe by the Black Death or the storm that crippled the Spanish Armada in 1588

- *Politico-cultural* wild cards, such as Hitler's rise to power or the Russian revolution of 1917

- *Techno-scientific* wild cards, such as Europe's first encounter with the New World in the late 15th century and the discovery of atomic energy in the 1930s.

It is almost in the nature of events like these that one cannot plan against them; surprise is a fact of life. However, by exploring around the edges of our normal planning futures—by closing one eye and squinting into the kaleidoscope of the future—we can at least narrow the range of events that can take us totally unawares.

The examples that follow are clearly just a selection from an almost infinite list of candidates. Clearly, too, we are not suggesting that the

United States revamp its defense-planning infrastructure to cope with these events, or their like. We present them as a way of illuminating the question, Where do we draw the line between those contingencies against which we hedge (even to the extent of commissioning studies or conducting "what-if" planning exercises), and those that fall off the table entirely? Our examples come from each of the three broad classes described above:

- Environmental wild cards

  - A highly lethal airborne virus (e.g., airborne *Ebola*)—either natural or human-engineered—emerges and kills millions.[28]

  - Astronomers identify an asteroid or comet on a collision course with earth.

  - A powerful earthquake devastates highly populated areas of coastal California.

  - Unchecked global temperature increases cause massive crop failure and large-scale coastal flooding around the world.

- Politico-cultural wild cards

  - An economic depression grips the developed world.

  - A major regional ally suffers revolutionary collapse and disorder.

  - Congress repeals or dramatically revises the restrictions on U.S. military involvement in domestic law enforcement.

  - Neofascists or extreme fundamentalists come to power in a nuclear-armed country.

  - A new cold war arises along "civilizational" lines.

---

[28]The popular movie *Outbreak* and Michael Crichton's novel *The Andromeda Strain* both deal with this frightening possibility. For a more factual, though still speculative, treatment, see Laurie Garrett, *The Coming Plague*, New York: Farrar, Straus, and Giroux, 1994.

- Techno-scientific wild cards

  — An energy source is developed that provides clean, inexpensive, and virtually limitless power.

  — A new technology promises to revolutionize daily life—and warfare—as dramatically as aviation and computers did in the 20th century.[29]

  — New technologies cut the cost of launching payloads into earth orbit by an order of magnitude.

  — Sensor technologies render the oceans transparent.

Implications

Hedging against the future's enormous uncertainties is part of the art of force planning, and we do not presume to provide definitive answers. However, a few examples of how U.S. defense planning might take these "X factors" into account may be helpful.

First of all, the Department of Defense can and should take steps to avoid future catastrophic technological surprise. Although the military is no longer the primary motor for technological innovation, it has sufficient resources to keep abreast of cutting-edge developments in both the private and nondefense public sectors. The U.S. Air Force in particular might consider developing a "technology warning system" that would enable it to flag both evolutionary and revolutionary advances of particular salience.

Second, the military could assemble a small, joint, planning cell responsible for sketching the basic outline of possible responses to unexpected challenges. Such a group could, for example, think through how the United States—with or without large-scale support from its security partners—could "denuclearize" a country that suddenly came under the control of a radically dangerous group or individual. These plans could be tested and refined in small-scale command-post exercises and war games.

---

[29]Biotechnology and nanotechnology are two obvious candidates.

Also, defense planners—and Air Force planners in particular—should explore the ramifications of widespread, inexpensive access to space. The Air Force has already committed itself to becoming a "space and air" force by 2025, signaling much greater emphasis on the importance of "space control" in future military operations.[30] Planning for this transition should focus not just on how the United States will exploit lowered costs to orbit payloads but how potential adversaries might as well.

Finally, and perhaps most important, the primary lesson of these wild cards—and the dozens of others that fertile minds could undoubtedly produce—is that rigid planning formulae based on a few "blessed" scenarios may be inadequate foundations for U.S. security. We suggest that U.S. interests will best be served by a strategy with built-in flexibility to hedge against the unexpected—prepared both to absorb unanticipated shocks and to exploit unforeseen opportunities.

IMPLICATIONS FROM THE REGIONAL ANALYSES

Introduction

We reproduce here excerpts from Project AIR FORCE's three regional area studies.

Asia

Our findings regarding Asia can be grouped around two major propositions. The first is that *the Asia-Pacific region will become the largest and perhaps the most important concentration of world economic power in the next century.* Four factors lead to this conclusion:

- The region is characterized by some of the highest rates of sustained economic growth in modern history, rates that are likely to remain at relatively high levels for at least another two decades.

---

[30]U.S. Air Force, *Global Engagement: A Vision for the 21st Century Air Force,* Washington, D.C., 1996.

- The wealth and prosperity of the United States will remain dependent on continued linkages with the Asian economies.

- China, Japan, and India will become important alternative centers of power in both economic and military terms, with China possibly emerging as a potential peer competitor to the United States.

- The Asia-Pacific region is home to a large and increasing concentration of technological capabilities with some emerging centers of high-technology excellence.

The second major proposition is that, despite its formidable economic power, *the Asia-Pacific region will remain a relatively turbulent region beset by internal conflicts and political transitions and will experience persistent insecurity flowing from both a changing external environment and new kinds of military technologies.* Again, four factors support this belief:

- Almost all the major countries in Asia are undergoing internal political transitions at the levels of both leadership change and societal transformation.

- The continent is faced with a morass of interstate conflicts over unresolved territorial and boundary issues, as well as competing claims to sovereignty.

- Asia at large is increasingly militarized in terms of burgeoning conventional capabilities and new weapons of mass destruction combined with new delivery systems.

- The long-term trend is for the traditional security regime that has maintained order in the Asia-Pacific region to be increasingly at risk.

These trends have five implications for the operations of the U.S. Air Force in Asia:

- Air and space power will remain essential for conventional and unconventional deterrence.

- Air power will become increasingly important for rapid reaction when crises break.

- Both because of and despite improving air capabilities among regional powers, U.S. Air Force assets will still be needed to fill gaps in critical capabilities, such as surveillance and long-range strike.

- Growing political constraints will inhibit en-route and in-theater access in the future.

- "NBC-shadowed" environments will pose new operational challenges to air power.

The Greater Middle East

Our work points toward six broad conclusions about the future security environment in the greater Middle East:

- Future sources of conflict across the Middle East will be more diverse, with shifting centers of gravity in security terms. Air Force planning must anticipate a much broader set of scenarios and missions.

- The resolution of the Arab-Israeli conflict—or its lack of resolution—will remain an important determinant of the future shape of the region.

- Many leading sources of conflict in the region will be intrastate, and security for Middle Eastern regimes will be, above all, a question of internal security. The United States must prepare for the probable loss of major security partners over the next few decades.

- Islam and nationalism will be key political drivers in the evolution of societies and the security environment. Both phenomena will complicate the outlook for security cooperation even short of revolutionary political change.

- Traditional distinctions between security in the Middle East and adjacent regions will erode as Europe and Eurasia are increasingly exposed to the retaliatory and spillover consequences of developments from Morocco to the Gulf.

- Capable niche competitors, wielding weapons of mass destruction and terrorism and employing asymmetric strategies, may well emerge, possibly supported by extraregional powers.

These findings yield the following implications for and constraints on the application of air and space power in the region:

- Persistent regional frictions and high resource stakes—oil and water—together with the limited capacity for self-defense of key allies in the region, suggest that the defense of borders will be a central task for U.S. air and space power. Attention to the low and high ends of the threat continuum—terrorism and weapons of mass destruction—should not obscure the continued relevance of large-scale conventional defense.

- Demographics, political stakes, and the modernization of economies point to the growing importance of cities as centers of crisis and conflict across the region. Beirut in 1982 may be just as important a model for the future of conflict in the Middle East as the desert war in the Gulf.

- Air and space power increasingly will be called upon to attack and defend economic targets and to wage economic warfare more generally. Middle Eastern economic infrastructures are becoming more important and potentially more vulnerable and will thus grow as potential high-leverage targets in future conflicts. Monitoring and enforcing economic sanctions and blockades against rogue regimes will also pose continuing demands for air and space power.

- The Air Force will face high demands for surveillance and reconnaissance across a broad and rapidly changing region.

- The United States will confront mounting tension between continued demands for regional presence and increasingly contentious and constrained relationships with host countries. In many cases, new arrangements for over-the-horizon deterrence will be required.

- Finally, the United States will face greater uncertainty of en-route and in-theater access in crises. Unpredictability of access and overflight argues for consideration of new hedging strategies and a portfolio approach to basing and security cooperation.

Europe and the Former Soviet Union

Europe is most likely to develop into two opposing poles, one formed by the EU in the West and center of the continent, the other consisting of Russia and possibly other countries reintegrated into a Russian sphere of influence. Although there is unlikely to be a West European superpower comparable to the United States today or to the USSR in its prime, Europe is becoming a more cohesive political and economic force.

Specific implications for the U.S. Air Force that would apply to all or most of the alternative strategic worlds include the following:

- With Russia's military in drastic decline, the United States and its allies will enjoy a decisive technological superiority over potential adversaries in Europe. This superiority will be particularly marked with respect to air power.

- NATO expansion and the proliferation of situations in which the United States might have interests without formal commitments (e.g., Bosnia), combined with continued low-level threats and instability, mean that U.S. forces will continue to be needed for conventional deterrence.

- The future situation in Europe will be fluid and will call for greater flexibility on the part of U.S. forces. For example, there might be cases in which U.S. forces could be asked to help deter attacks on countries, such as Bulgaria, in which NATO lacks bases and infrastructure.

- Future military operations and planning in Europe will be heavily influenced by the need to cooperate with allies. At least some of these allies are likely to continue to be increasingly assertive in pressing for enhanced influence in NATO, even though their actual military capabilities may still be modest.

- While Europe may evolve toward a stable West Europe–Russia bipolarity, there will be an unstable gray area between these two regions for a very long time that will be riddled with ethnic and other sources of conflict. The United States will need to maintain its capabilities for peacekeeping and other limited military operations.

- As threats from the south emerge, the United States may be increasingly called upon by its allies and by its own defense requirements to develop effective counterproliferation capabilities and options. Theater missile defense could also become a growing requirement.

* * * * *

We now turn to the first regional study—sources of conflict in Asia.

Chapter Three

SOURCES OF CONFLICT IN ASIA

*Ashley J. Tellis, Chung Min Lee, James Mulvenon,
Courtney Purrington, and Michael D. Swaine*

INTRODUCTION

The Asia-Pacific region is poised to become the new strategic center
of gravity in international politics. This transformation is momentous in world-historical terms in that for the first time since the beginning of modernity—circa 1500—the single largest concentration
of international economic power will be found not in Europe or the
Americas but in Asia. The implications of this development are as
far-reaching as they are poorly understood.

This chapter attempts to come to grips with the impending rise of
Asia insofar as its capacity to generate conflict makes new and increasing demands on U.S. air and space power. It does not describe
the manifold developments that promise to make the next century a
"Pacific century," but rather explores how the very circumstances
that make the rise of Asia so significant can also contribute to the potential for conflict within the continent. Since the United States will
continue to remain an Asian power, and will in fact be forced to engage the political ambitions and power-political capabilities of the
Asian states even more vigorously than it has done thus far, the
manner in which the emerging trends in Asia could lead to various
kinds of conflicts should be of great interest to both U.S. policymakers and strategic planners.

To make the range of issues more manageable, the vast geographic
expanse of the Asian continent has been conceptually divided into
three large "security complexes" for analysis in this chapter. A secu-

rity complex essentially encompasses "a group of states whose primary security concerns link together sufficiently closely that their national securities cannot realistically be considered apart from one another."[1] Understood in this sense, Northeast Asia, Southeast Asia, and South Asia are treated as separate security complexes because the relatively intense security interdependence of the states *within* each grouping makes these units useful for purposes of analysis—at least at the level of first-order approximation. It must be emphasized, however, that dividing Asia into such security complexes is undertaken primarily to ease the task of analysis and not because it is believed that such groupings constitute hermetically sealed agglomerations. In fact, the substantive analysis in the following sections will clearly suggest—and sometimes explicitly argue—that the traditional ways of distinguishing between security complexes have reached the limits of their success. U.S. policymakers ought to recognize that a good deal of instability in Asia will arise because amity and enmity patterns increasingly cross regional boundaries, thanks to the differential rates of economic growth and the availability of new military technologies that permit extended range and enhanced lethality.

This chapter is organized in the following way. First, a broad net assessment attempts to explain the conditions that have led to the rise of Asia; it defines the core U.S. national security interests in the continent; it provides a broad overview of the main trends occurring within Asia as a whole; and it concludes with a survey of the alternative strategic environments in the region, including an assessment of why one particular strategic future—continuing American preponderance—will probably remain the most likely strategic future until the first quarter of the next century.

We next provide more detailed analyses of emerging developments in Northeast Asia (China, Japan, and Korea), Southeast Asia, and South Asia, respectively. Each of these regional or country discussions follows a common format to better engage the core issues affecting political stability and to facilitate cross-regional comparison. Each discussion begins by identifying key current and emerging

---

[1] Barry Buzan, *People, States & Fear,* 2nd edition, Boulder, CO: Lynne Rienner Publishers, 1991, p. 190.

trends that characterize the area in question. The analysis then focuses on identifying specific *drivers* of change that affect the prospects for conflict over the short, medium, and long term. These temporal divisions are roughly defined as the 1997–2005, 2005–2015, and 2015–2025 time periods, respectively. Drawing from the analyzed trends and drivers, the analysis proceeds to identify, in concise form, the major potential *conflicts* that might emerge during these periods. The regional or country sections are thus designed to provide a summary, stand-alone, assessment of the current and future state of each of the major political entities in Asia.

The final section assesses the operational implications for U.S. air and space power flowing from the more detailed regional analyses offered earlier. The analytical treatment of these implications is not organized by region or country, but rather by the characteristic features and demands that are seen to emerge when all the regional contingencies are considered synoptically. This section is intended primarily as a summary statement of the principal features of the operating environment that will confront U.S. air and space power in Asia in the next century. A companion effort undertaken at RAND, which focuses on understanding the implications of this environment for U.S. Air Force acquisition, doctrine, and research and development, will result in a series of more detailed reports on these subjects in the near future.

OVERVIEW

The Asia-Pacific region is poised to become the new strategic center of gravity in international politics. This transformation is momentous in that for most of the modern era the continent subsisted mainly as an arena for Western exploitation and dominance. Asia functioned as the "object" rather than the "subject" of power and, hence, owed not only its political order but oftentimes even the eidetic image of itself to the acts and beliefs of others. Clearly, this was not always the case. Prior to modernity—which for practical purposes might be dated to 1492—and right through its early stages, the Asian continent hosted perhaps the most important concentrations of political power in the international system since the fall of Rome. However, these centers of power—exemplified by the Ming dynasty in China, the Mughal empire in India, and the Persian Empire in the

Near East—failed to survive military contact with the new rising states of Europe (and, later, the Americas).[2] This failure, the reasons for which are still debated in the scholarly literature, resulted in the demise of Asia as a autonomous arena in the international system, a situation that more or less persisted until the end of the Second World War midway in this century.

Explaining the Rise of Asia

Three factors in the postwar period essentially laid the basis for the resurgence of Asia. The first factor was simply the demise of the colonial order and the birth of dozens of new states, which created the possibility of new autonomous centers in international politics. As part of this process, several large entities, such as China, India, and Indonesia, were either restored to independent status or reincarnated in modern form, thus setting the stage for a rekindling of nationalism throughout the continent. The demise of the colonial order, however, was merely a permissive cause. It made the rise of Asia possible but not inevitable. Viewed in retrospect, however, inevitability was ensured by the second and third factors, respectively: the international order created and sustained by American preeminence in the postwar period and the presence of enlightened national elites in various Asian countries who embarked on national economic strategies that would produce sustained economic growth over time.

The new international order created and sustained by the United States remains the most important external cause of the rise of Asia in that it provided two complementary benefits—opportunities for wealth and assured security—which when synergized had explosive systemic effects.

To begin with, this order offered a structured opportunity for the war-torn states such as Japan and the smaller countries such as South Korea, Taiwan, and Singapore, as well as late industrializers such as China to benefit from a stable and open international trading

---

[2]The processes leading to the decline of Asia and the rise of Europe have been explored in William H. McNeill, *The Pursuit of Power*, Chicago: University of Chicago Press, 1982; and Paul Kennedy, *The Rise and Fall of the Great Powers*, New York: Random House, 1987.

regime. The relatively unfettered access enjoyed by these states to the international market, especially the gigantic consuming economies of North America and Western Europe, provided them an opportunity to specialize in accordance with their relative factor endowments and thereby secure the gains from trade that liberal economists have written about since the days of David Ricardo.

In the postwar period, the effective gains that accrued to the various Asian states were even larger than those predicted by the standard neoclassical models of free trade. This was because the United States, confident about its preeminent economic power in the early postwar period, chose not to institute a truly free trade system of the kind usually implied by the phrase. Rather, Washington opened its own markets to Asian products without insisting on a symmetrical openness on the part of Asian exporters, a strategy essentially driven by power-political considerations associated with the Cold War. The fierce competition during this period and the thin margins of safety that the Western allies were seen to possess essentially convinced Washington that strengthening the economic capabilities of its Asian allies and the neutral states in the international system was in America's larger interests. Toward that end, a large international aid program coupled with the development of a less-than-perfectly-free trading system turned out to be a useful solution. It enabled the allies to reinvigorate their capabilities and thereby contribute to the American-led effort to resist the Soviet Union, while allowing the neutral states to strengthen themselves sufficiently to resist both Communist lures and potential penetration efforts that might be mounted by Moscow.

The importance placed on strengthening both allies and neutral states thus combined to create a somewhat asymmetrically open international economic order. The Asian states, accordingly, were free to exploit America's open markets and absorb its vast capital and superior technology, even as they maintained relatively closed economic arrangements at home. While this was certainly not the kind of global institutional structure that would have satisfied any classical liberal, it suited Washington just fine insofar as it provided the United States with a cost-effective means of containing the Soviet Union: It rapidly strengthened the allied and neutral states and allowed them to garner such increases in strength under American alliance management, thereby denying Moscow the opportunity to prey upon the relatively weak and vulnerable clients while simultaneously enlarging the domain of power and influence enjoyed by the United States.

This strategy of encouraging the Asian states (among others) to participate in, and perhaps even exploit, the liberal international economic order was not embarked upon for altruistic reasons. In fact, Washington's calculations were self-interested and centered on preserving and maintaining American preeminence. For this reason, the open international trading order was complemented by the institution of an international political order as well. This political order was built on the foundations of multilateral security alliances in Europe and an interlocking network of bilateral alliances in Asia. In both instances, the object of these alliances was the same, at least in the first instance: to contain the Soviet Union (and, initially, China as well) and preserve Western security and autonomy. In the final instance, however, this alliance system had other, just as useful, effects. By providing an overarching defensive umbrella that structured the United States and its allies in a relationship of super- and subordination, the alliance structure served both to obviate destructive local security competition between the protected states (the bane of regional politics for the last several centuries) and to prevent these client entities from developing the kinds of military capabilities that could one day directly threaten the United States or its extended interests.

This lopsided security relationship was visible in its purest form in Asia—the United States committed itself to guaranteeing allied security without requiring the protected states to make comparable commitments in return. Even those states that were not directly protected, such as China, were shielded just the same, thanks to the positive externalities generated by American deterrence of the Soviet Union. As a result of such arrangements, the United States in effect provided the Asian states with guaranteed security *in tandem with* providing them the opportunities to procure significant gains from trade with minimal reciprocity, at least as far as comparable access to their own markets was concerned. The interaction of these two factors laid the foundations for creating an Asian juggernaut. The fact that security was assured meant that the Asian states could allocate less-than-maximum resources to producing safety, and they could concentrate much more of their national energies on nondefense production than would have been possible in the absence of an American security umbrella. While this result is seen most clearly in the case of Japan, it is nevertheless true in the case of Taiwan and South Korea as well. When these nondefense outputs were then channeled into an open trading system that demanded minimal reciprocity of access, the gains from trade incurred by the Asian exporters only multiplied.

The possibility of profitably participating in the open trading regime, however, required something more than simply an international regime and the security structures that protected it. It required enlightened national elites in Asia itself—elites who would not only recognize the opportunities provided by the U.S.-led international order but were also capable of developing the requisite domestic economic strategies that would help the Asian states get the most out of their participation in the international economic system. The existence of such national elites along substantial portions of the Asian periphery constitutes the third factor that made the rise of Asia possible.

These national elites contributed to the economic miracle in two ways—first, by developing specific national economic strategies that allowed their states to maximize external benefits from the international trading order; second, by developing the appropriate national institutions that allowed for the possibility of constantly "shared growth"[3] rather than repeated, divisive struggles over redistribution.

The national economic strategies devised by Asia's ruling elites centered substantially on maintaining highly regulated domestic market structures—with American acquiescence—which penalized consumption in order to force higher rates of saving. These accumulated savings were then directed to altering the structure of local factor endowments to make advantageous production of more sophisticated goods even more advantageous. As a result of this process, the Asian economies that began their "export-led" growth strategies by producing labor-intensive goods from small- and medium-scale light industries (garments, footwear, plastics, and toys) slowly shifted their attention and resources into process,

---

[3]A good survey of the institutions and techniques underlying this approach can be found in Jose Edgardo Campos and Hilton L. Root, *The Key to the Asian Miracle*, Washington, DC: Brookings Institution, 1996.

intermediate, and heavy industries to produce the electronics, computers, and automobiles that are synonymous with East Asia today.

The structuring of national institutions to allow for "shared growth" turned out to be a critical complement to these "export-led" strategies and reflected the corporatist approach to state-society relations that distinguishes many East Asian states from their Western counterparts. This approach, in effect, relied on the state (as a benign Leviathan) to institute procedural arrangements with critical groups in civil society, such as big business. These arrangements, in turn, helped to integrate weaker, but more numerous, sections of the populace through the development of relatively stable institutions, rules, and procedures that both limited the capriciousness of the state in matters of economic policy and encouraged rapid private economic growth. As part of these structural arrangements, political liberties (in the Western sense) were often traded off for economic rewards; these rewards were distributed not in the form of simple, transitory, entitlements but rather in the more durable form of expanding avenues for mass upward mobility and ongoing "opportunities to reap long-term, lasting benefits from the resulting economic expansion."[4]

---

[4]Campos and Root, p. 2. Unfortunately, the structure of the national arrangements that produced the "Asian miracle" also had certain weaknesses, some of which have become more visible in the context of the recent currency crises in Southeast Asia. All directed economies invariably immunize themselves against the discipline of the market and since the Asian economies, to one degree or another, were products of an effort at engineering growth in support of certain national objectives rather than being arrangements governed predominantly by internal market discipline, it should not be surprising to see occasional episodes of trouble. The recent financial crisis, which at root remains a product of bad lending practices resulting from a sheltered and politicized banking system that operated amidst an endless flow of cheap capital, remains a good example of how structural weaknesses can afflict even an otherwise successfully directed economic order. These problems, however, need to be put in perspective. The currency crisis, while shaking regional confidence, does not imply the end of the Asian miracle so long as the key ingredients that drove the miracle still persist: security provided by the United States; continuing access to global resources, wealth, and markets, especially in the United States; and national elites who, recognizing the nature of the challenge, respond appropriately to the task. Although the last element today may be the scarcest ingredient of all, the current crisis may well turn out to be a useful crisis if it forces the Southeast Asian states to recognize, as one commentary put it, that the Asia-Pacific region today is "entering the brave but infinitely duller world of trade-offs, a world of much harder choices and limited

As long as an Asian state, therefore, had a rational and calculating political leadership and responsive economic institutions, its ability to not only survive but actually thrive was all but assured under the international economic and political regimes created with the intent of maintaining American preeminence.

Assured security and unimpeded access to American markets in the presence of calculating nationalist elites and corporatist structures at home, then, created the Asian miracle. The first two elements of this mixture were produced as part of a deliberate American policy, while the third cluster of elements was tolerated throughout the Cold War as a "lesser evil" that must be permitted to preserve a robust *Pax Americana* capable of defeating the Soviet Union. This "grand strategy" succeeded brilliantly in that it contributed to the collapse of the Soviet Union and the reinvigoration of American allies and important neutral states. But it also produced another less desirable effect over time: the *relative* decline of American power. This phenomenon is often perceived to represent a real, long-term threat to U.S. preeminence, and it is precisely this perception that undergirds several of the more recent American arguments for new "fair trade" regimes as well as greater "burden sharing" in alliance defense. Irrespective of whether these calls are ultimately justified, the fact remains that the grand strategy that so successfully maintained American preeminence throughout the postwar period now threatens to undermine it. The provision of assured security and the traditional refusal to employ the "no-patsy"[5] principle have given rise to a set of new, economically powerful actors such as China and Japan, who could use their emerging economic and military capabilities—under some circumstances—in ways that may not enhance American strategic interests.

This reality by no means constitutes a criticism of U.S. grand strategy during the Cold War. That strategy was in fact appropriate for its

---

possibilities, a world Latin America entered a long time ago." Henny Sender, "Now for the Hard Part," *Far Eastern Economic Review*, September 25, 1997, p. 54.

[5]An excellent discussion of the "no-patsy" principle, which refers to the new demands for reciprocal openness in Asian markets, can be found in Julia Lowell, "The World Trading System in Crisis: The United States, East Asia, and the 'No-Patsy' Principle," in Jonathan D. Pollack and Hyun-Dong Kim (eds.), *East Asia's Potential for Instability and Crisis: Implications for the United States and Korea*, Santa Monica, CA: RAND, 1995, pp. 99–116.

time. It worked just as intended, even if it set in motion forces that could undermine the success of that strategy over the secular period. What is required now, therefore, is not despair about the wrath of some "iron laws of history" but rather a clear understanding of what U.S. interests in the region are today so that potentially unfavorable developments can be discerned before they occur and so that the requisite set of policy countermeasures can be developed to neutralize them in a timely fashion.

Surveying U.S. National Security Interests in Asia

The rise of new Asian powers clearly requires the United States to reflect anew on its core national security interests in the region. These interests will of necessity span many dimensions, but perhaps the best way of concentrating attention is to divide the several goals pursued by the United States into two categories: "vital interests," or those interests that "the people of a nation . . . must defend at the risk of their lives,"[6] and "significant interests," which (while valuable) do not compel quite the same intensity of public commitment.

The United States has three vital interests in Asia. Each is listed below in decreasing order of importance.

The first vital interest is to *prevent, deter, and reduce the threat of attack on the continental United States and its extended territorial possessions.* That this objective constitutes the principal American interest should not be surprising. After all, the state itself exists primarily for the production of internal order and the provision of external security. Preserving the security of the United States against foreign threat constitutes a first, obvious interest even though its remote consequences may not always be either apparent or uncontroversial.

In the simplest sense, this interest has two components. The first and most important involves preserving the continental United States (CONUS) and its possessions from threats posed by weapons of mass destruction (WMD) in Asia. These weapons can inflict extensive damage. The United States must pay careful attention to

---

[6]Walter Lippmann, *U.S. Foreign Policy: Shield of the Republic,* Boston: Little, Brown, 1943, p. 86.

the mature nuclear, biological, and chemical (NBC) warfare programs in Russia and China as well as the evolving programs in North Korea, Pakistan, India, Iran, and Iraq. It is equally important to pay attention to the sophisticated delivery systems, such as ballistic and cruise missiles and advanced attack aircraft, deployed today by the WMD-capable states and to prospective delivery systems that may be acquired by other Asian states over time. This includes spin-off technologies emerging from space and commercial aviation programs as well as other kinds of nontraditional, covert delivery systems.

The second component of this vital interest is to protect the CONUS and its possessions from conventional attack. Because of the vast distances involved in the Asia-Pacific region, this requires paying attention to the power-projection capabilities—both sea and air based—that may be acquired by some of the Asian states. In the time frames considered here, it also requires paying attention to other, newer approaches to conventional war-fighting such as strategic information warfare and the technologies and operational practices associated with the "revolution in military affairs." In all instances, U.S. interests require preventing potential adversaries from acquiring such capabilities; if prevention is impossible, deterring their use becomes the next logical objective; and, if even deterrence is unsuccessful, attenuating their worst effects through either extended counterforce options or effective defensive measures finally becomes necessary.

The second vital interest is to *prevent the rise of a hegemonic state in Asia.* Any hegemonic state capable of dominating the Asian land mass and the lines of communication, both internal and external, represents an unacceptable challenge to the safety, prosperity, and power position of the United States. For reasons well understood by geopoliticians since Sir Halford Mackinder, Asia's great wealth and resources would serve its possessors well in the struggles endemic to international politics. If the region's wealth and resources were secured by any single state (or some combination of states acting in unison), it would enable this entity to threaten American assets in Asia and, more problematically, in other areas such as the Middle East, and finally perhaps to challenge the United States itself at a global level. This entity, using the continent's vast resources and economic capabilities, could then effectively interdict the links presently connecting the United States with Asia and the rest of the world and, in the limiting case, menace the CONUS itself through a combination of both WMD and conventional instruments.

Besides being a threat to American safety, a hegemonic domination of Asia by one of the region's powers would threaten American prosperity—if the consequence of such domination included denying the United States access to the continent's markets, goods, capital, and technology. In combination, this threat to American safety and prosperity would have the inevitable effect of threatening the relative power position of the United States in international politics. For these reasons, preventing the rise of a hegemonic center of power in Asia—especially one disposed to impeding American economic, political, and military access—would rank as a vital interest second only to preserving the physical security of the United States and its extended possessions.

This interest inevitably involves paying close attention to the possible power transitions in the region, especially those relating to China in the near-to-medium term and to Japan, Russia, and possibly India over the long term. In any event, it requires developing an appropriate set of policy responses—which may range from containment at one end all the way to appeasement at the other—designed to prevent the rise of any hegemony that obstructs continued American connectivity with Asia.

The third vital interest is to *ensure the survival of American allies*—critical for a number of reasons. The first and most obvious reason is that the United States has treaty obligations to two important Asian states, Japan and South Korea. While meeting these obligations is necessary to maintain the credibility of the United States in the international arena, it is consequential for directly substantive reasons as well. In both instances, the assurance of U.S. protection has resulted in implicit bargains that are indispensable to the American conception of stable international order. Thanks to American security guarantees, South Korea and Japan have both enjoyed the luxury of eschewing nuclear weapons as guarantors of security. Should American protective pledges be seen as weakening, the temptation on the part of both states to resurrect the nuclear option will increase—to the consequent detriment of America's global antiproliferation policy.

Equally significant, however, is that Japan, and possibly South Korea as well, would of necessity have to embark on a significant conventional build-up, especially of maritime and air forces. The resulting force posture would in practice be indistinguishable from a long-range power-projection capability possessing offensive orientation. Even if such forces are developed primarily for defensive purposes, they will certainly give rise to new security dilemmas regionwide that in turn would lead to intensive arms-racing, growing suspicions, and possibly war.

What is finally problematic with this sequence of events is that even the least troublesome of these possibilities would result in the destruction of the East Asian "miracle." While such an outcome would certainly affect the strategic prospects of the East Asian region, the United States would not by any means be immune to its extended consequences. Since a considerable portion of American growth is directly tied to the vitality of the international trading system, the enervation of the East Asian economic regime would eventually lead to a diminution of American growth rates and, by implication, the quality of life enjoyed by its citizenry. For all these reasons, ensuring the survival of American allies in Asia represents a vital interest to the United States, an interest grounded less in altruistic considerations than in the hard realities of self-interest.

Promoting this interest requires that the United States pay close attention to the evolution of the threats facing its allies in Asia and take steps to meet such challenges expeditiously and after due consultation with the allied states. Ensuring allied security also involves paying requisite attention to the needs of those other states (mostly in Southeast Asia) that do not have treaty obligations with the United States but nonetheless rely on the U.S. presence in Asia for security. And, in the most demanding extension of all, ensuring allied security also requires that the United States be attentive to the prospect of securing new allies, especially because the imminence of regional power transitions may imply that today's allies—formal and informal—may not be friends tomorrow.

Besides these three vital U.S. interests in Asia, interests which should not only sustain American concentration but also engender a willingness to expend blood and treasure, it is possible to identify three other significant interests that merit attention on the part of policy-makers and planners.

The first such significant interest involves *preventing, minimizing, or neutralizing the proliferation of weapons of mass destruction and their associated delivery systems in Asia.* There is little doubt that WMD represent the principal means by which national security can be threatened on a large scale. Because these weapons can cause great damage in fairly compressed time frames, American policy has generally sought to prevent the further proliferation of these weapons and the systems used to deliver them. The emphasis is correct and ought to be continued even though there *may* be rare exceptions when regional security may actually be enhanced by tolerating some level of proliferation.

The Indian subcontinent may be one such example and, if so, it should be treated as truly the exception that tests the rule. The South Asian region constitutes an arena where high systemic insecurities coincide with few palpable American interests. As a result, the United States has few incentives to make the security commitments that might obviate the desire of the regional states for nuclear weapons. Nuclear weapons, therefore, might offer some modicum of security, but even if they do not, the United States has relatively little leverage to alter the prevailing trends in this area of the world. The challenge for the United States in this instance is twofold. On one hand, it may find it worthwhile to tolerate some movement on the part of the South Asian states toward low but relatively stable levels of nuclearization, *if that is seen to enhance local stability.* On the other hand, such toleration must not be allowed to impede larger U.S. antiproliferation policy either by increasing the level of laxity displayed toward the general problem or by hasty conclusions about antiproliferation strategies having reached the limits of their success before such judgments are truly warranted. In any event, tolerating a nuclear South Asia as the exception remains a significant U.S. interest in Asia, particularly because Southeast and Inner Asia as well as the Near East may confront similar problems in the distant future.

The second significant interest involves *preventing and possibly ending the outbreak of major war in high-risk areas.* Because national security is generally indivisible, a fact captured by the phrase "anarchy is seamless," an important American objective in

Asia should be the prevention or termination of major conflicts, whenever possible. This interest applies even in those areas where American interests may not be directly engaged by a local conflict. The rationale for U.S. activity with respect to prevention or termination of conflict in these cases in *not* merely humanitarian, though such considerations may well exist. Rather, it is first and foremost power-political. All conflicts have "demonstration" and "contagion" effects. The former refers to those effects that provide inspiration for future behavior as, for example, when Saddam Hussein's unfettered use of chemical weapons (CW) against the Kurds presaged both the later use of CW in the Iran-Iraq war and the current efforts at acquiring such weapons on the part of Iran. The latter refers to those advertent and inadvertent effects that may be precipitated in *third* countries as a result of war between two others—for example, when Palestinian pressure groups in Jordan effectively constricted Jordan's strategic choices after the successful Iraqi invasion of Kuwait. If one or more of such effects are seen to have consequences that imperil some long-range U.S. interests in the continent, it may be worth at least some investment of U.S. diplomatic energy and resources to prevent the wars that could give rise to such consequences.

Preventing or ending the outbreak of "distant wars" may also be worthwhile for other reasons. For one, a conflict could change the local balance of power in a given area *down the line*. Thus, even if a conflict does not engage U.S. interests or the interests of its allies immediately, American attention and possibly intervention—by diplomatic or other means—may still be warranted if the outbreak or persistence of such conflict threatens to tilt the local balance of power to the disadvantage of the United States at some future point in time. A Sino-Indian conflict or a renewed Iran-Iraqi war would be pertinent examples in this regard. Another important case where U.S. intervention may be warranted is when conflict between two third countries threatens to involve WMD. Here, a breakdown of the evolving taboo against WMD use as well as the pernicious demonstration effects that would surely accrue from successful WMD use remain sufficient reason for speedy U.S. efforts at preventing (or, if prevention is unsuccessful, rapidly terminating) such conflicts even if no tangible American interests are seen to be immediately at risk.

An Indo-Pakistani war would be the best example of such a possibility.

The third significant American interest in Asia is *sustaining political stability of key regional countries and promoting democratization whenever possible.* There is a compelling argument to be made for focusing American attention, resources, and support on a few key "pivotal states"[7] rather than on whole swaths of territory indiscriminately. Pivotal states are important states "whose fate is uncertain and whose future will profoundly affect their surrounding regions."[8] By this definition, it is clear that the Asian continent hosts the largest number of pivotal states—Russia, China, and Japan among the more developed countries and India, Pakistan, and Indonesia among the developing tier. The former category is noteworthy for obvious reasons: Russia continues to be a nuclear power of consequence; China is a rising state that not only possesses nuclear weapons but will probably be the world's largest economic power sometime in the next century; and Japan is not only an American ally but a significant trading state, the center for technological innovation in Asia, and the fulcrum for any policy of effectively managing China. The latter category is important for less-well-understood reasons. Pakistan and India are both nuclear-capable states: While the former may affect the global balance "if only by collapsing,"[9] the latter stands poised to become the world's fourth largest economy early in the next century. Indonesia is not only a large and populous state whose stability conditions the entire fate of Southeast Asia; it also lies astride the critical chokepoints that control transit from the oil-rich Southwest Asian states to the energy-hungry economies of East Asia. Every one of these states—in both categories—faces an uncertain future, yet each is in different ways "so important regionally that its collapse would spell transboundary mayhem" on one hand, while "its progress and stability would bolster its region's economic vitality and political soundness"[10] on the other hand.

---

[7]Robert S. Chase et al., "Pivotal States and U.S. Strategy," *Foreign Affairs,* Vol. 75, No. 1, January–February 1996, pp. 33–51.

[8]Chase et al., p. 33.

[9]Stephen P. Cohen, "Pakistan," in Edward A. Kolodziej and Robert E. Harkavy (eds.), *Security Policies of Developing Countries,* Lexington, MA: Lexington Books, 1982, p. 94.

[10]Chase et al., 37.

The issue of promoting democratization both in these states and outside them remains dear to the liberal world view within the United States. Yet the effect of democracy for ensuring international stability is murky and, at any rate, not sufficiently well understood. For this reason, the goal of promoting democracy—when pursued as part of American *foreign policy*—should not be absolutized, but rather should be tested like any other strategic goal. That is, its potential costs and benefits should be assessed against comparable values associated with other competing or complementary policies.

Key Structural Trends in the Asian Region

Having identified what are (or should be) the vital and the significant U.S. national security interests in Asia, we next focus on identifying the key structural trends the continent exhibits as whole. Understanding these trends is critical because they point to the kinds of challenges that will confront those American strategic interests identified previously. Equally important, they condition the kinds of conflicts that the continent may be expected to witness, all of which are identified in each of the subregional or country sections following this overview and detailed in the appendix.

The structural trends in Asia that should concern the United States can be summarized in two propositions. First, the Asia-Pacific region will become the largest and perhaps the most important concentration of economic power in the next century both as far as the United States is concerned and on its own terms. Second, despite its formidable economic power, the Asia-Pacific region will remain a relatively turbulent region beset by internal conflicts and political transitions and subject to persistent insecurity flowing from a changing external environment and new kinds of military technologies.

The proposition that *the Asia-Pacific region will become the largest and perhaps the most important concentration of economic power in the next century* is justified by four constituent trends.

First, the region is characterized by some of the highest rates of sustained economic growth in modern history, rates that are likely to remain at relatively high levels for at least another two decades. So long as the region does not experience a major war that disrupts both trade and domestic growth, and so long as the stabilizing effects of American regional presence more or less persist, it is likely that the region as a whole will continue to average growth rates in the region of 6–8 percent annually. With the exception of Japan, which, as a mature economy, will grow at about 2.5 percent, the four "tigers"— Hong Kong, Singapore, South Korea, and Taiwan—are expected to grow at about 6.5 percent, the Association of Southeast Asian Nations (ASEAN) states at about 8 percent, and even the late industrializers— China, India, and Vietnam—are expected to grow at between 6.5 percent and 7.5 percent over the next two decades.[11]

Such growth rates suggest that by the year 2010, the East Asian region alone will account for over 34 percent of the world's total output, with Western Europe and North America following with 26 percent and 25 percent respectively. If the output of the South Asian subregion is added to the East Asian total, the share of Asian output rises even more—closer to 40 percent—relative to Western Europe and North America. The data for world trade show similar Asian dominance. East Asia alone is expected to contribute almost 40 percent of the world's trade, with Western Europe and North America following with about 37 percent and 20 percent, respectively.[12] This high sustained growth will continue to be fueled by high rates of domestic savings, increased intra-Asian economic integration, increasing investment in infrastructure and human capital, a decreasing rate of population growth, and continuing export-led growth.

Second, the wealth and prosperity of the United States will remain dependent on continued linkages with the Asian economies. The Asian continent today represents the most important locus of American economic engagement. The 1993 data for merchandise trade, for example, show that the United States imports over 42 percent of its goods from the Asia-Pacific region, in contrast to about 20 percent

---

[11]International Monetary Fund, *World Economic Outlook*, Washington, D.C.: IMF, May 1994. Although these forecasts were developed prior to the current financial crisis in East Asia, there is little reason to doubt the validity of these projections *over the secular period.* In fact, to the degree that the current crisis provides an opportunity for the regional states to reform their financial sectors in an orderly fashion (perhaps under the aegis of external supervision), their prospects for robust growth over the long term will only be enhanced.

[12]Noordin Sopiee, "The Revolution in East Asia," *Strategic Analysis*, Vol. 19, No. 1, April 1996, pp. 5–25.

from Europe, about 19 percent from Canada, about 12 percent from the rest of North America, and about 5 percent from the rest of the world. The story is similarly revealing where merchandise exports are concerned. The Asia-Pacific region accounts for about 30 percent of American merchandise exports; Europe accounts for about 25 percent, Canada for about 21 percent, the rest of the Americas for about 16 percent, with the rest of the world accounting for about 5.6 percent of the total. When trade in invisibles and services is considered, a similar picture emerges: the Asia-Pacific region remains the single most important destination for the United States, a fact reflected by the data in Tables 5 and 6 below.

The Asia-Pacific region will also remain the most important arena for the export of American services as well as for direct investments in the oil, natural gas, minerals, and forestry industries. U.S. investments in infrastructure and advanced consumer goods will increase, and, thanks to the higher rates of return from investments in Asia (relative to the United States and Europe), the Asia-Pacific region will become increasingly important for U.S. manufacturing as well,

Table 5

U.S. Invisibles Trade by Region
(1995 flows in U.S. $ millions)

Region	Imports	Exports	Balance
Asia-Pacific	152	417	+265
Japan	154	225	+71
Hong Kong, Taiwan, Korea, and Singapore	98	268	+170
China	–2	23	+25
Australia and New Zealand	47	57	+10
Others in Asia-Pacific	4	18	+14
Europe	1,707	221	–1,486
Canada	565	487	–78
Mexico, Central and South America	1,838	193	–1,645
All other nations and international organizations	214	58	–156
World total	4,777	1,967	–2,810

SOURCE: *Survey of Current Business, November 1996*, United States Department of Commerce (compiled by the Bureau of the Census, Bureau of Foreign and Domestic Commerce, Bureau of Standards), Washington, D.C., 1996.

Table 6

**U.S. Services Trade by Region
(1995 flows in U.S. $ millions)**

Region	Imports	Exports	Balance
Asia-Pacific	122,479	145,579	+23,100
Japan	15,607	32,610	+17,003
Hong Kong, Taiwan, Korea, and Singapore	80,038	63,322	–16,716
China	NA	NA	NA
Australia and New Zealand	2,110	4,271	+2,161
Others in Asia-Pacific	24,724	45,376	+20,652
Western Europe	57,783	71,281	+13,498
Canada	12,605	18,129	+5,524
Mexico, Central and South America	25,013	30,825	+5,812
All other nations	NA	NA	NA
World total	NA	NA	NA

SOURCE: *Survey of Current Business, November 1996,* United States Department of Commerce (compiled by the Bureau of the Census, Bureau of Foreign and Domestic Commerce, Bureau of Standards), Washington, D.C., 1996.

particularly in the electronics and automobile industries. In summary, the Asia-Pacific region will be critical for U.S. prosperity, even as it will continue to function as the reason for both an increasing balance of trade and payments deficit and a steadily depreciating dollar.

Third, both China and Japan will become alternative centers of power in economic as well as military terms, with the former emerging as a potential peer competitor to the United States over the secular period. Both the Chinese and Japanese economies are already large and dominate the continent in many ways. Over the last two decades, Japan has initiated a makeover in its economy in an attempt to reduce the traditional structural vulnerabilities of its export-led growth. Investments have been directed at home in an effort to secure productivity increases, while assembly and manufacture in the United States has gradually edged out the previous emphasis on distribution. Japan has also sharply increased investments and foreign aid in the ASEAN region and within the East Asian "tigers" in an effort to gain cost advantages as well as to reduce vulnerability. All these efforts have resulted in the appearance of a Japanese economic dominance of East Asia, but the visible consequences notwithstanding, the Japanese state remains hobbled by deep structural disadvantages. It continues to depend on external rather than internal markets, which means that its economic vitality is always dependent on good political relations with its trading partners.

China, however, will not be burdened by such constraints over the long run. Though currently dependent on export-led growth for its prosperity, it has the requisite population and natural resources (except for fossil fuels) at home to sustain autonomous economic expansion over the longer term. For this reason, Chinese military capabilities will be more consequential than Japan's over the secular period, despite the fact that Japan today has the third largest military budget in the world. Japanese military forces today are unbalanced and even when fully developed will have to operate under the aegis of the United States if Japan seeks to maintain both continued access to its world markets and its newfound military power. China, in contrast, faces no such constraints over the long term and, hence, could become a true peer competitor of the United States in a way that Japan could not.

Fourth, the Asia-Pacific region is home to a large and increasing concentration of technological capabilities with some emerging centers of high-technology excellence. It is clearly important to recognize that the Asia-Pacific region does not host the merely labor-dominant economies of yesteryear. Increasingly, the Asian economies are becoming significant producers in a wide range of high-technology industries, and their dominance is most manifest in intermediate technologies. Today, Japan is the continent's most technologically "complete" state in that its domestic base is both comprehensive and deep. Even Japan, however, does not focus predominantly on conducting basic research and achieving raw ideational breakthroughs as do Europe and the United States. Rather, the emphasis is still (although this is changing) on applied research, with a view to commercializing basic science and technology (S&T) breakthroughs for a mass market. The other Asian states lag even further behind, but the trends toward greater incorporation of medium and high technology are evident.

These trends will gather steam over time for a variety of reasons. To begin with, the increasingly high cost of labor amid diminishing population growth rates has created greater incentives for producers to substitute high technology—either imported or home grown—for labor as means of reducing cost and enhancing productivity. Further, the relatively high saturation of European and American markets has led many Western corporations to trade their high technology for the right to participate in Asia's rapid growth, thereby leading to speedier technology diffusion than might have occurred otherwise. And, finally, the Asian states have increasingly begun investing in human capital and enhanced R&D efforts at home: more and more Asian students receive advanced degrees in the sciences from the United States; the Asian economies are increasingly investing in technical higher education; and Asian universities are consistently graduating a much larger fraction of science and engineering graduates in comparison to the United States. These trends taken cumulatively are not meant to suggest that the Asian economies are poised to overtake the Western economies as centers of leading-edge S&T. Rather, the processes of technology diffusion have reached the point where Asia is no longer synonymous with a labor-intensive economic regime, and technology surprises, especially in certain niche areas and in the military realm, are increasingly probable. It should not be startling, therefore, that Japan, for example, already feels confident about developing a stealth fighter as a follow-on to its Rising Sun (FSX) fighter; that India already casts the largest solid-fuel rockets outside the United States and Russia; and that China has already begun intensive efforts to assess how the "revolution in military affairs" might enable it to attain sophisticated military capabilities more rapidly.

Similarly, the proposition that *despite its formidable economic power, the Asia-Pacific region will remain a relatively turbulent region beset by internal conflicts and political transitions and will experience persistent insecurity flowing both from a changing external environment and new kinds of military technologies* can be decomposed into four constituent trends.

First, almost all the major countries of Asia are undergoing internal political transitions in both leadership change and societal transformation. It is rare in human history that such dramatic transitions have occurred synchronically within a given region, but the Asian continent appears to be on the cusp of precisely such a wrenching transformation. China, for example, is experiencing a transition from the traditional form of command politics to a new, yet to be institutionalized, pattern of logrolling and strategic bargaining at the national level. This transformation coincides with the disappearance of the founding generation that created the modern communist state. Even as these patterns evolve, China is completing the first phase of its transition to a modern market economy wherein purely entrepreneurial capitalism must give way to more institutionally ordered forms of market behavior if its economic transformation is to be successfully completed.

Japan appears poised to undergo a transformation of almost similar magnitude, and its long-term effects are perhaps just as uncertain as the Chinese experiment. The era of one-party dominance seems to have come to an end. What the new form of parliamentary democracy will bring cannot be clearly discerned, except that neo-mercantilist growth strategies appear to be well and alive, at least for now. While the commitment to the U.S.-Japan Security Treaty appears to be fairly robust at present—in part because of the progressive adjustments made to the structure of U.S.-Japanese treaty obligations—the best analysis suggests that the current domestic realignment process "could also lay the foundations for repolarization by permitting the rise of a stridently nationalistic force, especially in the context of deteriorating economic relations with the United States."[13] Over the long term, therefore, the rise of a real participatory democracy as opposed to a bureaucratically dominant state would reopen difficult questions on the nature of Japan's national economic strategy, the character of relations with China and Korea, and the future of security ties with the United States, including the relevance of nuclear weaponry.

Russia and South Korea are also undergoing similar transitions. Russia is struggling with its transformation to a Western-style democracy even as it attempts to restructure its economy from the command model to new market structures. Given its large nuclear arsenal and its significant latent power capacity, the direction determined by

---

[13]M. M. Mochizuki, *Japan: Domestic Change and Foreign Policy*, Santa Monica, CA: RAND, 1995, p. xiv.

domestic Russian politics will shape the environment both in Europe and Asia. The Korean transition is perhaps less momentous in contrast but certainly just as complicated. South Korea is attempting to complete the transition from an authoritarian past to new institutionalized patterns of democratic rule in the face of continued threats of war from the North. The North itself increasingly faces the prospect of decay and possibly even a precipitous meltdown that may result in highly provocative international behavior and perhaps even war involving nuclear brandishing and, in the limiting case, nuclear use. The Korean peninsula thus appears to face the challenge of reunification in some form down the line, a political transition that only coincides with the rise of a new generation of Koreans who, having enjoyed prosperity and peace, now urgently clamor for new political arrangements that offer greater autonomy, freedom, and life outside of ties with the United States.

In the developing world, the transitions are similarly conspicuous and just as pronounced. Pakistan, India, and Indonesia are all experiencing profound leadership and societal changes. In each case, the founding generation is on the verge of passing away; there are increasingly clamorous calls for effective mass political participation; and all three states are making the transition from relatively controlled economic institutions to new market structures.

Second, the continent at large is faced with a morass of interstate conflicts over unresolved territorial and boundary issues as well as competing claims to sovereignty. This trend is not surprising given that most of the political entities in Asia inherited boundary disputes that often date back to the colonial era. These disputes have thus far remained unresolved only because the Asian states were relatively weak for most of the postwar period. In any event, the Cold War resulted in an enforced "pacification" of these disputes, even when these contentions might have been resolved in any given case. On both counts today, these constraining conditions have disappeared. The end of the Cold War has resulted in the demise of all systemic restraints, and the newly generated wealth in Asia has provided its possessors with even greater capabilities to attempt to enforce their claims. Not surprisingly, then, the specter of unresolved disputes leading to armed conflict once again stalks the Asian continent.

The spatial extent of these disputes is just as disconcerting as their intensity, because each country in almost every major dyad in Asia either mounts its own or is faced by territorial claims. With the exception of the North-South Korea dispute, which is more a quarrel about who rules over a certain territory than about territory per se, all major and several minor actors are embroiled in territorial or sovereignty disputes. These include the Sino-Japanese dispute over the Senkaku Islands; the Russo-Japanese disputes over the Northern Territories and the Kuriles; the Sino-Russian disputes over the Inner Asian boundary; the Sino-Indian border dispute over the Aksai Chin and the northeastern territories; the Indo-Pakistani dispute over Kashmir; the Chinese-Southeast Asian dispute over the Spratly Islands; and the sovereignty disputes over the Southeast Asian straits. The political dimensions of these claims in many instances are reinforced by the perceived economic value of the territory in question: As competition for resources becomes more critical, the salience of these disputes will only increase, even though—mercifully—most of these disputes appear to be placed on the back burner at the moment.

Third, the Asian continent at large is witnessing an increased militarization in the form of burgeoning conventional capabilities and new weapons of mass destruction together with associated delivery systems. The increased availability of wealth, rising fears about changing regional power capabilities, growing perceptions of long-term American disengagement, and the increasing incidence of boundary and sovereignty disputes are among the reasons why the Asia-Pacific region has witnessed growing arms procurement and force structure changes in recent years. Whereas the Indian subcontinent led the way in this regard during the 1980s, the locus of activity has shifted to East Asia proper during the 1990s. The rate of change has been truly astonishing, as is evident from the fact that between 1987 and 1992, defense expenditures grew by 125 percent in Malaysia, by about 100 percent in Singapore, by about 70 percent in Thailand, and by about 50 percent in the Philippines. China, too, continues its program of military modernization and is estimated to have increased its military expenditures by well over 10 percent per annum since 1990, with an intention of sustaining such increases throughout the 1990s.[14]

Increased military expenditures are only one aspect of Asia's militarization. Another interesting development centers on changing force structures and strategic orientation. Unlike the postwar period, when regional actors focused mainly on countering landward threats in close proximity to their international borders, the new focus of Asia's military modernization is on countering open-ocean contingencies some distance removed from the land boundaries of the contesting states. Thus, China has acquired new long-range air superiority aircraft such as the Su-27 together with production technologies, and it seeks air-to-air refueling capabilities even as it contemplates acquiring organic afloat aviation in the form of aircraft carriers. The Japanese have acquired potent anti-air warfare platforms built around the Aegis SPY-1 radar and threat management system, combined with new fighter ground-attack aircraft such as the Rising Sun. Malaysia has acquired new air combat aircraft such as the MiG-29 and the F-18 Hornet, together with the first active radar air-to-air missiles in Asia (the AIM-120); Thailand has acquired a vertical/short takeoff and landing (V/STOL) aircraft carrier; and Taiwan is in the process of acquiring new air combat aircraft such as the F-16 and the Mirage 2000 together with new sea denial capabilities centered on diesel-electric submarines. In South Asia, India is slated to acquire a contingent of nuclear-powered attack submarines, while Pakistan is already integrating new diesel-electric submarines which, in another Asian first, will be refitted with conventional air independent propulsion systems.[15]

The new maritime orientation in Asia is complemented by further distension in WMD capabilities. China is already a nuclear power, and India and Pakistan have active nuclear programs and have declined to join either the 1967 Nuclear Nonproliferation Treaty or the

---

[14]For a survey of these developments, see Desmond Ball, "Arms and Affluence: Military Acquisitions in the Asia-Pacific Region," *International Security*, Vol. 18, No. 3 (Winter 1993/1994), pp. 78–112.

[15]A discussion of which military technologies in East Asia are truly "destabilizing" can be found in Ashley J. Tellis, "Military Technology Acquisition and Regional Stability in East Asia," in Jonathan D. Pollack and Hyun-Dong Kim (eds.), *East Asia's Potential for Instability and Crisis*, Santa Monica, CA: RAND, 1995, pp. 43–73.

Comprehensive Test Ban Treaty. These three states have both air-breathing and tactical ballistic missile delivery systems either operational or close to it. China's mature strategic nuclear capabilities are being increasingly supplemented by new theater and tactical nuclear systems. In the wings are increasing numbers of potential nuclear states such as Japan, South Korea, and Taiwan. A substantial number of Asian states are also suspected of pursuing chemical and biological weapons programs. Iraq, Iran, Syria, Taiwan, North Korea, Vietnam, Myanmar, China, Pakistan, South Korea, India, Indonesia, Afghanistan, Thailand, and the Philippines have been identified at one time or another as seeking chemical weapons (CW) capabilities, while Iraq, Iran, Syria, Taiwan, North Korea, Vietnam, China, Pakistan, India, and Laos have been accused of pursuing biological capabilities as well.[16]

Fourth, the inevitable long-term trend is that the traditional security regime that maintained order in the Asia-Pacific region will be increasingly at risk. This outcome is perhaps likely given the growing Asian wealth, military capabilities, and self-confidence conjoined with the relative decline of American power. Both traditional U.S. allies—South Korea and Japan—will seek to revise the terms of their security arrangements. Important Japanese elites have already issued calls for a new, more "normal," Japan, while the South Koreans have held off similar calls for revision only because final closure on the reunification issue has not been achieved. China has already begun displaying increasing ambiguity about the desirability of future U.S. involvement in Asia, while other rising powers such as India have not displayed any compensating interest in moving under a U.S.-led security umbrella. The Southeast Asian states have been the most vocal champions of U.S. presence in the region thus far (though unwilling to act as hosts), but there is no evidence that such encouragement will continue after the Chinese rise to ascendancy is complete or that the Southeast Asian states would matter very much if major allies like Japan and South Korea lose faith in American guarantees.

---

[16]U.S. Congress, Office of Technology Assessment, *Proliferation of Weapons of Mass Destruction: Asssessing the Risks*, Washington DC: U.S. Government Printing Office, 1993.

What do these trends, viewed cumulatively, imply for the United States? The Asian states will constitute the new core concentration of economic power in the international system for the first time since the rise of the modern era. This event may also presage a much more consequential development when viewed against the larger canvas of global history: It may signal the beginning of the end of Western pre-eminence and a return to the earlier condition when the European subsystem was simply one of several regional concentrations of political-military power. Irrespective of whether this outcome eventually obtains, the fact remains that the United States (and Europe) will experience further relative decline in the future just as Asia will experience further growth in political and economic power. This in turn implies that the Asia of tomorrow—if it successfully completes its internal evolution—will be a more confident entity, harder to influence and control, and much more aware of its own uniqueness and identity. The Asian states will seek to transform some of their new-found capabilities into instrumentalities that bequeath them greater control over their own destinies, even if in the final analysis a truly autarkic existence is neither possible nor desired.

This transformation will be, by most current indications, difficult for the United States. Perhaps the greatest challenge will be simply ideational, that is, getting American policymakers and security managers—many of whom, after all, are linked to Europe by historical experience, cultural affinity, and ideological predilection—to recognize that the strategic center of gravity in international politics may be steadily shifting from a familiar and recognizable direction to a "brave new world" with different languages, cultures, and belief systems that share less with the West than is usually expected.

Prognosticating the Strategic Future

The coming transformation of Asia is real, but until the year 2025 it is likely that the international political universe will still be defined by the United States as the single most important actor in global politics. American hegemony, as manifested in the period after World War II, will probably disappear, but the United States will still remain preponderant with the most balanced set of political, economic, and military capabilities among all states. This conclusion appears counterintuitive, given previous discussion about Asian trends and the rising power of the continent. But the major Asian states individually still face considerable constraints on their ability to translate economic strength into politically usable power even though they will, as a bloc, have grown faster relative to Europe and North America and will constitute the largest single economic unit in the international system. This conclusion becomes salient when the causal drivers, the range of strategic possibilities, and the limitations facing the individual Asian states are sketched out.

Understanding the prospects for the triumph of certain strategic futures over others requires an understanding of the drivers—or the causes—that enable such triumph. In the Asian continent, it is possible to identify five such drivers.

The first driver will be the future U.S. role in Asia. Because the rise of Asia is itself a complex product of American preeminence, and because its prognosticated growth rates all implicitly assume that the global trading order and local peace will continue indefinitely, the choices made by the United States with respect to its global leadership will fundamentally determine the future of Asia. This of necessity will include decisions pertaining to preserving regional security (including that in Asia) and sustaining the international trading order (on which continued Asian prosperity depends so much).

The second driver will be the success of domestic transformations in the key Asian states. This variable will determine the nature of the international political objectives sought by the rising Asian powers as well as the levels of efficiency produced in their own economic institutions. It will also affect the changing patterns of state-society relations in each of the major Asian states and that, in turn, will condition the ability of elites to expand their state's power in the face of other domestic claims on national resources.

The third driver will be the kind of indigenous technological capabilities developed in Asia. This variable will determine how much the Asian states will depend on the United States and the rest of the world. It will also condition the range of threats that various Asian states can mount against one other, against American forces and facilities in the theater, and, ultimately, against the United States itself.

The fourth driver will be the extent, kind, and pace of WMD and strategic conventional technology diffusion in Asia. Because WMD and strategic conventional technologies hold the promise of providing political autonomy as well increasing the levels of threat perceived by others, this variable will be significant in conditioning the future of Asia as a political space. It will also affect the success of America's global antiproliferation policy and its conceptions of an ordered international system in general.

The fifth driver will be the political relations between the major Asian states. The relations between Russia and China, China and Japan, Russia and India, China and India, Russia and Japan, and Japan and India will be critical determinants of the future political order in Asia. The character of these relationships will determine whether Asia can become a more-or-less autonomous order-producing entity either through collective security arrangements or common ideational orientation, or through continental or maritime alignments that produce peace through a balance of power (which may require support from external actors for its success).

These five drivers taken together will determine which of the four principal alternate strategic futures facing Asia comes about. These futures are (1) continued American hegemony or Pax Americana; (2) American preponderance, but not hegemony, in the context of new, multiple, regional power centers; (3) regional dominance (either Sino- or Japan-centric) in competition with the U.S.; and (4) regional collective security arrangements with no U.S. participation.

It is quite likely that current American hegemony, a carryover since World War II, will persist in some form or another until 2015 or thereabouts. Thereafter, and most likely for at least another decade, the current preeminence could give way to a new strategic environment defined by American preponderance in the context of the new, multiple, rising regional power centers in Asia. Over the longer term—*if current trends hold*—Chinese regional dominance in the continental arena, coupled with systemic challenges at the global level, would slowly become manifest: This would in effect imply that China now functions as true peer competitor of the United States. What is simply unlikely at any point is the fourth possibility— regional collective security arrangements with no U.S. participation—because continuing rivalries between the Asian powers coupled with more continuity than change in international politics imply that a liberal Kantian order is all but ruled out in the region.

The second future—American preponderance—appears most likely as an alternative to current U.S. hegemony because broad domestic support for continued American primacy will ensure that the United States will make the necessary adjustments to maintain its preponderance—even as the Asian powers continue to be stymied by multiple constraints. China, for example, seeks respect and security and will continue to acquire the appurtenances necessary for them, but any manifest exercise of such power will provoke a continent-wide balancing that would negate its nascent efforts at producing regional primacy. Moreover, the vast magnitude of its domestic demands will ensure that the bulk of its state resources will be allocated to developmental rather than power-political objectives for at least another couple of decades. Japan is in many ways a poor candidate for regional dominance. The historical evidence suggests that no trading state can ever maintain primacy in competition with large continental-sized states unless it has a secure empire it calls its own. Japan not only has no such empire today, it also has substantial resource constraints. Even those resources it does possess—skilled labor and large capital surpluses—are dependent on secure access to overseas markets that cannot be guaranteed by Japan's own military capabilities for both historical and practical reasons. India is certainly an actor of potential importance. Before it obtains anything more than local dominance, however, it will have to demonstrate a capacity for more highly sustained growth rates than its historical record justifies. And, it will have to service its vast developmental responsibilities, just like China, before it can confidently embark on any continental role. For these reasons, the rise of India as a true Asian great power—one that marries political confidence with robust economic growth and significant power-projection ability—is several decades away at best.

Thanks to such constraints, the United States will continue to dominate the global international system, but as a preponderant power over the truly long term (beyond 2025) rather than as the hegemonic state it is today. While Asia will be stronger than it is currently, it will still not be strong enough either collectively or in the form of a single dominant Asian state at least until 2015 and possibly until 2025. The relative weakness of Asia can then be summarized as a function of three particular characteristics: (1) the specific constraints facing each major Asian state; (2) the continuing rivalry between individual Asian states coupled with the lack of an effective political mechanism for ensuring coordinated collective action; and (3) the lack of balanced capabilities—political, economic, and military—in any single Asian state and continuing limitations of depth.

Therefore, for purposes of assessing the potential for conflict, each of the following regional or country sections treats the international system as continuing to be characterized by significant, though slowly diminishing, American primacy.

CHINA

Introduction[17]

China is undergoing rapid and revolutionary change along every dimension of national power: economic, political, military, technological, and social. A systematic program of market-led economic reform and opening to the outside inaugurated in the late seventies has produced growth rates of nearly 10 percent per annum since the 1980s. This explosion in growth has resulted in major increases in living standards for most of the population, a loosening of political controls over society (and rising expectations of further change), strong and expanding economic and diplomatic linkages to nearby Asian countries, and a determined effort to construct a more modern and comprehensive military establishment. However, this growth has also created severe disparities in income, periods of high inflation, increasing numbers of displaced and unemployed urban and rural workers, lowered respect for political authorities at every level of government, and growing corruption throughout the polity and society. To complicate matters further, China is also facing an unprecedented transition to a new leadership generation. Although largely united in their commitment to the maintenance of economic

---

[17]This introduction is drawn from Michael D. Swaine, "Strategic Appraisal: China," in Zalmay Khalilzad (ed.), *Strategic Appraisal 1996*, Santa Monica, CA: RAND, MR-543-AF, 1996, pp. 185–187; and Michael D. Swaine, "Arms Races and Threats Across the Taiwan Strait," in Gerald Segal and Richard H. Yang (eds.), *Chinese Economic Reform: The Impact on Security*, London: Routledge Press, pp.158–187.

growth and the enhancement of national wealth and power, these new leaders possess less authority and arguably less vision than their predecessors.

These events pose major implications for the future security of the Asia-Pacific region. Indeed, China today arguably constitutes the most critical and least understood variable influencing the future Asian security environment and the possible use of U.S. military forces in that region. If current growth trends continue into the next century and most of the problems mentioned above are overcome, China could emerge as a major military and economic power in Asia, capable of projecting air, land, and naval forces considerable distances from its borders while serving as a key engine of economic growth for many nearby states. Such capabilities could embolden Beijing to resort to coercive diplomacy or direct military action in an attempt to resolve in its favor various outstanding territorial claims or to press other vital issues affecting the future economic and security environment of the region. The possibility of military conflict across the Taiwan Strait in particular has become a more urgent concern in some quarters, largely as a result of rapid, and in many ways revolutionary, domestic changes occurring on both sides of the Strait.

The above developments could eventually reorder the regional security environment in decidedly adverse directions, producing various conflict scenarios. For example, a confident, chauvinistic China could apply unprecedented levels of political and military coercion against an increasingly independent Taiwan in an effort to reunify the island with the mainland, thereby prompting a confrontation and even military conflict with the United States and possibly Japan. Equally negative outcomes would likely emerge from a reversal or wholesale collapse of Beijing's experiment in combining political authoritarianism with liberalizing market-led reform. National fragmentation, breakdown, and/or complete chaos could result, leading to severe economic decline and a loss of government control over the population and over China's national borders. Such developments would almost certainly generate massive refugee flows and send economic shockwaves across the region, producing major crises for neighboring countries. A weak, fragmented Chinese political and social environment could also lead to the adoption of a highly xenophobic, anti-foreign stance by many Chinese elites and social groups, possibly resulting in confrontations with the outside over a variety of territorial and other issues.

Major Trends

Trends in four domestic areas will likely exert an enormous influence over China's external stance in the future and provide drivers of possible conflict scenarios in Asia:

- The changing composition of the central and provincial civilian and military leaderships, the nature and extent of elite support for continued reform, and the open-door policy toward Asia and the West.

- Evolving public attitudes and behavior toward political reform, toward the authority of the communist regime, and toward divergent intellectual views of China's changing security environment.

- The effect of continued reform and development on the changing pattern of economic capabilities and controls, external economic ties, and the military modernization effort.

- The pace and composition of military modernization, especially in naval and air power projection, presence and denial capabilities, and China's overall stance toward greater transparency of its military intentions.

In addition, developments on Taiwan, particularly within the political and social spheres, could serve as a catalyst for various conflict scenarios with mainland China. Major trends in each of these five areas are presented below.[18]

Political Trends. During the past 15 years, a wholesale transformation has taken place in the composition, outlook, and regional orien-

____

[18]The preceding paragraphs and much of the analysis presented in the following trends sections have been drawn from Michael D. Swaine, *China: Domestic Change and Foreign Policy*, Santa Monica, CA: RAND, MR-604-OSD, 1995; and Michael D. Swaine, "Chinese Military Modernization: Motives, Objectives, and Requirements," paper prepared for the Joint Economic Committee, Washington, D.C., July 18, 1996.

tation of China's political leadership. The most basic features of this leadership transformation include:

- The civilianization and specialization of leading party and government figures, replacing the party-army political "generalists" of the past with development-oriented bureaucrats and technocrats.

- The emergence of strong unifying forces among this new leadership, centering on a common pragmatic approach toward continued economic reform, yet complicated by increasing overall support for a highly chauvinistic, state-centered form of patriotic nationalism.

- The existence of several potential causes of leadership conflict over the medium and long term, including both latent policy divisions and narrower power rivalries, and a resulting concern for order and stability. In the short term, the leadership structure will be primarily authoritarian in nature. In the longer term (e.g., 2025), however, a multiparty/faction coalition could develop, divided into three groups: a nationalist, neo-conservative group composed of military and civilian elites (businessmen, ideologues), united behind issues of national reunification, national dignity, and Chinese culturalism; an atavistic Communist group ("communism with a smile"), marked by suspicion of the West and a belief in social order but also pro-growth in economic outlook; and a third, pro-Western, democratic party with nationalist elements.[19]

- The emergence of three major leadership and specialist approaches toward China's regional and global security environment and resulting national security strategy:

  — A mainstream, balance-of-power, realpolitik approach that combines suspicion of the United States with a recognition of the need for continued cooperation with the West and the maintenance of a placid regional environment.

---

[19]Lest this discussion imply that a future China will be more democratic and therefore less aggressive on national reunification issues such as Taiwan, it must be pointed out that democracies often have just as many difficulties dealing with sovereignty issues as authoritarian regimes.

— A more conservative variant of the mainstream that stresses increased regional turbulence and uncertainty and Western hostility toward China and draws upon the above-mentioned neo-conservative school of thought.

— A distinctly minority nonmainstream view that recognizes the growing importance of global interdependence and the consequent need to qualify or reject the realpolitik approach for a more cooperative approach to the West and more extensive participation in emerging multilateral forums.

Of the two latter approaches, the hardline, neo-conservative variant of the conventional approach, associated with elements within the military, is more likely to gain greatly in influence.

Social and Intellectual Trends. Five broad social and intellectual trends and features have the greatest implications for future adverse Chinese external behavior:

- Rising expectations of higher living standards among an increasing number of social classes, tempered by growing economic uncertainties and anxieties in some sectors and regions.

- Widespread political cynicism, passivity, and low class consciousness among the mass of urban and rural dwellers, combined with signs of increasing nationalist pride in China's recent achievements.

- The absence of genuinely representative social organizations to mediate between state and society.

- A deep chasm between the attitudes and beliefs of the general populace and more politically aware social or intellectual groups, reinforced by a popular aversion to social and political disorder.

- Increasing movement of Chinese workers and social groups, both within China and to nearby regions in Asia.

These trends and features present some closely interrelated implications for overall social stability and government policy over the next 10–15 years and beyond:

- The danger of widespread social upheaval in the event of a weakened, paralyzed government or a significant, prolonged decline in economic growth levels.

- Increasing incentives for government policies keyed to further economic reform, combined with greater pressures to incorporate genuine social interests into the policy process, especially those of the urban middle class.

- Possible popular support for a more assertive and chauvinistic foreign policy that seeks to utilize the greater leverage provided by China's increasing economic, diplomatic, and military clout.

- The emergence of large Chinese enclaves in various sensitive areas near China's borders, including those previously controlled by the Chinese government, such as the Russian Far East.

Economic Trends. Five major positive and negative economic trends and features of the past decade will likely prove especially significant to future regional behavior:

- High national growth levels, through major increases in private and semi-private production, trade, and investment, largely resulting from economic reform.

- Major decentralization of economic decisionmaking and the emergence of significant levels of local government and enterprise autonomy over spending and investment.

- Rapid increases in personal income and savings levels and provincial growth rates, leading to significant disparities across key sectors and regions.

- Major decreases in state sector output and profitability and resulting declines in government revenues, combined with increasing public expenditures.

- Explosive growth in foreign economic relations, leading to growing economic linkages with global and regional economies, especially in China's coastal areas.

These economic trends and features suggest major changes in the composition, geographical focus, and pattern of control over economic development that have major direct and indirect implications for China's future domestic stability and external behavior. Five implications are especially important:

- Deep-rooted structural incentives for further reform, combined with major obstacles to successful completion of its final stages.

- Increased potential for internal regional tensions, kept in check by continued growth.

- Possible constraints on long-term government financing of high levels of defense modernization.

- Growing Chinese dependence on foreign economic relations for continued domestic growth and social stability.

- A larger role for economics in determining cooperative or conflictual relations with nearby Asian nations.

Military Trends. In the military sphere, six key trends present major implications for China's external behavior over the short, medium, and long terms:

- A new generation of more-professional military leaders has emerged during the past decade, largely replacing the military politicians of the revolutionary generation. These officers are younger, better educated, and more professionally trained than in the past. The attention of China's emerging professional officer corps is now focused primarily on military modernization through continued economic reform, technological advancement, and improvements in force structure and operational doctrine, and the maintenance of domestic stability and unity.

- The emergence of a less immediately and seriously threatening, yet arguably more complex and uncertain, security environment has led to a significant transformation in China's strategic outlook and resulting force requirements, from that of a continental power requiring a minimal nuclear deterrent capability and large land forces for "in-depth" defense against threats to its northern and western borders, to that of a combined continental/ maritime power requiring a more sophisticated, flexible conventional and unconventional force structure.

- China's diverse security concerns provide the foundation for a newly emerging post–Cold War defense doctrine, comprising such modern concepts as "local or limited war under high-technology conditions," and "active peripheral defense." These concepts assume that local or regional conflicts or wars of relatively low intensity and short duration could break out virtually anywhere on China's periphery, demanding a rapid and decisive application of force through high-tech weaponry. Many such conflicts are seen to pose the possibility of escalation and expansion in intensity, duration, and geographic area; Chinese military modernization goals are thus designed to prevent such developments.

- China's effort to create a conventional force structure with medium- and long-range force projection, mobility, rapid reaction, and off-shore maneuverability capabilities and a more versatile and accurate nuclear weapons inventory has achieved some significant successes. However, force modernization remains plagued by deeply rooted financial, organizational, technological, and managerial problems that suggest that the pace and extent of military advances will remain limited, at least over the next 10–15 years. Moreover, China's senior leadership has not accorded the effort a high priority in China's overall economic reform and development program, which remains keyed to civilian growth.

- The People's Liberation Army (PLA) has been permitted to engage in a wide range of money-making activities, largely to make up for funding shortfalls resulting from the continued priority placed on civilian economic growth. As a result, military leaders have converted many defense industries to the production of civilian goods, established private enterprises—including many in the foreign trade, transportation, vehicle production, pharmaceutical, hotel, property development, textile production, and mining sectors—and invested heavily in key nonmilitary sectors of the economy. Such activities have come to play an important role in the defense modernization effort.

- The recent successes of Taiwan President Lee Teng-hui's ongoing effort to achieve greater international recognition of Taiwan as a separate political and diplomatic entity from the mainland have apparently prompted Beijing to focus greater attention on acquiring more potent maritime air and naval capabilities for use in a variety of possible actions against the island. Such actions conceivably could include low-level intimidation through various military displays, a naval blockade, a limited missile or air attack, limited ground incursions, or even, over the long term, a full-scale invasion.

These major military trends present several implications for future Chinese behavior and capabilities in the Asia-Pacific region:

- It is unlikely that Chinese military modernization will decisively alter the strategic balance in Northeast Asia over at least the medium term (5–10 years), given both the above-mentioned internal modernization difficulties, the continued high priority placed on civilian development, and the clear military advantages enjoyed by other major powers in the region. However, a drastically heightened external threat environment could force a major reallocation of spending priorities in a variety of areas (see, for example, the discussion of Taiwan below).

- Nonetheless, China will likely display increasing confidence in its ability to use conventional military instruments to assist in resolving complex political, diplomatic, and territorial issues, even under conditions of rising regional concern over Chinese military modernization. Over the long term, sustained successes in Chinese air, naval, and ground force modernization could increase Chinese leverage and lower Chinese hesitation to press more aggressively to resolve regional issues in its favor. In the WMD area, medium- and long-term advances in China's nuclear weapons arsenal probably will result in an improved second-strike capability (although still not on the scale of historical U.S. and Soviet/Russian inventories) against the continental United States and Russia (including the likely ability to penetrate a ballistic missile defense system); a possible preemptive first-strike capability against intermediate-range counterforce targets in countries such as Japan, Korea, India, and Russia;[20] and the ability to employ a large number of short-range nuclear and

---

[20]This will likely also include an ability to strike counterforce targets, including U.S. military facilities, with conventional warheads.

other WMD-armed missiles for preemptive or tactical use in a battlefield environment.[21]

- A potential for increasing (and possibly adverse) military influence over the civilian leadership exists, despite a trend toward military detachment from politics. Military forces could become drawn into the fray in a post-Deng succession contest, to support contenders for power or to ensure overall stability. The military might also intervene to resolve policy debates in its favor. Alternatively, the military leadership might become completely paralyzed in such circumstances given an absence of clear directives from above and its own internal debates. Any form of military involvement in elite politics will likely accelerate the trend toward more patriotic nationalist, and possibly neo-conservative, policies, given the growing presence of such views within Chinese military leadership circles.

- However, the problem of military capabilities against Taiwan is the most likely flash point over at least the medium term (5–10 years). As a result of the recent tensions over Taiwan, China's weapons programs will likely place an increased emphasis on acquiring capabilities designed to strengthen the credibility of Beijing's military options against the island and to deter the United States from deploying aircraft carriers in an effort to counter such options.[22]

---

[21]Such WMD capabilities will not equate to a positicn of nuclear parity with the United States and Russia during the time period covered here, absent a major reduction of American and Russian warheads to levels below those proposed by a START III agreement. Moreover, China's willingness to deploy its nuclear forces in the manner suggested above (e.g., to constitute a preemptive first strike) would require a change in its "no first use" and "no use against non-nuclear powers" doctrine.

[22]Specific military systems relevant to such capabilities include (1) large amphibious landing craft, especially those capable of traversing wide, shallow mud flats as are found on the west coast of Taiwan; (2) medium-range fighter/interceptors and attack helicopters; (3) short- and medium-range ballistic missiles; (4) conventional attack submarines; (5) improved command, control, communications, and intelligence (C3I) and carrier detection systems; (6) long-range, stand-off, anti-ship weapons, including cruise missiles and anti-carrier torpedoes; and (7) fixed-wing and helicopter troop and equipment transports.

Trends on Taiwan.[23] Dominant trends and features evident in five arenas will have the greatest impact on Taiwan's approach to China policy and to foreign and security affairs:

- Lee Teng-hui's accession to power as Taiwan's first locally born and nationally elected president has furthered the Taiwanization of the political process. Within the ruling Nationalist Party, discussions of the status issue no longer assume that a "One China" solution is the *only* possible basis for a resolution of the conflict.

- Indeed, a broad consensus appears to have emerged that the current status quo—Taiwan's de facto independence—is the baseline condition for a debate about Taiwan's status.

- Significant foreign exchange reserves, investment in neighboring economies, the considerable role played in many countries by Taiwan capital, and the benefits in the industrialized world of a democratic image have given the island's leadership greater confidence in its capacity to leverage wealth for political gain.

- Where one interest—the Kuomintang's (KMT's)—once defined Taiwan's approach to the China issue, and two interests—the KMT's and the Democratic Progressive Party's (DPP's)—eventually supplanted the old approach, multiple interests on the island now have distinct and often conflicting stakes in Taiwan's mainland policy. Internal divisions muddy the KMT's policy; DPP politicians appear to disagree on the credibility of the Chinese threat, the likelihood of foreign support, and the pace for a push toward independence.

- Taiwan remains highly trade dependent, the level of its offshore investment continues to accelerate, and the pace of restructuring its economy to a more capital-intensive focus remains slow. Business interests now include those with mainland investments to protect, as well as those at home facing stiff competition from mainland-relocated Taiwanese industry.

On the Taiwanese side, the most serious miscalculation would consist of a declaration of formal independence or some other action(s)

---

[23]This section is drawn from Evan A. Feigenbaum, *Change in Taiwan and Potential Adversity in the Strait*, Santa Monica, CA: RAND, 1995.

viewed by the Chinese as a prelude to independence. Most analysts believe that Beijing would almost certainly use military force against Taiwan under such circumstances.[24] Moreover, such a Chinese resort to force would likely occur regardless of the state of the military balance at the time or the adverse consequences such action would pose for Chinese reform policies and Beijing's relations with other powers. Such a Taiwanese miscalculation would probably be associated with the emergence to power of the DPP.

Drivers of Conflict. The above trends include a range of possible drivers or precipitants of conflictual or aggressive Chinese behavior in the Asia-Pacific region. These drivers could interact to produce four basic alternative Chinese security postures, as highlighted below.

Continuity: Gradual Emergence as a Major Power, Yet Still Committed to Reform and the Open Door. One set of drivers is associated with the continuation of several existing political-social, economic, and military trends and features. Even in the absence of highly adverse or alarming changes in Chinese attitudes and capabilities, the steady accumulation of Chinese influence and the strengthening of Chinese nationalist views—all part of China's emergence as a major power in Asia—might precipitate a variety of conflict scenarios.[25] This would prove especially true in the context of perceived external provocations designed to challenge or constrain China's emergence as a major power or to deny the assertion of its interests, especially

---

[24]Paul Kreisberg provides several examples of possible Taiwanese political actions that would probably drastically raise tensions or trigger a Chinese attack. (Paul Kreisberg et al., *Threat Perceptions in Asia and the Role of the Major Powers: A Workshop Report*, Honolulu, HI: East-West Center and Alexandria, VA: Center for Naval Analyses, 1993, p. 82.) In the same volume, also see "Conclusion," p. 177; and Vernon V. Aspaturian, "International Reactions and Responses to PRC Uses of Force Against Taiwan," pp. 140–142.

[25]We are by no means predicting such conflict as an inevitable outcome of existing trends but instead merely point to such a possibility given that the central tenets of China's regional security stance are not those of a status quo power. They assume the eventual expansion of Chinese influence or direct control over nearby territories claimed by other Asian countries, as well as a greatly increased ability to shape events across much of the Asia-Pacific region, through the combined use of more potent economic, military, and diplomatic instruments of national power. However, the continued Chinese need for a placid regional environment, and its growing economic linkages with foreign economies, suggest a basis for future Chinese caution and pragmatism toward both the Asia-Pacific region and the West.

regarding territorial issues. Key drivers of a "continuity" trend line would likely include:

- In the leadership realms, the emergence of a stable, collective leadership structure dedicated to continued economic growth and social order. In the short term, this leadership structure will be primarily authoritarian in nature. In the longer term (e.g., 2025), however, a multiparty/faction coalition could develop (see political trends above).

- In the foreign policy realm, a continuation of the strongly status- and power-oriented (and potentially destabilizing) nationalistic impulses motivating China's search for increasing power and influence in Asia.

- In the economic realm, the continuation of stable, reasonably high growth rates with manageable inflation.

- In the military realm, the continued, gradual improvement of Chinese rapid deployment and force projection capabilities, particularly in the areas of naval and air power.

- Externally, provocative actions taken by Taiwan, the United States, or several other Asian states could greatly increase the chances that existing domestic trends would result in conflict scenarios. On Taiwan, such actions might include:

  — A formal declaration of independence by Taiwan

  — Further expansion of Taiwan's "pragmatic diplomacy"

  — Increased support for Taiwan's "pragmatic diplomacy" in the United Nations

  — Significant support for Taiwan's "pragmatic diplomacy" in the United States and Japan

  — DPP control of one or both major branches of Taiwan's government: the presidency and the legislative Yuan

  — Some form of convergence between DPP moderates and ethnically Taiwanese KMT softliners

  — Further breakdown of the ruling Kuomintang, leaving the party a rump of its former self

— Shifts in Taiwan's attitude toward the ongoing cross-Strait dialogue, especially in light of the increasing marginalization of "one China" absolutists, even within KMT ranks.

In the United States, such actions might include:

— The adoption by Washington of an explicit "two Chinas" policy toward Taiwan and the PRC

— A formal commitment to employ U.S. forces in the defense of Taiwan against a military attack

— The placement of U.S. forces on Taiwanese soil or the sale of major offensive or defensive weapons to Taiwan, including a theater missile defense (TMD) system

— A U.S. decision to deploy forces into North Korea in the event of a collapse of the Pyongyang regime.

Elsewhere in Asia, such actions might include:

— Major oil or liquefied natural gas (LNG) discovery in the Spratly Islands, especially in the Vietnamese areas

— Military buildup among ASEAN claimants, focusing on power projection capabilities (air and naval)

— Major military efforts by Southeast Asian claimants to secure control over large sections of the Spratly Islands in the South China Sea

— Increased dependence of several ASEAN states on the Chinese economy, emboldening China to pursue further aggressive moves in the region

— A Japanese decision to acquire significant offensive power projection capabilities

— Worsening of Sino-Japanese relations, based on increasingly fractious economic competition and historical fears

— Discovery of significant oil or LNG deposits in the disputed Senkakus

— Weakened or hostile U.S.-Japan relations

—   Outbreak of chaos in North Korea

—   Increased intervention and corruption in Hong Kong by mid- or lower-level bureaucrats, undermining confidence in the Hong Kong economy and possibly leading to demonstrations

—   A serious downturn in the Hong Kong economy, either because of intervention by China or normal business cycles, causing severe economic pressures on the Chinese economy

—   Severe internal disarray in Russia across all sectors (political, economic, military, social)

—   Resumption of Russian influence over Central and East Asia (Russia overcomes problems)

—   Decline of Sino-Russian rapprochement, in particular an end to military technology transfer

—   Increased Chinese migration and settlement of the Russian Far East

—   The rise of aggressive fundamentalist movements in Central Asian states along China's borders, leading to transnational Muslim uprisings in Xinjiang

—   Continued Indian naval buildup

—   Expansion of Sino-Burmese military ties.

Discontinuity One: A Highly Assertive China, Committed to Regional Dominance. The likelihood of Chinese conflict behavior would increase significantly if several of the above trends and features produced major decreases in rates of Chinese regional power accumulation and, as a result, markedly more aggressive Chinese behavior, even in the absence of external provocation. Under this scenario, the priority emphasis on rapid civilian economic growth would give way to the state-centered nationalist goals of the defense of national sovereignty and territory and the attainment of big-power status. A combination of at least five domestic drivers would increase the chances of such a fundamentally adverse shift in Chinese foreign policy:

- Stable, high growth rates with manageable inflation

- A fiscally strong central government

- A high level of conservative (especially military) involvement in politics

- Accelerated, "crash" development of air and naval power projection capabilities

- The emergence of a highly conservative, hardline viewpoint on China's security environment as the new "mainstream" view.

Discontinuity Two: A Weak, Insecure, and Defensive China, Concerned with Preventing Foreign Intervention and Social Chaos. A marked downturn in China's internal fortunes could also precipitate more aggressive or assertive Chinese behavior. Several factors could drive such a downturn and a resulting defensive, hypersensitive Chinese regime:

- The failure of the successor leadership to establish a consensus on dealing with a range of obstacles to the final stages of economic reform, such as the future disposition of huge state enterprises, the establishment of a more effective national banking system, and an effective program of national tax reform.

- The inability to generate future growth through expansion of the domestic economy and utilization of China's very high domestic savings, rather than a continued reliance on exports.

- A lack of confidence in the economy by China's emerging entrepreneurs, manifested by slackening investment in the private sector. The first visible sign of this lack of faith would probably be an upsurge in the flight of capital.

- The failure to implement a genuinely effective program of national tax reform designed to ensure a stable and increasing level of revenue for the central government, commensurate with overall national growth levels.

- Prolonged, declining levels of official government spending on military modernization and other military-related activities, manifested either as a constant defense budget or a defense budget growing slower than military costs.

Discontinuity Three: A Chaotic China. Finally, an extremely chaotic domestic situation, resulting from a period of *prolonged and very severe* economic and social decline, exacerbated by unresolved (and possibly violent) conflicts among both civilian and military successor leaderships at the central level, could also produce conflictual Chinese behavior. Such a dangerous scenario could draw subnational elites into the conflict and might even lead, under certain circumstances, to the sporadic use of regional forces in support of contending factions.

The most critical domestic indicators of this adverse scenario would likely include those noted in Discontinuity Two, exacerbated by

- negative economic growth rates over several years;

- stockpiling and widespread shortages of goods moved in inter-provincial trade, particularly those regulated by the center;

- a collapse of the tax collection system. Reactions to such a problem could include greatly accelerated inflation or sporadic and reduced pay for central and local government employees;

- an exchange rate in free-fall and the collapse of normal trade relations. China's trading partners would become loath to extend credit and would insist on foreign currency; exporters would be scrambling to unload merchandise to acquire foreign exchange, preferably in an overseas account;

- accelerated efforts by individual provinces or regions to adopt independent or protectionist fiscal, trade, and investment polities, perhaps leading to

- prolonged, unresolved leadership conflict.

Conflicts. Given the above trends and drivers, the following conflict scenarios are most likely for each of the three time periods covered:[26]

---

[26]This listing is by no means exhaustive. It presents only three representative scenarios deemed to be possible under the three time periods covered by this study.

Short Term (2000–2005): China-Taiwan crisis involving blockade, missile campaign, or limited invasion.

Description. Despite strengthening economic, cultural, and social contacts across the Strait, Taiwan's domestic political process generates steadily increasing pressures for greater international recognition and a clearer domestic expression of de facto independence from Beijing. In this context, Taiwan's highly popular president, leading a largely pro-independence political coalition, continues to chip away at the legal fiction of "one China" in a variety of ways, without actually declaring independence. A more confident, nationalist Beijing decides that it must either press Taiwan through military force to agree to some variant of its formula for peaceful reunification or take the island outright. Three alternative Chinese strategies are possible: (1) gradual pressure to provoke Taiwan; (2) blockade; and (3) sudden attack.

Why Possible? This scenario could conceivably emerge out of a continuation of present trends in China and Taiwan, including ongoing nationalism and Taiwanization, and Chinese air and naval modernization. Moreover, perceived provocations by the United States would greatly increase the chances of such a scenario. This scenario is also possible during the other two time periods covered in this study, and under the conditions of either a strong, assertive China or a weak, defensive China concerned with foreign intervention, given the critical importance of the Taiwan issue to questions of Chinese national unity and China's emerging great-power status, and Chinese suspicions regarding foreign manipulation of the issue.

Importance for the United States. Chinese military pressure or an outright attack on Taiwan would present a major crisis for U.S. policy in Asia and would likely lead to the deployment of U.S. forces to the immediate area. This could result in a direct clash with Chinese forces. Depending upon China's level of military development, such a clash could threaten U.S. carrier and air forces.

Medium Term (2006–2015): Ethnic Border Tension (Siberia).

Description. Years of Chinese migration and settlement into Russian Far Eastern territories adjoining China have displaced many Russian residents and created local Chinese support for a reversion of much of the region to China. This sentiment is increasingly expressed by local Chinese elites and through demonstrations in cities near the Russian border. A strong, prosperous, and unified Chinese government privately conveys its sympathy for the demonstrators, and Chinese small arms increasingly appear among Siberia's Chinese residents. Some Chinese leaders also privately speak with some bitterness of the "unequal" treaties of the 19th century that led to the "seizure" of Chinese lands by Imperial Russia. However, there are also hints of Chinese discussions with Moscow regarding a possible purchase of the "disputed" territories. A weak, economically strapped, and divided Russian government openly demands that China cease all efforts to foment secession in the Russian Far East and reinforces local police and military units. China responds by placing elements of several group armies closer to the Manchurian border with Russia.

Why Possible? This scenario could result from the resolution, over the medium term, of many of China's internal development problems and the emergence of a more militarily capable and nationalist regime, as well as the continuation of existing trends regarding Chinese immigration into the Russian Far East. Hence, both continuities in current trends and the first discontinuity outlined above could precipitate such a scenario.

Importance for the United States. This scenario would not present a major challenge to U.S. policy or forces in Asia. However, this scenario would likely promote major regional concern and demands for U.S. efforts to stabilize or contain any possible conflict.

Long Term (2016–2025): Spratly Islands/Strait of Malacca Tensions.

Description. Tensions in the South China Sea are sparked by a Chinese decision to expand its level of influence in the region through regular deployments of naval forces into the southern Spratlys and through the Malaccan Strait. Although the Chinese do not forcibly displace any of the other Spratly claimants from occupied islands, the rapidly increasing Chinese military presence sends shockwaves through the area, prompting major efforts from Indonesia, Malaysia, Singapore, and Vietnam to increase their forward-deployable air and naval assets. India also expresses great concern over the Chinese actions. These actions raise the level of tension in the area and produce some sharp exchanges with Chinese representatives at the

ASEAN Regional Forum (ARF) security dialogue. Privately, many Southeast Asian countries implore the United States to pressure the Chinese to reduce their activities to the pre-escalation levels.

Why Possible? This scenario, which could also occur during the medium term, could become even more likely over the long term as a result of the emergence of a more militarily capable and nationalist Chinese regime.

Importance for the United States. This scenario would pose a serious challenge to critical U.S. interests in the Asia-Pacific region, including a commitment to the peaceful resolution of disputes; to the stability and unity of ASEAN; and to unhindered maritime passage through a critical line of communication and commerce.

JAPAN

Introduction

As Japan approaches the 21st century, it finds itself at a crossroads, faced with critical choices concerning the future of its economy, its alliance with the United States, what roles it should play in the international system, and its relations with Asian neighbors. It also is entering into a period of great uncertainty in terms of its strategic environment. Both the manner in which Korean unification will unfold and what external stance a unified Korea will adopt are sources of considerable anxiety. Another source of apprehension concerns how long the United States will choose to remain militarily engaged in East Asia. But even more critical over the longer term, Japan faces the prospect of a dramatic power transition in favor of China over the next decade. Will a highly assertive China seeking regional domination emerge during the next three decades, or will China's growing links with the international economy result in the emergence of a status quo Chinese state?

Given such uncertainty in its external environment, Japan is hedging in its security relations with the United States and in its relations with other Asian countries. Such behavior is highly convenient for Japanese policymakers, who wish to postpone difficult and controversial foreign policy decisions at present given the fluid state of Japanese politics. The choices that Japan eventually makes in the next five years, however, will have critical consequences for the regional security environment and far-reaching ramifications for U.S. Air Force strategy well into the next century.

Major Trends

Political Trends. *The process of political realignment will likely result in a period of political instability and weak governments over the short term, but could result in stronger governments over the long term—with critical foreign policy implications.* Japanese politics are undergoing a dramatic process of realignment and transformation.[27] Examples include the end of a long-standing pattern of stable rule by a single, conservative party (the Liberal Democratic Party) and formation of a non-LDP coalition government in 1993, the declining electoral fortunes of the former main opposition party (Social Democratic Party), the creation of new political parties, and formation of new political coalitions crossing former ideological boundaries (e.g., the LDP-SDP-Sakigake coalition government in 1994). Political realignment, made possible by the end of the Cold War, was given further impetus by growing societal demands for political reforms to reduce corruption and liberalize the electoral system. Moreover, realignment was linked to the interests of the economic bureaucracies and the ambitions of ostensibly reformist political elites. In turn, political opportunism, including political alliances between former electoral foes, has encouraged growing public apathy and distrust of all major political parties. Growing public mistrust has also been fueled by a series of political scandals and by revelations of political corruption involving elected government officials and bureaucrats.

Japan's highly fluid domestic political environment could lead to a series of weak coalition governments. This in turn will further promote political instability until the process of realignment is completed. But over the long term, this fluidity could lead to the emergence of stronger governments seeking new directions in Japanese domestic and foreign policy. As a result, the evolution of the political system will have an important impact on several major foreign policy

---

[27]This process is discussed in greater detail in M. M. Mochizuki, *Japan: Domestic Change and Foreign Policy*, Santa Monica, CA: RAND, 1995.

debates now under way, each having major implications for Japan's long-term relations not only with the rest of Asia, but also with the United States.

One critical foreign policy debate concerns Japan's search for an appropriate role to play in international affairs in light of the power shift in its favor during the 1980s and the end of the Cold War. A second concerns how Japan should approach relations with Asia. A third revolves around economic development, including the liberalization and deregulation of the Japanese economy. While no consensus has yet been reached on any of these debates, their outcomes will have a decisive impact on Japan's basic foreign policy and U.S.-Japan relations over the next 25 years.

Current political trends in Japan are highly critical for the U.S. Air Force, because they could both diminish the deterrent effectiveness of a U.S. presence and constrain U.S. en-route and in-theater operations in the event of a major regional conflict. As a result, Japan's ability to respond to an international crisis in a timely fashion and render assistance to its ally, the United States, will be affected by today's political trends. Even more problematic, political turmoil could affect whether Japan insists on "prior consultations" in the event of a breaking crisis in the Far East, thereby imposing severe constraints on the ability of U.S. aerospace power to function as a rapid reaction force. Any prolonged delay by the Japanese government, any attempt to place limitations on the use of U.S. military capabilities, or any exercise of veto rights in a worst case scenario would have critical consequences for the U.S. Air Force war-fighting capabilities and hence the outcome of a crisis. Political instability, in conjunction with the Japanese public's strong "allergy" to Japan's involvement in armed conflicts, could therefore have a decisive impact on

- whether Japan could be expected to insist upon prior consultations in the event of a crisis requiring the deployment of U.S. troops stationed in Japan;

- what types of logistical and other indirect support Japan would likely provide;

- whether Japan's Self-Defense Forces would themselves directly participate in such a conflict;

- what types of participation could be expected (minesweeping, escort duties, direct combat roles), if Japan responded positively to a crisis overseas; and

- what calculus potential military adversaries of the United States, its allies, and its friends would make in a crisis, given the uncertainty about how Japan would respond.

Japan's response in the event of another major regional conflict in the Persian Gulf or in East Asia would also have great political significance. In the event Japan's future response were seen in the United States as "too little, too late," as it was during the Gulf War,[28] strains on the alliance relationship would become severe. Repetition of a Gulf War situation would likely undermine American public support for the alliance if Japan again were seen to contribute little in "human" terms, while at the same time U.S. forces were sacrificed while defending Japanese security interests in the Middle East, Strait of Malacca, South China Sea, Taiwan Strait, and especially Korea. Moreover, in the context of ongoing economic friction and the lack of an overarching threat that the Soviet Union posed during the Cold War, the alliance relationship itself could prove domestically unsustainable in the United States. U.S. troops would be seen by the U.S. public as performing "mercenary tasks" for Japanese interests with few tangible benefits for the United States. This view in turn would also have devastating consequences for U.S. strategy in East Asia.

Economic Trends and Features. *Low growth rates over the long term, with the possibility of a stagnant economy if Japan does not address critical structural problems.* The Japanese economy is at a crossroads. Since the collapse of the "bubble economy" in 1990, Japan has been mired in a structural economic recession. While the Japanese economy has shown signs of a partial recovery—in part because of the recent depreciation of the yen, countercyclical measures designed to stimulate the economy (although basically "pork" in nature), and large trade surpluses—reports hailing recovery may be

---

[28]See Courtney Purrington and "A. K.," "Tokyo's Policy Responses to the Gulf Crisis," *Asian Survey*, Vol. 31, No. 4, April 1991, pp. 307–323; Courtney Purrington, "Tokyo's Policy Response to the Gulf War and the Impact of the 'Iraqi Shock' on Japan," *Pacific Affairs*, Vol. 65, No. 2, Summer 1992, pp. 10–21. "A. K." is an anonymous Japanese military officer.

premature. Instead, the possibility remains of a stagnant economy in the long term. Problems that need to be addressed include a "hollowing out" of the Japanese economy; heavy debt among Japanese banks arising from bad loans made during the "bubble" years and a sharp decline in the value of equities owned by Japanese banks; inefficient service sector industries protected from foreign competition by excessive regulations; overcapacity in certain industries; long-term appreciation of the yen; and an aging population. At the very least, long-term growth rates are likely to remain low in comparison to Japan's economic performance during the Cold War and in comparison to the growth rates of its rapidly developing Asian neighbors.

Future trends in the structure and direction of Japanese economic growth will play an important role in influencing the process of political realignment. A prolonged downturn of the Japanese economy could strengthen the position of those Japanese who argue for a more assertive form of economic nationalism, keyed to the expansion of links to Asian markets and a reduced reliance on the United States. Conversely, the resumption of stable and moderate growth levels could increase the chances for a more stable transition to a more liberal political leadership.

A rapid expansion of Japanese direct investment in Asia and transfer of production abroad, in large part driven by a rapidly appreciating yen, has begun a "hollowing out" process of the Japanese economy in such areas as textiles, consumer electronics, chemicals, and even in the automobile sector.[29] The globalization of Japan's production activities is also weakening Japan's manufacturing *keiretsu* system, as manufacturing firms loosen and in some instances cut traditional ties with domestic subcontractors. Although some subcontractors have followed manufacturers overseas in order to survive, in many instances these subcontractors also work for other manufacturers (both Japanese and non-Japanese). Finally, a process of *kakaku hakai* (price destruction) driven by cheap foreign imports by discount stores is straining Japan's distribution system, resulting in a changing balance of power between manufacturers and retailers, fa-

---

[29]For an up-to-date study of Japanese investment in Asia, see Eileen Doherty (ed.), *Japanese Investment in Asia,* San Francisco, CA: The Asia Foundation and U.C. Berkeley Roundtable on the International Economy, 1995.

voring the latter. As a result, Japan not only may import increased amounts of finished products from the rest of Asia, but may even procure more manufactured components from South Korean and Taiwanese companies to remain competitive against U.S. and European rivals.

Japan's process of structural adjustment is significant, because interstate conflict can arise from states seeking to protect declining industries from foreign competition. Labor and capital interests in declining sectors of an economy will tend to lobby for protectionist policies, while similar interests in internationally competitive sectors will tend to favor free trade.[30] When the former are more powerful politically, their preferences for protectionist policies are more likely to be adopted and in turn lead to interstate political conflict. This risk of conflict is not only acute between Japan and advanced economies in the West, but also among Asian states themselves. Such conflict is significant, because it could harm alliance relations with the United States and exacerbate relations with traditional rivals (e.g., China and Korea).

Persistent and large trade surpluses with Asia (except China) and the United States. Despite early signals of a fundamental structural transformation under way in the Japanese economy, it is also possible that declining economic sectors in Japan, in tandem with bureaucratic interests seeking to maintain their influence over the domestic economy, may postpone or even attempt to derail such an industrial adjustment. Resistance will be especially strong if economic growth remains stagnant. As a result, growing trade imbalances between Japan and Asia may not be rectified, with the costs of adjustment foisted upon the United States—likely leading to rising conflict not only between Japan and other Asian states, but also between Japan and the United States. The reluctance of Asian states to further liberalize their economies could lead to a protectionist backlash in the United States. Continued U.S. trade imbalances could in turn increase domestic pressure to disengage militarily from Asia because of tensions arising from the usage of

---

[30]Helen Milner, *Resisting Protectionism: Global Industry and the Politics of International Trade,* Princeton, NJ: Princeton University Press, 1988.

scarce financial resources to protect nations running large trade surpluses with the United States.

By running large trade surpluses, states pursuing neo-mercantilist trade strategies can further promote economies of scale for national industries and the accumulation of national wealth. Interstate conflict can therefore arise from persistent imbalances between trading partners. China and Japan account for most of the U.S. global trade deficit. Whether or not these two Asian powers liberalize their markets and serve as engines of growth for the region will be especially important in determining whether U.S. relations with the region are increasingly marked by cooperation or conflict and whether Asian states themselves can establish durable forms of economic cooperation.

On an aggregate basis, Japan continues to run a trade and current account surplus with the rest of Asia and the United States. Between 1990 and 1994, Japan's trade surplus with Asia more than doubled, from $25 billion to $57 billion. Behind this large trade surplus lay Japanese exports not only of finished products but also of industrial equipment, components, and manufacturing technology. Although Japanese imports from the rest of Asia have steadily risen, Japan's exports to the region have risen much quicker. In fact, exports from some Asian states to Japan have stagnated or declined in recent years.[31] As a result, Japan in 1994 ran an even larger current-account surplus in trade with Southeast Asia than with Organization for Economic Cooperation Development (OECD) members.[32] China is the only major country in East Asia that enjoys a large trade surplus with Japan.

While the collapse of Japan's bubble economy and burgeoning economic growth in Asia (i.e., growing demand for Japanese machinery, components, and the like) provides a partial explanation for rising

---

[31] South Korea's deficit with Japan continues to rise despite its own trade barriers, largely because of a reliance on Japanese machinery and components. Taiwan also has experienced a strong and increasing trade deficit with Japan in recent years.

[32] According to Ministry of Finance trade statistics for 1994, Japan's trade surplus with OECD members was $70.05 billion, versus $72.007 billion with SE Asia. Japan's trade surplus with the United States was $54.9 billion, versus $60.868 billion with the Asian newly industrialized economies (NIEs). Japan's trade deficit with China was $7.683 billion, however.

trade imbalances between Japan and the rest of Asia, both formal and especially informal barriers continue to limit Japanese imports of Asian manufactured goods, a particular source of friction between Japan and South Korea.[33] Moreover, the structure of Japan's trade with the rest of Asia still tends to be vertical in nature, with Japan typically supplying manufactured goods to Asia, while tending to import food and raw materials and textiles.

Further rounds of yen appreciation, however, could change existing trade patterns in Asia by stimulating increased Japanese imports from the rest of Asia, especially as the rising value of the yen is likely to spur a new round of Japanese manufacturing investment in China and Southeast Asia. Japanese companies are increasingly manufacturing products in Asia, not only for local consumption in other Asian countries and for export to Western countries, but also for re-export back to Japan. These developments might eventually ameliorate Japan's large trade surpluses with the rest of Asia and generally heighten prospects for economic integration. But if these developments are not realized, then Japan's political relations with the rest of Asia and especially the United States may be increasingly marked by discord.

Increasing rivalry over the locus of advanced technologies among Japan, its primary Asian competitors, and the United States. Competition over the locus of high-technology industries in the world economy could exacerbate political relations among Japan, other Asian states, Europe, and the United States. Technological innovations have facilitated flows of capital, goods, persons, and knowledge across borders and therefore may promote integration between economies. But politics need not adjust to technological change.[34] Instead, interstate competition can undermine both technological innovation and the scope of international markets. Because technological innovation is not only important for long-run economic growth prospects in a nation but is often critical to its military power, states compete over leadership and control of advanced technologies.

---

[33]*New York Times*, "New Asian Anger at Tokyo's Trade," April 13, 1993.

[34]Eugene Staley, *The World Economy in Transition*, New York: Council on Foreign Relations, 1939, p. 52.

Accordingly, advanced states such as the United States and Japan are increasingly concerned with limiting the diffusion of technologies abroad for both security reasons and to maximize the "rents" obtained from possessing innovative technologies at the high-value end of the product cycle.[35] The motivation for limiting technological diffusion to other countries can be benign (i.e., maximizing welfare gains at home). Or the motivation can be to maximize relative gains, because the possession of advanced technologies is critical to a state's long-run power position in the world. For corresponding reasons, lesser-developed states seeking to move up the technological ladder and to establish a national presence in a given sector attempt to create an "artificial" comparative advantage through neo-mercantilist policies that de facto limit the monopolistic rents an innovator can obtain. The resulting rivalry over control of the commanding heights of technology, or over technologies further down the product cycle, can create severe tensions even among allies, and, especially, exacerbate political and economic conflict among traditional geopolitical rivals.

Japan, China, South Korea, Taiwan, and the ASEAN states possess complementary factor endowments, creating the potential for a self-contained Asian division of labor.[36] But for economic and political reasons, other Asian countries are reluctant to accept a hierarchical differentiation of functions biased in Japan's favor, including vertical patterns of trade and dependence on Japanese technology, along the lines of a "flying geese" pattern of development. Instead, Korea and Taiwan have sought to move up the technological ladder and to compete head-on with Japanese companies, not only in consumer electronics and automobiles, but even in certain high-technology sectors. Japanese companies have in turn responded to such competition by expanding industrial production in Southeast Asia to maintain competitiveness in their own domestic market and abroad. China and Southeast Asian states often insist upon technology transfers to local firms, just as Japan did vis-à-vis certain U.S. multinationals seeking to establish operations in Japan during the 1960s

---

[35]Robert Gilpin, *The Political Economy of International Relations*, Princeton, NJ: Princeton University Press, 1987, p. 99.

[36]This point was made by Robert Gilpin, 1987, p. 399.

and 1970s. Japanese firms, however, have been generally wary of such transfers.

The danger of heightened technological competition among Asian states, or between Japan and the United States, lies in exacerbating other forms of rivalry already present. The degree to which such political conflict will be mitigated by the response of multinationals to such sectoral protectionism—foreign direct investment in the home markets of competitors or developing states—remains uncertain. What is clear, however, is that in a world of fragmented markets, many technologies—those that are costly to develop, involve large economies of scale, and hence require mass markets to provide a profitable return on capital invested—will not achieve their full potential. These limitations will in turn impede prospects for Asian growth and integration and hence have a negative impact on the potential for long-run regional stability.

Differential rates of growth favor Japan's historical rivals, especially China. Uneven growth trends in East Asia could represent a major source of instability for the region. Shifts in the locus of economic activities in the global economy as a result of uneven growth will result in changes in the distribution of wealth and power among states. Under certain circumstances, where relative gains concerns are high, the attendant redistribution of power and its effect on the wealth of a given state can lead to conflict between rising and declining powers (in relative terms) as they seek to maintain or even improve their standing in the international system. In particular, China's potential emergence as a preeminent regional power looms largest in the Japanese calculus, although the potential emergence of an unfriendly, unified Korea with close relations with China also remains a concern.

Uneven growth is especially significant when states expect that differential gains in power in another state's favor will be one day used against them. States will therefore be reluctant to engage in cooperative endeavors with other states except as related to balancing behavior. However, in instances where states expect long-run, friendly interactions with another state, uneven economic growth is not necessarily destabilizing. But in a region marked by historical enmity and suspicions, sovereignty and territorial conflicts, as well as diverse cultures and civilizations, the potential for relative gains eventually serving as a severe impediment to regional economic cooperation looms large.

At a time when Japan is experiencing anemic economic growth, China and South Korea have had average annual growth rates exceeding 7 percent. If one extrapolates from World Bank purchasing power parity estimates as a basis for projecting the future size of China's economy, China's Gross National Product (GNP) would be $4.34 trillion in 2002, while in 2007 it would be $6.09 trillion, or approximately one-third larger than Japan's projected GNP (projection based on expansion of China's economy at 7 percent annual rate and 2 percent annual rate for Japan).[37] Given such a shift in China's favor, improving relations with Korea in Japanese calculations is vital. Japanese elites are understandably concerned over Korean unification, given extant historical enmity between both countries, the potential economic challenge a unified Korea would eventually pose for Japan, and uncertainty regarding the future alignment of a unified Korean state.

To the extent that Japan expects long-run peaceful interactions with China, such a power transition could be peacefully managed. Rising economic integration in the region could serve as an important stabilizing factor mitigating relative gains concerns. For example, Japanese relative gains concerns vis-à-vis China may be eased by China's continued dependence on external sources for technology and capital investments necessary for successful economic reform.[38] However, to the extent disparities in growth rates exacerbate Japanese fears that a non-status quo Chinese power will eventually seek to dominate the region, continued economic integration and cooperation will be imperiled. Much will depend upon the extent to which China can be enmeshed within the international economy

---

[37] *World Development Report, 1994.* China's GNP was roughly 2.37 trillion in 1992 (figures obtained by multiplying China's per capita GNP in 1992 of $1,910 (using 1992 dollars) by a 1992 population of 1.162 billion and then adjusting corresponding figure for 1995 dollars). The above growth figure assumes that China will continue its economic reform efforts and that obstacles to continued growth will be surmounted.

[38] According to the Japanese Foreign Ministry, Japanese Overseas Development Assistance (ODA) to China has increased from approximately ¥105 billion in 1990 to approximately ¥155 billion in 1995. China has now replaced Indonesia as the single largest destination for Japanese ODA. See *Asian Wall Street Journal*, "Nuclear Testing in China Moves Japan to Anger," May 19–20, 1995, pp. 1–2.

and regimes and, even more, upon the future evolution of Chinese reforms and internal politics.

The relative importance of Asia for the Japanese economy is growing, while the relative importance of Japan for most Asian countries is declining. Since the appreciation of the yen in 1985, Japanese direct investment in Asia has expanded more than fourfold. Japan has made a considerably high percentage of its Asian direct investments in manufacturing industries, even compared to its investment patterns in other regions. Asia's share of Japan's total direct investment abroad rose from 12.2 percent in fiscal 1989 to 18.4 percent in fiscal 1993, and rose to approximately 25 percent in fiscal 1994.[39] Although the United States remains the single largest destination for Japanese exports and capital, Asia is rapidly replacing North America as the most important economic region for Japan.

Given Asia's superior growth prospects, Japanese capital flows into the region will likely continue to increase. The latest round of yen appreciation, which began in 1994, as well as Japan's increasing labor costs and decreasing labor supply, will hasten increased Japanese capital flows into the rest of Asia, as Japanese companies seeking to remain competitive with East Asian and U.S. rivals establish more manufacturing operations in the region.[40] With further appreciation of the yen, foreign investment will be comparatively cheaper. Moreover, the anticipated rapid growth of Asian markets and profitability of Japanese investments there (compared with Japanese investments in North America) will further encourage such trends. As a result, Japanese banks, in search of potential sources for revenue growth and improved asset quality, are increasing their lending exposure to Asia.[41]

---

[39]*Journal of Japanese Trade and Industry,* "Current and Future Investment Outlook in Asia," No. 2, 1995, pp. 8–10.

[40]This development will likely result in increased Japanese imports of manufactured products from offshore Japanese companies (as well as other Asian companies) and could alter the triangular pattern of trade that has developed in Asia since the mid-1980s and lead to more intraregional trade self-reliance as Japan and especially China serve as engines of regional growth.

[41]*The Nikkei Weekly,* "Asia Loan Demand Hands Lifeline to Struggling Banks," October 10, 1994. North America remains the single largest lending destination for Japanese banks, taking a 39 percent share.

Although Japan represents the single largest source of foreign direct investment (FDI) in Asia, Japan is unlikely to achieve a dominant economic position in Asia. The overall scale of Japanese FDI activity in the region is dwarfed collectively by that of other Asian countries, Europe, and North America. For example, Japanese FDI as a percentage of total FDI exceeded 40 percent in only three East Asian states between 1987 and 1991: Thailand (44.3 percent), South Korea (49.0 percent), and Indonesia (67.8 percent).[42] In China, Japanese FDI accounted for only 10.4 percent of total FDI. As a percentage of gross domestic capital formation, Japanese FDI exceeded 3 percent in only three East Asian countries during this period: Thailand (5.6 percent), Malaysia (5.9 percent), and Singapore (8.4 percent).[43]

The importance of Asia as a trading partner for Japan has also grown rapidly in recent years. In 1990, two-way trade with East Asia exceeded that with the United States. But because of the continued persistence of vertical patterns of trade between Japan and its Asian trading partners, Japan imports a small percentage of East Asian exports of manufactured products. Even if Japan continues to open up its economy to increased imports of manufactured products, the size of its market is simply too small to absorb surplus production in a rapidly growing Asia. Although the value of Japanese imports of Asian goods measured in dollars nearly doubled between 1987 and 1993, Japan's overall importance as a destination for Asian exports declined during from 15 to 12.4 percent. But this decline in the importance of the Japanese market for Asian exports should also be weighed against an even more significant decline in the relative importance of the U.S. market. Whereas the United States absorbed 27.3 percent of non-Japanese Asian exports in 1987, it absorbed only

---

[42]Japanese FDI figures obtained from various years of International Monetary Fund (IMF), *Balance of Payments Yearbook*. Gross domestic capital formation figures obtained from IMF, *International Financial Statistics*.

[43]Japan-led integration will also encounter a number of political obstacles. As Asian economies move up the technological ladder, as in the case of Korea and Taiwan, or attract Japanese FDI, as in the case of Southeast Asia, they are becoming increasingly dependent upon Japanese technology, machinery, and components. But for political reasons, Asian states, especially China, South Korea, and Taiwan, will likely be unwilling to accept excessive long-run economic dependence on Japan. Instead, Asian states will likely continue to encourage extraregional economic linkages with U.S. and European multinationals to balance Japan's regional influence, and to encourage the United States to maintain a military presence in the region.

21.6 percent in 1993.[44] The main reason for the declining importance of the U.S. and Japanese markets was the rapidly expanding volume of intra-Asian trade (excluding Japan), which rose from 27.4 to 37.1 percent in the period.

Even with further import liberalization, changes in tax policy and other measures designed to enhance domestic consumption, and stronger economic growth in Japan, this downward trend in the importance of Japan's market for the rest of Asia will likely continue given the rapidly expanding volume of intra-Asian trade. Thus, there is little evidence for the emergence of a Japan-dominated trading zone in Asia because of both the inherent limits in the size of the Japanese economy and a lack of willingness on the part of Japan to attempt such dominance as long as it continues to benefit from maintenance of the status quo in its trading relationships within and outside the region.[45]

Japan's expanding economic linkages with Asia, however, could pose certain challenges for the United States. Given such trends, Japan could adopt a more independent foreign policy stance apart from the United States. Even more critical, perhaps, China could replace the United States as Japan's most important trading partner within the next decade if a relatively benign Asian security environment persists. Such an occurrence would in turn have a strong impact on Japanese crisis behavior in the eventuality of a regional conflict involving China, in turn constraining potential U.S. politico-military responses and reducing the deterrence functions of a U.S. presence. Finally, persistent U.S. trade deficits with Japan and its Asian trading partners could also inflame bilateral relations with Japan (undermining the trust necessary for alliance maintenance) and encourage Japanese elites to seek closer ties with Asia at the expense of trans-Pacific ties with the United States.

Military-Security Trends. *Hedging behavior and an ongoing Japanese security debate concerning what contributions (including*

---

[44]Europe's importance as a destination for Asian exports remained at 16 percent during the period.

[45]Supporters of the creation of a yen zone and an exclusive East Asian economic grouping, however, are increasing among Japanese firms, because of trade friction with the United States and rapid appreciation of the yen.

military) Japan should make toward maintenance of international order. In contrast to the Cold War era, when sharp cleavages existed in Japanese politics and society on critical foreign policy issues, including the U.S.-Japan alliance, there is now a remarkable degree of consensus supporting Japan's security posture. But the present consensus is likely to erode in the next decade. As in Germany, a debate is under way in Japan (albeit less mature) concerning what roles Japan should play in the international system. Constitutional and other legal constraints severely limit the potential roles Japan could play in the event of a regional conflict. However, the scope of what roles Japan's Self-Defense Forces (SDF) can perform within the context of both the alliance and the United Nations has broadened in recent years, in part because of a relaxation of public opinion following the end of the Cold War and widespread international criticism of Japan during the Gulf War. Nevertheless, public opposition to direct Japanese involvement in armed conflicts overseas remains strong, especially any conflict in which nuclear weapons could be used. Even more important, the Japanese public would be extremely wary of being dragged into any Northeast Asian conflict in which Japan itself could be attacked because of the presence of U.S. troops on Japanese soil.

Currently, most Japanese elites and public opinion support maintenance of the status quo in terms of Japan's defense policy.[46] In other words, they support maintenance of the alliance and a conventional interpretation of Article 9 of the Constitution as banning the right to exercise collective self-defense. This group, including most bureaucrats within the Foreign Ministry and Defense Agency, in part reflects bureaucratic inertia and satisfaction with a status quo that has adequately provided for Japan's security for nearly 50 years. The group also includes former leftists, who view the alliance in a post–Cold War context as a "cap in the bottle" preventing a recurrence of Japanese militarism and providing a splendid justification for reducing the size of the SDF in a regional security environment lacking an overarching threat. Finally, the group also includes most

---

[46]The next three paragraphs are drawn from an unpublished paper by Courtney Purrington and Shigeki Nishimura, entitled "Redefining the U.S.-Japan Alliance for the Next Century." The paper was presented at the Conference on U.S.-Japan Relations, Center for Strategic and International Studies, Washington, D.C., May 2, 1997.

Ministry of International Trade and Industry (MITI) officials, Finance Ministry officials, and business elites. Many within the Finance Ministry favor a reduction in the size of Japanese military spending to cope with a growing fiscal deficit and therefore view cost savings derived from alliance burdensharing in positive terms. During the Cold War, these elites supported alliance maintenance because it guaranteed Japan's integration into the U.S.-led world economy. They believe that Japan should maintain current patterns of security responsibility sharing with the United States.

A majority of these elites believe that Japan should become a "global civilian power." This approach can be seen as a direct outgrowth of the so-called "Yoshida Doctrine" that guided Japanese foreign and defense policy during the Cold War. Such continuity, however, masks a hedging strategy in Japan. Over the short run, this vision would complement the international roles played by the United States, viewed as a declining global power. This vision would allow Japan to defer critical foreign and defense policy decisions until the eventual outcome of certain key issues becomes more certain. These issues include the future disposition of the Korean peninsula, the future of reform efforts in Russia, whether or not a friendly and status quo China emerges, and the future course of the "liberal" international trading system. Instead, Japan would simply assume a more prominent role in supporting the maintenance of international order over the near term. Should a benign regional security environment emerge and today's present globalization trends continue in the world economy, Japan's soft power resources would allow it to play a leading role in the shaping of both a new regional and world order. Over the longer term, these Japanese elites could be therefore characterized as holding a non–status quo view of the international system.

Advocates of a vision of Japan as a "normal" power generally support a redefinition of security responsibilities on a more equitable basis between Japan and the United States, as well as reinterpretation of the Constitution so that Japan could exercise the right of collective self-defense and participate in UN-sanctioned multinational forces. These elites, consisting of traditional pro-American academics and politicians, military strategists within the Foreign Ministry and Defense Agency, and some business leaders, do not necessarily desire Japan to become more independent of the United States. Indeed, given uncertainty posed by China, many of them view a strengthened alliance with the world's leading maritime power as vital to Japanese security interests. Nor do these elites desire Japan to become a "great" military power again. Instead, U.S. and Japanese armed forces would become more interdependent, and a "normal" Japan would assume more of the regional security burden.

Few Japanese elites at present support Japan's emergence as a great military power. Barring the ascension of a nationalistic Japanese government (following a prolonged period of economic recession, political turmoil, collapse of global economic regimes, weakening in U.S.-Japan economic ties, and abrogation of the alliance), such a development will be unlikely, given the large benefits Japan derives from the present international order.

Growing dissatisfaction over the status quo in the alliance relationship among Japanese elites. Although there is no significant group that now advocates a dismantling of the U.S.-Japan security system, there is growing dissatisfaction over the present security framework. Those dissatisfied include not simply former leftists, pacifists, and Okinawa citizens (who assume a disproportionate share of the costs of hosting U.S. forces stationed in Japan), but even Japanese elites who are traditionally pro-American. Many traditional supporters of the alliance suspect that the United States wants Japan to remain a junior alliance partner, highly dependent upon it for security protection. They suspect that the United States either retains mistrust stemming from World War II and/or that the United States seeks to remain the dominant global power and is therefore reluctant to share leadership with Japan. They suspect that the United States simply wants Japan to ante up those financial resources necessary to support a weary global titan ("taxation without representation") that is no longer financially capable of unilaterally bearing the costs of maintenance of the international order, in part because of its own fiscal irresponsibility. One popular explanation for U.S. behavior is that the United States is seeking to contain Japan because it suspects Japan may seek to become an independent great power and challenge U.S. leadership.

The "Asianization" debate among Japanese elites, including the relative importance of Asia versus the United States. Such resentment could eventually feed into anti-U.S. sentiment and even result in a nationalistic backlash that would support further "Asianization" of Japanese foreign policy. In its most extreme form, the development of "malevolent Asianization" could take place as a concerted drive with other Asian states to exclude the United States from Asia. Whereas continuity is therefore likely in Japanese foreign and defense policy over the next five years, such resentment could result in significant changes over the longer term, especially within the context of Japan's ongoing process of political realignment and restructuring of the Japanese economy.

A rediscovery of Asia is taking place within Japan, with parallels to the 1930s, in the context of debate over what roles Japan should play in international affairs in an era of post-American hegemony. At the popular level, this search for a national identity is reflected in an "Asia boom," or rediscovery of Asia through travel and study of Asian cultures, history, and languages. This debate coincides with increasing Japanese economic interests in Asia. Mainstream elite debate revolves around whether Japan should encourage America's integration into East Asia through support of U.S. regional objectives, or whether Japan should promote an exchange of Western and Asian values by leading Asia's "restoration." The debate includes the merits of Japanese civilization and whether Japan represents an alternative path to modernity that could serve as a model for the rest of Asia.

Many civilian power advocates believe that Japan should place more importance on relations with Asia or promote the "Asianization" of Japanese foreign policy. While somewhat concerned about the rise of China, these elites optimistically believe that deepening interdependence and common cultural ties in East Asia will result in a relatively benign regional security environment over the long term. Accordingly, they believe that multilateral security (e.g , UN and ARF) should play an increasingly prominent role in Japanese security at the expense of bilateral ties with the United States.

Slow growth in military expenditures in the absence of a clear regional threat. Although Japanese military expenditures continued to grow in the 1990s in absolute terms, they did so at a much slower rate than in the 1980s. The rate of annual increase in the Japanese defense budget has declined steadily since 1990, from a 6.1 percent increase in that year to an increase of only 0.9 percent in 1994.[47] Moreover, since 1991, the share of the defense budget devoted to weapons procurement has declined by 3.9 percent. This change reflects increased expenditures for certain components of Japan's defense budget—including personnel, operations and maintenance, and support for U.S. forces—and stabilized procurement expenditures after the rapid increases of recent years. The change also reflects the impact of anemic economic growth, which began in the early 1990s, and the impact of a strong yen, which has lowered the price of imported weaponry.[48]

Barring abrogation of the alliance or an armed attack against it, Japan is unlikely to increase its military expenditures dramatically in the next decade and acquire a large military force with major offensive capabilities. First, a majority of public opinion will likely continue to support keeping the size of the SDF at present levels (about 238,000 troops) or even reducing its numbers. Public opinion would also oppose the procurement of weapons systems that would enable Japan to project military power, including long-range bombers and missiles, aircraft carriers, long-range logistics support, and sufficient amphibious and airlift capabilities to mount an invasion of neighboring countries. Given such popular opinion and legal constraints, the Japanese government will most likely lack the political will to carry out a major expansion of Japan's defense capabilities. Second, the number of young Japanese of military age will continue to decline, making it difficult to recruit enough volunteers to meet a recently reduced authorized ground troop personnel level of 145,000 (barring a severe economic recession). Moreover, public opinion would be highly opposed to any attempt to impose conscription. Third, slow economic growth and tight constraints on government spending will further make it unlikely that Japanese defense expenditures will exceed 1 percent of GNP—the traditional ceiling. Fourth, given slow budget growth prospects, it will be difficult for Japan to procure a large number of new major weapons systems; comparatively few fi-

---

[47]At the same time, the military expenditure's share of GDP is expected to move slightly downward, from the traditional limit of 1 percent to 0.9 percent.

[48]For more detailed information on decreases in specific types of weapons systems, see, for example, "JDA Aircraft Buys Suffer," *Aviation Week and Space Technology*, April 3, 1995, p. 64.

nancial resources will remain for operations and maintenance, procurement, and research and development because of unusually high expenditures on personnel (about 44 percent of the defense budget) and host-nation support for U.S. forces (about 11 percent of the defense budget). Furthermore, procurement costs are much higher for indigenous systems, given a lack of economies of scale, leaving few financial resources to devote to research and development. As a result of these constraints, the Japanese government recently decided to cut back procurement of the FSX fighter, developed jointly with the United States, from 120 planes to 80 planes.

Despite such limitations, Japan nevertheless has the financial, industrial, and technological resources to become a major military power should its regional security environment worsen, international economic institutions collapse, and the alliance be abrogated. Japanese hedging against the possibility of a more hostile regional security environment and abrogation of the alliance can be seen in recent plans: (1) to improve the intelligence capabilities of the SDF, including the use of satellites; (2) to procure transport aircraft that can fly greater distances and carry more than existing C-1 and C-130 aircraft; (3) to acquire air-refueling tankers for patrol planes; and (4) to perhaps acquire "defensive" aircraft carriers. Moreover, Japan possesses stockpiles of near-weapons-grade plutonium. It could, therefore, become a nuclear superpower quickly, if it had the political will to do so. Choice of the nuclear card will remain unlikely, however, given the legacy of World War II, the enormous benefits Japan currently derives from maintenance of the status quo, and the continued willingness of the United States to extend a nuclear umbrella over Japan.

Drivers of Conflict and Regional Instability. The foregoing trends point to a range of potential drivers, or possible precipitants, of conflict between Japan and other regional states. Even more significantly for the United States and regional stability, these trends point to a range of drivers that would have an adverse impact on the maintenance of the U.S.-Japan alliance or impede the proper functioning of the alliance in the event of a crisis. In the absence of the alliance, a number of regional conflicts would become more likely, including several involving Japan, arising from long-standing animosities, divided nations, territorial conflicts, leadership transitions that could give way to more nationalistic and assertive regimes, and power transitions in East Asia. The stabilizing functions of a U.S. presence would be negated if adversaries of the United States, its allies, and its friends calculated that Japan would not provide support for U.S. forces stationed in Japan or would not allow U.S. forces to conduct military operations against an adversary from bases in Japan. With a weakening of the deterrent function of the alliance, potential adversaries would view aggression as involving less risk, raising the potential for armed conflicts in East Asia. Moreover, the ability of the United States to wage war would be crippled against a major Northeast Asian aggressor, given the highly adverse effect that a weakened alliance would have on U.S. Air Force operations and logistical support.

The first potential driver of conflict or regional instability would be an extended process of political realignment and the emergence of a politically unstable and ineffectual Japanese government unable to cope with critical choices facing its economy and regional security environment. As already discussed, such a development would make it difficult for Japan to cooperate with the United States in a timely manner should an international crisis arise. If Japan's response was expected to be "too little, too late," it would affect the calculations of potential adversaries of Japan and the United States and also constrain the range of possible diplomatic, economic, and military responses the United States could make in a crisis. A weak and ineffectual Japanese government would also encourage China to be more aggressive in its pursuit of its claims to the Senkaku Islands.

The emergence of a series of weak governments would make it difficult for Japan to make hard choices concerning the restructuring and deregulation of its economy. Such indecisiveness in turn would encourage heightened economic conflict with the United States (unable to continue to absorb excess Asian production as it attempted to pay off its large, accumulated deficit) and strain the alliance. Maintenance of the alliance would become increasingly difficult to justify to the American public in light of its costs, especially if Chinese external interactions with its neighbors were relatively tranquil.

The second potential driver of conflict would be the emergence of great-power nationalism in Japan over the long term (2015–2025). Although a much less likely development, a combination of trends already identified could produce such an outcome. This development would follow a period of prolonged political instability; failure to restructure and deregulate the Japanese economy, with highly adverse consequences for long-term economic growth prospects (stagnant or negative growth) and high unemployment; great strains in U.S.-Japan relations; development of an autonomous Japanese security policy and offensive conventional weapons; abrogation of the alliance; and a major shift in the locus of Japanese interests away from the United States and toward Asia. Most likely, Japan would become a state possessing nuclear weapons. Because of the legacy of past Japanese behavior in Asia, however, Japan's neighbors would be alarmed by such a development, which also would increase the costs for the United States of maintaining stability in East Asia, if it still chose to do so.

Great-power nationalism likely would be accompanied by a revival of prewar Japan's strategy of attempting to construct a coprosperity sphere primarily through coercive means, given Japan's dependence on imported resources. This nationalism would involve a resurrection of Japan's prewar goals toward the Asia-Pacific region, centered on the attainment, through either direct military seizure or indirect intimidation, of unchallengeable control over major sources of raw materials and markets throughout much of the region. Such a transformation in Japan's relations with other Asia-Pacific countries would require the acquisition of highly sophisticated offensive and defensive conventional capabilities and a limited nuclear capability. It would become more likely not only as a result of a fundamental breakdown in the U.S.-Japan alliance relationship and global trading system, but also in response to strong insecurities associated with such events as the acquisition of nuclear weapons by a unified Korea, the breakdown of order in China, and the development of a Sino-Korean military entente.

Any Japanese attempt to achieve hegemony through military means would almost certainly prove quixotic, however. Traditional East Asian suspicions of Japan—in large part mitigated by Japan's strong economic links with Asia, restrictions on the size of Japan's armed forces, limitations on its procurement of weapons systems with power projection capabilities, and Japan's lack of nuclear weapons— would be rekindled if Japan again attempted to become a dominant military power in the region. Japanese nuclear ambitions would likely set off alarms in other Asian capitals—particularly Beijing, Seoul, and Taipei—and risk undermining Japan's regional economic links, especially in the absence of a stabilizing U.S. military presence in the Western Pacific.

Any Japanese attempt to achieve hegemony through military means would most likely result in the creation of an anti-hegemonic coalition aimed at the containment of Japan and perhaps result in armed conflict with other states, including China, Russia, and even the United States. In the event of the implosion of China, a weakened Russia, and a more isolationist United States, all three states would remain major nuclear powers—a factor that would likely prove sufficient to prevent a reoccurrence of Japanese military aggression in East Asia. Even a nationalistic Japan would therefore be unlikely to attempt to resort to force to resolve its territorial conflict with Russia. Moreover, even a divided Korea is much more powerful than it was at the beginning of the 20th century when it was occupied by Japan. Finally, Japanese energy supplies from the Middle East would be highly vulnerable in the event of hostile relations with China. Any Japanese adventurism would therefore most likely be directed at Southeast Asia.

A third potential driver of conflict or regional instability would be a failure by Japan to liberalize its economy. The consequences of this development for U.S.-Japan bilateral relations, and alliance maintenance and trust in particular, have already been discussed. Economic conflict, whether between the United States and Asia or between Japan and its Asian neighbors (which have emulated Japan's economic development strategy), could lead to a protectionist backlash in the United States. Continued U.S. trade imbalances could in turn increase domestic pressures to disengage militarily from Asia because of tensions arising from the usage of scarce financial resources to protect nations running large trade surpluses with the United States.

A breakdown of U.S.-Japanese cooperation in international economic institutions could have even more critical consequences for global trade and investment and hence regional and world economic growth over the longer term. Lowered growth prospects in China and Southeast Asia could result in domestic political instability and increase the incentives for East Asian states to resort to war to achieve their objectives. Sino-Japanese, Korean-Japanese, and Chinese armed conflict with a Southeast Asian state (with potential Japanese involvement) would all become much more likely, given preexisting historical animosities and overlapping territorial claims in the region.

The key economic challenge for Asia during the next 15 years, which poses critical security implications, is the question of who will absorb its exports. If the U.S. and European markets prove incapable of continuing to absorb Asian exports, given disparities in present growth rates and accumulated foreign debt in the United States, the importance of economic liberalization within Asia would be accentuated. The United States may be increasingly unable to serve as an engine for regional growth, given that it has become the world's largest debtor state and has lost its former huge net earnings on foreign investment, and instead may need to run a large trade surplus to service its debt. Europe, faced with political pressure to open its market to Eastern Europe, also appears an unlikely candidate to further increase imports.

Japan's support for a successful implementation of the recent Asia Pacific Economic Cooperation (APEC) free-trade commitment will therefore prove critical, because continued pursuit of neo-mercantilist strategies by East Asian states would eventually result in the alienation of each from all. Declining shares in world markets outside Asia could conceivably result in zero-sum, neo-mercantilist conflict between Japan and other Asian exporters. Only the emergence of huge consumer markets in the region, facilitated by trade liberalization, could compensate for possible stagnant or even declining exports to developed countries outside Asia. Furthermore, if Chinese economic growth should stall, economic liberalization in the rest of Asia would become even more important. Japan's liberalization of its economy will therefore be critical to prospects for long-term stability in East Asia.

A fourth potential driver of regional conflict or instability would be an attempt by Japan to develop tight-knit economic, political, social, and even military ties with other Asian countries and exclude U.S. influence from Asia. Trends that could lead to this development include Japan's growing economic, political, and social ties with other Asian countries, the declining economic influence of the

United States in Asia, the declining salience of the shadow of the past between Japan and its Southeast Asian neighbors, growing desires for an East Asia economic grouping as a counterweight to trade friction with the West, and rising political friction between the United States and several East Asian regimes. This development would require the abrogation of the Japan-U.S. alliance and continuity in Japanese defense policy, including maintenance of Japan's nonnuclear principles and nonpossession of offensive weapons, for Japan to avoid alarming its neighbors.

The significance of such "malevolent Asianization" lies less in its prospects for sustainability and more in the danger that could arise from miscalculation by Asian regimes and the United States, each pursuing hedging strategies or short-sighted bargaining positions that in the end could result in an outcome that would not be in the long-term interests of any Asia-Pacific country. A process of malevolent Asianization, directed at the United States, would ultimately consume itself and lead to a breakdown of Asian economic cooperation, to Sino-Japanese rivalry, and perhaps even war, or a form of hegemonic dominance by China or Japan.

Anticipating Conflict in East Asia. Based on the general trends and the specific drivers identified in the previous discussion, it is possible to envisage the following military conflicts involving Japan directly or indirectly (as an ally of the United States):

Short Term (Present Year–2005): In this time period, Japan is extremely unlikely to become involved in a major military conflict that it provokes with its neighbors. Reasons include a probable continuation of the alliance during this period, a lack of incentives to resort to force as the Asian power benefiting most from maintenance of the status quo,[49] and probable continuity of public opinion in favor of maintaining Article 9 of the Constitution and opposing the possession of offensive and nuclear weapons.

Japan is also unlikely to become involved in a dyadic conflict that one of its neighbors provokes during this period, both because of the

---

[49]The only exception is the disposition of the Northern Territories. The potential costs of armed conflict with a nuclear-armed Russia would, however, greatly exceed any gains from seizure of the islands.

deterrent qualities of Japan's alliance with the United States and because of Japan's preeminent economic position in Asia. As long as China continues to place a high priority on economic development, China will be unlikely to attempt to resort to force to resolve its territorial dispute with Japan over the Senkaku Islands, especially given the importance of Japanese technology and capital for China's modernization efforts. This conflict would be unlikely even in the event of prolonged political instability in Japan. An attempted seizure of the Senkaku Islands would also solidify the Japan-U.S. alliance, provoke a nationalist backlash in Japan, and encourage the formation of a grand Asian alliance led by Japan and the United States against China. Moreover, reunification with Taiwan represents a much higher priority for China. Japanese-Korean military conflict is also highly unlikely during this period, except for the possibility of minor skirmishes over conflicting territorial claims in the Sea of Japan.

The most likely conflict scenarios involving Japan in this period would be conflicts resulting from Japan's being dragged into a conflict by virtue of its alliance with the United States. An armed attack against Japan (including the possible use of WMD) by either North Korea or China could stem from Japan's provision of logistical support to the United States and/or because Japan allowed U.S. forces to conduct direct military operations against an adversary from Japanese soil. Japan might also be attacked if it provided air and naval support for U.S. forces against an East Asian state, although such support would be questionable in a conflict involving China. These conflict scenarios would most likely take place in the event of the emergence of a strong Japanese government and a revitalization and redefinition of the alliance relationship with the United States.

As already discussed, the most significant trends in Japan with major consequences for regional stability for the near term are (1) those that could have an adverse impact on the deterrent qualities of a U.S. regional presence by encouraging greater risk-taking behavior by other Asian states, or (2) those that could result in Japan placing severe limitations on the conduct of U.S. military operations from Japanese soil.

Medium Term (2006–2015): In this time period, Japan would continue to be unlikely to become involved in a dyadic conflict for reasons identified above. Toward the end of this period—should trends and events result in the emergence of Japan as a major military power following the abrogation of the alliance, in conjunction with a neo-imperialistic scramble for resources among the great powers following a breakdown of the liberal trading system—Japan could become a party to resource conflicts in Northeast and Southeast Asia, especially those involving energy resources.

Although the chances of conflict would remain low, barring a breakdown of global and regional trade patterns, Japanese-Korean relations could also become more problematic during this period, which would be especially likely under three conditions: (1) The United States withdraws its military presence from Asia; (2) a more confident and nationalist Korea emerges following unification (especially if it possessed WMD capabilities); and (3) no true atonement for past Japanese behavior has yet taken place. Nevertheless, aside from possible minor skirmishes over fisheries and other resources in the Sea of Japan, Japanese-Korean armed conflict would be unlikely during this period. In the face of a relative power shift in China's favor, Japan would be wary of encouraging the development of a Sino-Korean entente or alliance directed against itself. Armed conflict between Japan and Korea would be most probable in the event of a conjunction of four developments: (1) U.S. disengagement from Asia; (2) a breakdown of the global trading system; (3) the eventual ascendance of great-power nationalism in Tokyo; and (4) the emergence of a chaotic China—all of which would create opportunities and incentives for Japan to undertake aggressive actions against its neighbor.

Prospects for dyadic Sino-Japanese armed conflict would be low during this period, although a weak and insecure China could attempt to seize control of the Senkaku Islands during this period for "rally 'round the flag" purposes. Such an event, however, would be more likely in the subsequent period examined by this study. Dyadic Sino-Japanese conflict over Taiwan could become possible toward the end of this period, but only in the event of the emergence of a chaotic China, or a weak and insecure China, in conjunction with the ascendance of great-power nationalism in Tokyo.

The most striking development that could take place in this period—with profound implications for regional security and U.S. policy—would be the emergence of a Sino-Japanese entente in the context of malevolent Asianization discussed earlier. Although Asian national-ism could serve as a unifying force against "unreasonable" U.S. de-mands and actions, such pan-nationalism could only supplement and not substitute for real common interests on the part of Asian states.

Sustained Sino-Japanese cooperation would be difficult in the ab-sence of a U.S. regional military presence as a stabilizing force, given historical enmity and geopolitical considerations. Sino-Japanese collaboration would be inherently unstable, because it would involve a pairing of a non–status quo China seeking to increase its overall ability to shape regional events and a nonnuclear and defensively oriented Japan. The same constellation of domestic forces in Chinese politics that would support confrontation with the United States—that is, a high level of conservative (and possibly military) involvement in politics—would also likely adopt an aggressive stance on the South China Sea and Taiwan issues. Moreover, such conservative elements would be especially suspicious of Japan's regional ambitions, if Japanese politics again become dominated by those elites favoring a "continental" Asia strategy and also in view of Japan's past historical conduct in Asia. Adoption of a pro-Japanese foreign policy by conservative elements in China would at best represent temporary pragmatism on their part.

In the absence of an alliance with the United States, Japan would likely view rising Chinese power with alarm, especially if China's economic growth continued at rates nearly double or triple those in Japan. With some parallels to the 1930s, the same right-wing or left-wing groups favoring an exclusivist Asian vision for Japan would also likely favor a great-power vision. If Japan, however, chose to procure nuclear weapons and considerably upgrade its force projection ca-pabilities, it would alarm China and other Asian neighbors. As a re-sult, China and Japan would compete for economic, military, and political influence in Korea, Taiwan, and Southeast Asia.

Long Term (2016–2025): In this time period, conflicts involving Japan would resemble those that could occur toward the end of the last time frame. In the face of the emergence of a highly assertive China, committed to regional dominance, Japan could seek a mari-time alliance with ASEAN, India, and perhaps Russia. The geo-graphic scope of possible clashes between China and Japan would expand to include not only Northeast Asia but also Southeast Asia and the Indian Ocean. Sino-Japanese rivalry over Korea especially would become acute.

THE KOREAN PENINSULA

Introduction

At century's end, the Korean peninsula is poised for another major transition based on an acceleration of systemic atrophy in North Korea and attendant political-military outcomes.[50] Although it is difficult to forecast the timing and magnitude of change going into the "unification tunnel,"[51] stability could be affected through one or more of the following developments: regime collapse or replacement by force (i.e., a military coup); breakdown in command and control hierarchies (either between the party and the military or within the military); civil unrest or uprisings coupled with refugee flows; variants of state collapse; enhanced low-intensity conflicts; and the possible outbreak of major war.[52]

It is important to recall that throughout most of the Cold War era, stability on the peninsula was maintained largely through three principal factors: tight military alliances, a balance of forces between the South and the North, and strong domestic regimes. A major contributing factor toward stability on the peninsula during the Cold War was that *simultaneous* transformations did not occur in each of the three factors noted above. Incidents such as the discovery of tunnels under the Demilitarized Zone (DMZ) in the mid-1970s, the 1976 tree-cutting incident in the DMZ that resulted in the deaths of several U.S. and ROK personnel, the assassination of President Park

---

[50]The official term for South Korea is the Republic of Korea (ROK); North Korea is the Democratic People's Republic of Korea (DPRK). The official acrnoyms as well as the terms South and North Korea are used jointly in this chapter.

[51]The term "unification tunnel" refers to the development of events on and around the Korean peninsula that will ultimately result in the formation of a unified Korean state. It does not follow, however, that the process will be linear or without conflict.

[52]It should be emphasized that future scenarios and developments on the Korean peninsula that are depicted in this study are not predictions or forecasts. Rather, certain scenarios are developed to look into the potential political and military implications.

Chung Hee in 1979 by his intelligence chief, the 1983 Rangoon bombing by North Korean agents that caused the death of 17 high-ranking ROK officials, and the initial eruption in 1993–1994 of the North Korean nuclear crisis all contributed to rising apprehension on the peninsula. Nevertheless, although tension rose significantly after each of these events, no direct military clash occurred between South and North Korea.

With the end of the Cold War, not only have shifts taken place in each of these areas but a new factor has emerged with potentially profound implications for stability on the peninsula and Northeast Asia—regime atrophy and the possibility of collapse in the North. Stability on the peninsula could be affected by a volatile mix of the following developments: (1) accelerated economic decline in the North (the North Korean economy registered its seventh consecutive year of negative growth in 1996, or about a 30 percent contraction since 1989); (2) dwindling or narrowing strategic options for the Pyongyang regime; (3) the unwillingness or inability of China or Russia to extend long-term economic assistance; (4) shifting political dynamics within the Kim Jong Il regime; and (5) continuing concern surrounding North Korea's weapons of mass destruction (WMD) capability.[53] The key question is whether efforts by South Korea and the United States to foster long-term stability on the peninsula through a combination of deterrence and engagement toward the North will ultimately bear fruit in the form of moderated North Korean behavior. The critical danger, however, is not whether a policy of engagement is appropriate or even if it is politically viable. Rather, the key issue is whether systemic atrophy will reach such a

---

[53]Despite the Agreed Framework of October 1994, which was put into place to freeze North Korea's potential nuclear weapons program, doubts persist on whether North Korea has given up its nuclear ambitions. Hwang Jang Yop, the former central committee secretary for international affairs of the Korean Workers' Party who defected to the South through Beijing in April 1997, stated in a press conference in July 1997 that while he had no concrete evidence that North Korea had nuclear weapons, it was his belief that North Korea was prepared to launch an invasion against the South and that he was working on the assumption that North Korea probably had nuclear weapons. However, notwithstanding the significance of Hwang's testimony (since he is the most senior North Korean official to defect to the South), his belief that North Korea has already successfully developed nuclear weapons has not been verified by either the U.S. or South Korean governments.

stage that, irrespective of U.S. and South Korean incentives, the system in the North will ultimately collapse under its own weight.

If internal dynamics in North Korea can be construed as the nucleus of South-North stability, fundamental change within the North Korean system cannot but affect the peninsula's center of gravity. Most problematic for U.S. and ROK security and defense planners, however, is that as the internal situation in the North continues to worsen, the net utility of "timely corrections" is likely to become increasingly marginalized to the extent that North Korea may be tempted to fundamentally alter the correlation of forces on the peninsula through selective or full-scale applications of force. Alternatively, if a "hard landing" occurs in the North, it could result in potentially serious military spillovers.

Critics of the hard-landing school (or proponents of the soft-landing school), however, emphasize that precisely because of the looming specter of a North Korean collapse and all of its negative and destabilizing aftershocks, the United States should take the lead in fostering peaceful change on the peninsula. From a conceptual and even a policy perspective, promoting a soft landing in the North makes eminent sense because it is not in the interest of the United States, South Korea, Japan, or other regional power to foster a North Korean collapse. But if North Korea collapses, it is likely to do so *independent* of the strategies employed by the United States and South Korea. Diplomatic engagement, economic assistance, and even political breakthroughs could *postpone* a North Korean collapse, but are unlikely to *prevent* it, since the root causes of collapse are entrenched within the North Korean system. Moreover, the very prescription that proponents of a soft landing have called for—such as economic reforms along the lines of China or Vietnam to prevent a North Korean collapse—will, in all likelihood, have the opposite outcome of accelerating the regime's demise given the extremely high political and social-control costs associated with enacting any wide-ranging and meaningful economic reforms.

From a historical perspective, three key developments on the Korean peninsula over the last 100 years have had international consequences. First, in the aftermath of the Sino-Japanese War of 1894–1895 and the Russo-Japanese War of 1905, Japan displaced China as the dominant regional hegemon. The outbreak of these two wars can be traced to a confluence of factors, but retaining, denying, or extending control over the peninsula was a major determinant. Second, and some five decades later, the outbreak of the Korean War in 1950 resulted in the globalization of the Cold War. Equally significant, it added a fourth major power—the United States—directly into East Asian power politics by extending U.S. security guarantees to Japan and South Korea. Third, mounting political and economic challenges in North Korea, coupled with Pyongyang's limited diplomatic maneuverability, are likely to result in another fundamental transformation on the Korean peninsula at the tail end of the 20th century—with substantial regional repercussions.

This history does not suggest that contingency planning has not taken into account the range of threats emanating from the North such as multiple forms of low-intensity conflict, ballistic missile proliferation, and infiltration/insurgency operations. Nevertheless, political and military disruptions short of full-scale war (otherwise referred to as operations other than war or OOTW) have not received the attention they deserve by the defense communities in either Seoul or Washington. To be sure, the specter of a North Korean collapse or implosion, or at the very least, significant political shakeout, did not fully register until the collapse of East Germany in 1989–1990, the breakup of the Soviet Union in 1991, and the passing of Kim Il Sung in 1994. However, with the emergence of new sources of instability, conceptualization of future contingencies and realistic policy options must begin anew. Traditional approaches to security on the Korean peninsula such as deterrence and defense will continue to be relevant until such time that a military threat ceases to exist or is superseded by events. But the net utility of those approaches to security going into the unification tunnel is likely to decline as transformation dynamics impose new demands on U.S. and ROK strategies.

Seen from this perspective, an emerging challenge lies in the ROK's articulation of a long-term national security strategy. Clearly, managing the North Korean problem will consume the lion's share of South Korea's attention until such time that the military threat from the North is reduced substantially or a more enduring peace mechanism is formed. Nonetheless, if unification occurs at an accelerated pace, the ROK and the major powers could find themselves in the post-unification era sooner than currently expected. Therefore, how the ROK envisions its own future role in Northeast Asia, the impact of domestic political forces on shaping key foreign and defense policy platforms, future force modernization objectives and programs, new alliance management dynamics with the United States, and other major security issues will rise to the fore. Since the post–Korean War era, the ROK's defense posture has been strongly tied to the U.S.-ROK alliance—including, but not limited to, the presence of some 37,000 U.S. forces in South Korea. As the ROK heads into the unification tunnel, however, it has to begin the process of laying out a security blueprint for the post-unification era. For its part, the United States has noted on several occasions that U.S. forces could continue to be deployed on the peninsula after unification, since Korea would be the only mainland Asian country where the United States could have a forward presence. In the short to mid term, domestic political developments in South Korea could also complicate security planning dynamics, including alliance management with the United States.

Over the long run, however, post-unification deployment of U.S. forces could become increasingly affected by domestic politics both in Korea and in the United States, in addition to a unified Korea's overall foreign and security policies. The question of U.S. troop deployments would be one of a range of major security issues to be broached by the two governments, although political pressure could increase in the U.S. Congress to withdraw U.S. ground forces from Korea after unification. At the same time, increasing nationalist sentiments in a unified Korea and the desire for greater autonomy could result in a significant reduction in the size of U.S. troop deployments. In addition, the possibility cannot be ruled out that China might pressure a unified Korea to disallow stationing any U.S. troops. Beijing could react extremely negatively to the possibility of a continuing U.S. military presence in Korea after the disappearance of the North Korean "buffer zone." The specific attributes of post-unification deployment are difficult to pinpoint at this juncture, although a unified Korea's overall security would be enhanced by a strong defense relationship with the United States given the specter of a rising and more influential China and other changes in the regional balance of power. From an operational perspective, if some U.S. forward presence is maintained in a unified Korea, the role of the U.S. Air Force could increase if there is a significant reduction in ground forces or alternative basing modes.

A unified Korea's strategic choices would have to deal with other crucial issues. For example, if it turns out that North Korea did succeed in developing a small number of nuclear weapons, those weapons and delivery vehicles and any other weapons of mass destruction would need to be dismantled. In essence, the ROK has to begin serious deliberations on post-unification dynamics, the role a unified Korea would play in the Northeast Asian balance of power, the foundations for a forward-looking alliance with the United States, longer-term force modernization goals, and a national security strategy that takes into consideration the likely strategies and policies of its more powerful neighbors. The United States also has a critical stake in future outcomes on the Korean peninsula and resultant implications for Northeast Asia's strategic balance. Owing to the convergence of fundamental challenges such as near- to mid-term developments in the North as well as managing unification dynamics, security planning between the United States and the ROK may have to be revamped substantially over the next several years.

Strategic Trends and Drivers

In sharp contrast to geopolitical dynamics on the Korean peninsula during the Cold War, prospects for instability and conflict have increased through the convergence of four major trends: (1) accelerating systemic decline in the North coupled with narrowing strategic options for the North Korean leadership; (2) increasing political clout of the already formidable North Korean armed forces by determining and driving key strategic goals and the potential for enhanced political struggles within the apex of the North Korean political-military structure; (3) a fundamental reappraisal of the major powers' strategies and policies toward the two Koreas with greater attention to crisis management dynamics and prospects for increasing Chinese activity vis-à-vis developments in North Korea; and (4) a hardening of South Korea's overall position toward North Korea on account of increasing political uncertainty in the North coupled with Pyongyang's attempts to enhance its strategic space through insurgency, terrorism, or a full-scale conventional war.

These four trends strongly suggest that, in whatever form they may ultimately materialize, *military stability* on the Korean peninsula could be disrupted. To be sure, accounting for some type of a military conflict has always been at the center of contingency planning on the part of the ROK and the United States. Nevertheless, the stakes are greater today than at any other time since the end of the Korean War in 1953, given that internal developments within the North are likely to drive strategic dynamics on the Korean peninsula. The point here is not to argue that war is inevitable, only that the most desirable outcome—peaceful and democratic unification through a mutually acceptable political process between Seoul and Pyongyang—is the least likely outcome. As a result, despite expectations that diplomatic negotiations will ultimately bear fruit on such fronts as South-North dialogue and the four-party talks, unification of the two Koreas based on genuine negotiations between the South and the North could ultimately prove to be ephemeral despite the best of intentions. Moreover, unless and until one side is willing to make fundamental concessions, prospects for a negotiated settlement will continue to remain limited.

The biggest threat to stability on the peninsula over the next several years stems from strategic calculations the North Korean leadership will make to regain its political and military momentum. Many have argued that North Korea's errant behavior over the last several decades (but particularly since the end of the Cold War) reflects its deeply imbedded sense of insecurity. If South Korea, the United States, Japan, and other actors provide adequate assurances—in the form of diplomatic engagement, economic assistance, and military confidence-building measures—Pyongyang will not only negotiate in good faith, it will enact meaningful and much-needed economic reforms. Nevertheless, the concept of a "soft landing" is fundamentally flawed since it assumes that North Korea in its present form has the political capacity to undertake pragmatic economic reforms without political fallout or fundamental threats to regime survival. Many proponents of the soft-landing school argue strongly for greater engagement with the North in the belief that stronger institutional linkages between North Korea and the outside world will constrain North Korean behavior, build political support for the technocrats within the system, and compel the North to craft a more pragmatic, nonthreatening exit strategy from mounting domestic challenges. Nevertheless, given the absolute personification of state and regime in the form of the ongoing Kim dynasty, pragmatic shifts in North Korea are not only highly unlikely but would unleash forces detrimental to regime survival. In a nutshell, the key dilemma confronting the North Korean regime is that if the state is to survive, measures must be taken that could ultimately result in its demise. And, conversely, strengthening the regime is likely to weaken state capacity even further to the extent that maintaining centralized control is likely to become increasingly problematic, if not volatile and violent.

The window of time is narrowing in earnest in the North. From Pyongyang's perspective, offsetting worsening economic conditions with an influx of foreign aid and direct investment but *without* political side effects is not only the preferred approach, it is, in many respects, the only viable approach. However, this strategy is unlikely to succeed because any significant amount of economic aid is likely to be linked with promises of positive behavior on the part of the regime. Perhaps more important, structural decay has reached a point where current and expected foreign assistance is unlikely to fundamentally improve North Korea's economic crisis and may ultimately lead to state collapse.[54] No foreign country, either individually or collectively, is willing to provide the North with a "mini-Marshall Plan." Even if such a comprehensive aid package were to materialize, it would cause severe political problems for Pyongyang, so that ultimately it would not be able to digest any massive influx of foreign economic aid or investment. If the aforementioned analysis is correct, Pyongyang is unlikely to enact meaningful economic reforms for fear of disrupting the regime's hold onto power. But as domestic pressure mounts, coupled with only marginal support from the outside, the regime may calculate that the only viable means to

---

[54]Conceptually, the very idea of a collapse is open to various interpretations. Within the range of possible regime transitions in the North, three basic models can be considered: (1) replacement or elimination of Kim Jong Il and his core group of supporters from the *nomenklatura*, (2) a change in the fundamental political and ideological characteristic of the regime (for example, renunciation of socialism and a centralized planned economy), or (3) severe atrophy and ultimate breakdown of the North Korean state along the lines of the former Soviet Union. Moreover, other variations from these three basic "collapse models" could also be considered, but in its basic form, a North Korean collapse would correspond to one or more of the outcomes noted here.

correct the correlation of forces on the Korean peninsula is through military provocation against the South, ranging from enhanced insurgency operations (as evinced by the infiltration of North Korean commandos in a mini-submarine in mid-September 1996), selected terrorism (such as the likelihood of North Korea's involvement in the assassination of a South Korean diplomat in Vladivostok in October 1996), sporadic low-intensity conflicts, or full-scale war. A more detailed assessment of the four major trends followed by key drivers and prospects for conflict on the peninsula is provided below, although primary emphasis is placed on systemic transformation within North Korea given its broader implications.

Trend One: Acceleration of a "funnel phenomenon," marked by entrenched systemic decay or atrophy in North Korea. The most pronounced aspect of such a decline is in the economic sector. Although economic stagnation in and of itself is unlikely to result in a North Korean collapse, a prolonged downturn compounded by increasing food shortages (because of the failure of collectivization and severe side effects from unprecedented floods in 1995 and 1996), a de facto breakdown in the all-important ration system, acute shortage of energy and oil supplies, and inability to rejuvenate key industrial sectors other than defense industries cannot but affect political stability. In 1996, the North Korean GNP was about $23 billion and its total trade volume was estimated at $2.1 billion. In contrast, South Korea's GNP in 1996 was $450 billion with a total trade volume of about $200 billion.

North Korea's economic decay poses several challenges to the Kim Jong Il regime. To begin with, it has become impossible for North Korea to compete with the South in economic terms. (The North Korean economy until the mid-1960s outperformed that of South Korea's because of the concentration of natural resources in the North and the initial successes of postwar reconstruction in North Korea. However, since the South Korean economy began to take off in the early 1970s, the gap has grown between the two economies.) Notwithstanding longer-term structural problems confronting the South Korean economy, the South-North economic competition has clearly ended in favor of the South. In addition, North Korea's economic decline has coincided with Kim Jong Il's rise to the center of North Korean politics. Just as Kim Jong Il's control over the party, the military, and the intelligence agencies began in earnest in the mid to late 1980s, decades of economic mismanagement, a sharp decline in Soviet and Chinese economic assistance, and structural problems associated with overinvestments in the military sector began to surface.

Indeed, Kim Il Sung's death in July 1994 created a crucial dilemma for Kim Jong Il: While the entrenched structural problems of the North Korean economy were based on the economic policies instituted by his father, Kim Il Sung, since the 1960s under the all-consuming ideology of *Juche* (self-reliance), he could ill afford to blame North Korea's economic woes on his father since such a move would be equated with his own delegitimization. Therefore, the ability of North Korea to enact meaningful economic reforms ultimately will be decided not on an economic but a political rationale. Kim Jong Il is unlikely to depart from the status quo even as the overall situation continues to worsen at an accelerated pace. *The relevant drivers here are twofold: deteriorating economic conditions and the regime's inability to arrest, control, or fundamentally alter economic decline.* As the economic situation worsens and as the regime's strategic options begin to dwindle in earnest, even stopgap measures such as attracting much-needed foreign economic assistance and direct investments are unlikely to fundamentally alter the health of the North Korean economy.

Trend Two: Increasing political influence of the military and its impact on strategic choice. Perhaps no other state in the world is as militarized as North Korea, which has a standing army of 1.1 million troops, and some 4.5 million reserves (500,000 of which could be called into active service in a relatively short time) and paramilitary forces, and is a police state second to none. That the military enjoys political prestige and exercises considerable political influence is certainly not surprising. However, its overall political influence has increased substantially with the death of Kim Il Sung, and the military plays a crucial role in buttressing Kim Jong Il's regime. Unlike his father, Kim Jong Il has no military background and although he is the supreme commander of the Korean People's Army (KPA) and has formally assumed the position as general secretary of the Korean Workers Party (KWP), it remains to be seen whether he will be able to maintain effective control over the military in the long run or in a major political or military crisis.

In this respect, three key issues need to be examined. First, even as the core leadership in the armed forces remains loyal to Kim Jong Il, increasingly intrusive political control and interference by Kim could contribute significantly to resentment within the professional officer corps. If Kim Jong Il further tightens political control to stamp out real or imaginary opposition "grupas" (or groups) in the KPA (as has been reported but not confirmed) and opts to enact wide-ranging and potentially bloody purges, opposition within the top military hierarchy could develop and strengthen. Second, while conventional wisdom dictates that the KPA is unlikely to directly challenge Kim Jong Il (it is the major beneficiary of his regime), the KPA's survivability is not dependent on Kim Jong Il. For Kim Jong Il, however, regime survival without the KPA's backing is virtually impossible to imagine. Thus, while the KPA can live without Kim Jong Il, he cannot survive without the military. Third, how will the KPA influence key strategic choices as North Korea's window of opportunity begins to narrow? Currently, it appears that North Korea has little choice but to hunker down domestically and to ride out its economic difficulties. However, as the regime's strategic options continue to narrow and the costs associated with maintaining the status quo heighten, pressures will mount within the system. Corrective measures may well be taken to alleviate acute shortages, but, again, wholesale reforms are unlikely.

It is at this point that North Korea will have to seriously address key strategic options with increasing input from the armed forces. It appears that the North has the following options:

Option 1: Maintain the status quo on political, military, and economic fronts with even firmer political control.

Option 2: Introduce partial economic reforms while retaining centralized planning mechanisms with no change in the Leninist party structure. Variations include (1) enacting gradual but ultimately fundamental economic reforms along the Chinese model (e.g., retaining the current leadership structure but with a "gentler and kinder" face); or (2) implementing wide-ranging and fundamental economic reforms with some loosening of party controls, (e.g., partial decentralizing of decisionmaking process and more open debate within the higher councils of government).

Option 3: Oust Kim Jong Il and his extended family through a military coup and install a pragmatic leadership willing to undertake key economic reforms while retaining the central role of the armed forces and the party.

Option 4: Undertake destabilizing actions against targets within South Korea through insurgency operations, terrorism, and selective military strikes short of an invasion (such as an artillery attack on a South Korean military unit or launching one or more ballistic missiles against an industrial or energy plant in the South), in the hope that internal cohesion can be strengthened without inviting a foreign response.

Option 5: Launch a full-scale war against the South through *blitzkrieg* operations and threaten the employment of nuclear, biological, or chemical (NBC) weapons, in the belief that such a move would deter the United States from sending timely reinforcements to the South.

Even as the domestic situation in North Korea worsens, Pyongyang is likely to reject the second option because of the key political costs associated with introducing meaningful economic reforms and the military's objection to wide-ranging budget cuts. If North Korea is to undertake realistic economic reforms, the inordinate amount of resources it devotes to the KPA must be curtailed, but Kim Jong Il is unlikely to do so in the face of the KPA's role as the backbone of his regime. The litmus test for North Korea will come when its strategic options become exhausted when its systemic atrophy will reach unmanageable levels. This turning point will confront the regime with its most difficult challenge since 1948, not unlike the situation surrounding Erich Honecker in the final phase of the German Democratic Republic. Therefore, the possibility of conflict on the Korean peninsula could grow as North Korea's viable strategic options begin to narrow at an accelerated pace and the military is tempted by the need to use its assets—the only remaining "force multiplier" available to the North—to safeguard the regime. *To summarize, the key driver here is the army's increasing political influence as North Korea's strategic options begin to narrow in earnest; in other words, the key driver is the army's ability to define viable options in military terms, including the need to regain the strategic initiative through the use of force against the South.*

Trend Three: As the situation in the North continues to worsen, the strategies and policies of the regional powers—the United States, China, Japan, and Russia—will reflect crisis management dynamics. Nevertheless, the overtones are likely to be very different from previous crises on the Korean peninsula given the likelihood for some type of a military intervention in North Korea by one or more regional powers. Although any direct military involvement of the regional powers in North Korea would be highly situation-specific, it stands to reason that developments in the North could precipitate active Chinese responses. For example, assuming some type of a collapse occurs in the North but prior to the ROK's establishment of political control there, the possibility cannot be excluded of a significant "transfer" of KPA forces into China and the creation of a political enclave with some political influence, particularly if Beijing renders its support for a provisional DPRK government within China's borders. This would pose key problems for the ROK and the United States, particularly if China decides to intervene militarily "at the request of the DPRK provisional government" to "maintain social and political order." This specific scenario is perhaps far-fetched, but the possibility cannot be discounted. The real issue here is that active crisis management strategies must be developed by the regional powers for the first time since the outbreak of the Korean War. Problems ranging from refugee flows (with implications for China, Russia, and Japan), potential military disruptions (such as sporadic skirmishes along the Russo-North Korean and Sino-North Korean borders), ballistic missile threats (Japan), and even all-out war will have to be considered by the major powers as events begin to rapidly unfold in the North. *The key driver here is the degree to which Chinese and Russian decisionmakers will feel threatened by a North Korea either on the verge of collapse or in the aftermath of collapse and will feel the need to take preemptive action to safeguard Chinese or Russian interests along their respective borders with North Korea.*

Trend Four: Finally, domestic political factors, including a range of political realignments, could affect South Korea's crafting of a consistent and effective North Korea policy. In addition, if structural economic problems continue to worsen in South Korea—including slower economic growth, sustained currency devaluation, and rising foreign debt—political stability could be affected. To be sure, regardless of whether the ruling party or the opposition wins the December 1997 presidential election, the overall strategy of engagement and deterrence is unlikely to be revamped fundamentally. Nevertheless, if an opposition candidate emerges as the victor (such as Kim Dae Jung), new initiatives toward the North are likely. Proposals could include an early inter-Korean summit, major economic assistance to the North in return for its full participation in the four-party talks, an arms control package, significant modification of the National Security Law, and extensive opening of economic and social exchanges with the North. Such initiatives, however, could contribute to a polarization of the public debate on relations with the North. Moreover, the engagement strategy that has been largely shaped and led by the United States could come under increasing political attack in South Korea. Indeed, serious political divisions could occur if the new government forges ahead with extensive economic assistance to the North without linking such aid to progress in South-North talks or if U.S.-North Korean ties improve without reciprocal change in the inter-Korean relationship.

Ultimately, the key political test in South Korea will rest in the extent to which the government can craft an effective but politically acceptable North Korea strategy in terms of domestic politics, alliance relations with the United States, and ties with other major powers. In summary, *the key driver here is the potential for increasing polarization of the security and unification debate within South Korea, particularly if events begin to accelerate in North Korea. If North Korea continues to ignore South Korea while cultivating its ties with the United States or even Japan, South Korea is likely to respond to the engagement strategy with even greater ambivalence.*

Military Implications

When the Berlin Wall crumbled in November 1989, a remarkable development was Gorbachev's unwillingness to prop up the East German regime and the relatively passive reaction by the German Democratic Republic (GDR) armed forces. (To be sure, Honecker did contemplate the use of force to quell the uprisings, but in the end, the GDR army did not respond.) Indeed, throughout the period leading to formal unification in October 1990, there was no military clash between the *Bundeswehr* and the GDR forces, or for that matter, between the Group of Soviet Forces Germany and NATO forces. Moreover, the rapid demobilization of the East German army (including virtually all of its senior military staff) proceeded without any major problem. In contrast to German unification, however, political change on the Korean peninsula is likely to be more volatile, with the possibility of some form of a military clash. There are conflicting reports on the overall combat readiness of the Korean People's Army, but the fact remains that a 1.1 million strong military is likely to react very differently than in the German case. Moreover, the KPA enjoys significant political clout, and the degree to which its senior leadership exercises real influence should not be underestimated.

While the ROK ground forces will have the major task of blunting a major North Korean invasion, border incursions, and other forms of low-intensity conflict, the picture becomes more complex once a variety of elastic and unconventional scenarios are considered. Depending on the pace and depth of political-military change in the North, the following sets of events could be considered.

Peacetime Activities. 1. *Enhanced Political-Military Deception.* Not unlike the period immediately preceding the outbreak of the Korean War in June 1950, North Korea could accelerate a series of inter-Korean dialogue proposals (such as economic cooperation, exchange of separated families, scholarly exchanges, etc.), comprehensive arms control initiatives, and a high-level political meeting (inclusive of a summit between the two leaders). At the same time, however, Pyongyang could also intensify intelligence operations within South Korea with a special focus on progressive or pro-North Korean student groups, labor unions, and political activists. As in the past, such activities will surge prior to major elections (parliamentary and presidential) or at times of domestic political turbulence in the South.

2. *Limited Probes and Provocations.* With increasing openness in the political, security, and unification debate in the South, North Korea will take advantage of probing and influencing public opinion, media coverage, and elite opinion in South Korea. Initiatives designed to elicit a negative response from the ROK government—such as direct party-to-party talks, abrogation of the National Security Law, and the unconditional release of "patriots" with pro-North Korean senti-

ments—could be set into motion. At the same time, assuming that relations between North Korea and the United States (as well as Japan-North Korean ties) improve, Pyongyang will call for direct negotiations with the United States to replace the armistice agreement with a permanent peace treaty. Pyongyang realizes that decoupling South Korea from the United States is virtually an impossible task. Therefore, it will attempt to maximize its diplomatic leverage by emphasizing that only direct negotiations between Washington and Pyongyang will result in the type of positive change desired by the United States.

Internal Turmoil and External Deflections. 1. *Tighter Military Control.* Assuming that the political and economic situation in the North continues to worsen, the KPA will have a greater say not only over military policy but over grand strategy toward the South. Like the People's Republic of China (PRC), where the PLA has acquired increasing influence over the last several years, the KPA profile has been on the rise. However, the KPA's role in sustaining the regime is greater than in China's case given the greater concentration of political power at the apex of the party leadership and the regime's critical dependence on the army for maintaining domestic control (and quelling any opposition to the regime), and because the KPA is the largest recipient of government funds, up-to-date technologies, and crucial energy supplies.

2. *Partial Breakdown of Command Authority.* As the military's influence increases with greater political turmoil, a side effect is divisions in loyalty within the KPA and the major internal security organizations. For instance, whereas the army will do the bidding of the top leadership to maintain public order, sentiments within the rank and file may not always coincide with the top military or party leadership. The major danger is not that the army will ignore the party leadership per se, but that critical orders may not filter down within the system. Moreover, if sharp divisions emerge with increasing frequency in the politburo, the army may begin to set its own agenda. If the top military leadership has to choose between preserving Kim Jong Il in power versus retention of the army's overall position, it may well opt to preserve its own interests. The net external result will be conflicting signals with increasingly ambiguous party-military relations.

3. *Military Coup.* The most direct means for the army to salvage its position in a deteriorating political situation is to take direct control through a military coup or to install a leader of its own choosing. Although military coups are extremely rare in communist countries, the highly centralized nature of the North Korean system dictates that any major power vacuum would be filled by the most influential player. While the origins are admittedly quite different, the South Korean army's decision to launch coups in 1960 and 1979 following a major weakening of civilian authority could be repeated in a North Korean version. However, even if the army assumes direct control, it does not imply that it will pursue a more reformist line. Indeed, this is the central dilemma for the KPA, since assuming power on its own would have to translate into some perceived benefits by the population at large, especially in economic terms. Within the spectrum of possible events, the army could choose to promote economic reforms through the promotion of technocrats within the party and the bureaucracy, but ultimately any major attempts at reform would have to consider a partial, if not a substantial, reduction in the army's budget as well as its share of increasingly rare technological and energy resources.

Enhanced Operations Against the ROK.   1. *Sporadic Border Incursions and Clashes.* Assuming that political relations between the two Koreas worsen over a period of time with specific breakdowns (such as the nuclear agreement between the United States and North Korea), the North could opt to undertake military probes in the form of selected border incursions. It could also increase surveillance flights close to the border or sorties that make quick penetrations of the Korean Air Defense Zone. Exchange of fire across the DMZ in such an instance cannot be ruled out. Pyongyang could also increase the combat readiness of some of its forces deployed along the DMZ. If such incursions persist, the United States and the ROK would have to consider appropriate response options, but given the overriding political constraints, it remains in doubt whether the U.S.-ROK Combined Forces Command (CFC) would commit to take specific retaliatory military action. The primary objectives of North Korea in such an instance would probably be threefold: (1) testing of response reflexes by U.S. and ROK forces and their respective command, control, communication, computers, and intelligence (C4I) systems, (2) psychological warfare against the ROK, and (3) indirect pressure on the United States to enter into direct negotiations with North Korea over a number of issues such as the signing of a peace treaty.

2. *Infiltration and Sabotage.* North Korean sabotage was most evident in the mid to late 1960s when, among many operations, it mounted an unsuccessful raid on the Blue House in 1968 and then captured the U.S.S. *Pueblo* in 1969. In the 1970s, North Korea deemphasized sabotage operations and shifted its emphasis to underground tunneling below the DMZ and political recruiting in the South. (However, this does not mean that North Korea did not undertake any sabotage or assassination operations against the South during this period. President Park Chung Hee was the target of an assassination attempt in August 1974 and the First Lady was killed.) In the early 1980s, North Korea began a comprehensive infiltration campaign targeting politicians, journalists, businessmen, student and labor movements, and even sections of the armed forces.[55]

Military Operations. 1. *Selective Targeting and Destruction of ROK Air and Naval Assets.* One of the most difficult military challenges confronting the CFC is the specter of limited military strikes by the North short of an all-out invasion. Clearly, whether North Korea would choose to initiate limited military strikes is highly situation-specific in the face of the theoretical retaliatory options available to the ROK forces and the U.S. Forces, Korea (USFK). However, under rapidly deteriorating South-North relations, the North may opt to employ limited strikes because the political constraints on launching retaliatory strikes would be extremely high in South Korea as well as in the United States. For example, elements of the North Korean navy might use midget submarines to target a small number of ROK

---

[55]After the assassination of President Park Chung Hee by Korean Central Intelligence Agency (KCIA) Director Kim Jae Kyu in October 1979, there was a wholesale purge within the KCIA by the then Martial Law Command through its Defense Security Command. An unfortunate side effect of this purge was that the counterintelligence office was gutted. The net result was that by the late 1980s, as North Korea began to mount extensive infiltration operations in the South, counterintelligence faltered. Another major factor was the changing political environment in the South after democratization, when redirecting the nation's intelligence operations became a major political issue. As a result, while the National Security Law remains in force, its provisions have been weakened and an Intelligence Oversight Committee has been created within the National Assembly.

patrol craft or launch a limited artillery attack on an ROK military base or facility near the DMZ. At the same time, an ROK reconnaissance aircraft or helicopter could be fired upon. While the ROK and the United States would have to seriously ponder the appropriate military response, the major challenge is the inherent risk in escalation, a point that the North Koreans have exploited throughout the post–Korean War period. Beyond direct but limited military strikes, North Korea could opt to undertake sabotage operations against selected ROK targets such as major industrial and power plants or communications facilities.

2. *Preemptive Invasion of the ROK.* In the foreseeable strategic window, North Korea could also decide to launch a major conventional and unconventional attack on the South, especially as the domestic political situation worsens. Ironically, the threat of major war could increase at a time when North Korea's overall position vis-à-vis the South continues to decline. Therefore, if the North calculates that regime survival can be increased (at least in the short run) through conflict, the leadership may decide to take preemptive action. To be sure, an all-out invasion by the North would most likely result in the regime's ultimate collapse, but it would also destroy much of the progress South Korea has made since the post-Korean War era.

Conclusion

While a majority of the scenarios depicted here may not materialize, it would be extremely naive on the part of the political leadership in the United States and the ROK to believe that change on the peninsula will be evolutionary, nonviolent, and most important, manageable at an acceptable cost. Clearly, it is extremely difficult to forecast just how North Korea will evolve over the next several years, but most of the debate on the future of North Korea boils down to two contrasting schools of thought—the "negotiation school" and the "collapse school."

At its heart, the negotiation school believes that with the right incentives, North Korea will gradually reject its most orthodox policies and ultimately join hands with the South. Throughout the period leading to the signing of the Agreed Framework in October 1994, political leaders, policymakers, and analysts who subscribed to this school argued that force and pressure would only convince Pyongyang that unification by force was the sole remaining and viable option. In the aftermath of the accord, major proponents of this school argued that having successfully capped the nuclear threat, the next step was to freeze other key security threats such as North Korea's robust ballistic missile program.

Notwithstanding elements of success in the accord and follow-on measures, the key weakness in the negotiating school is twofold: (1) It does not take the endgame scenario into full consideration. For example, what will actually transpire once the North peels off its isolationist and aggressive policies and decides to join the community of nations? In other words, it places too much emphasis on *extending fundamental change* without taking into account the actual political, military, economic, and social fallout if and when the situation in the North begins to deteriorate sharply. Moreover, it argues that change within the North is dependent *not upon the internal dynamics of the regime as such but how the regime chooses to respond to an array of external developments. As a result, the outside world, and not North Korea, has to create an atmosphere conducive to real reforms.* (2) It assumes that the North Korean leadership is divided into "moderates" and "conservatives" as well as "technocrats" and "bureaucrats" and that so long as the "moderates" are able to emerge as the stronger group, meaningful economic reforms, a more open foreign policy, and a less threatening military posture are well within reach. It places an inordinate amount of importance on figures who allegedly support a "softer, gentler" version of North Korean communism and who, with the right incentives on the part of the ROK and the United States, will be able to ultimately dominate the policymaking process.

The major problem with the negotiating school's logic is that whereas certain elements of North Korea's behavior could be modified on the basis of negotiations [such as working with the Korean Peninsula Energy Development Organization (KEDO) and responding to U.S. requests on ballistic missiles and the missing-in-action (MIA) issue], it cannot alter the fundamental dynamics of North Korea power politics. Ultimately, almost everything comes back to the central question of how the Kim Jong Il regime and the *nomenklatura* that supports it will choose to respond. Will they open up the regime at the expense of their own survival and authority? What are the realistic possibilities of the KPA supporting genuine economic reforms? Can economic reform be seen as a central tenet and goal of the current regime? Regardless of the ultimate outcome of the series of bilateral U.S.-North Korea talks, future South-North dialogue, and potential multilateral diplomatic undertakings, fundamental and meaningful change in the North can only take place after substantial domestic political change in Pyongyang. But as the regime in the North grapples with its exit strategy, its overall options will begin to narrow at an accelerating pace, and with it, bring new and potentially more dangerous implications for defense planners in the United States and South Korea.

In this regard, the key threat to stability on the Korean peninsula is the potential for the outbreak of some type of a military disruption, including a range of low-intensity conflicts, operations other than war, sustained military probes and actions, military fallout from a North Korean hard landing (even civil war), and in the worst-case scenario, a full-scale conventional war launched by the North to offset its dwindling strategic options.

Despite worsening economic conditions in the North, which many believe is key in preventing North Korea from launching a major conventional offensive toward the South, if North Korea does undertake major military operations, they will be premised not on economic grounds (i.e., whether it has the ability to wage war for an extended period of time) but on strategic calculations premised on a "high-gain, high-risk" strategy. A complete bolt-out-of-the-blue surprise attack along the DMZ is unlikely, although the drivers that could result in a military disruption on the Korean peninsula are clearly visible today and may become increasingly clearer as the domestic situation in North Korea deteriorates. Ironically, prospects for military disruption on the Korean peninsula are the highest since the end of the Korean War. The world is confronted by an economically weak North Korea, uncertainty over the longer-term sustainability of the Kim Jong Il regime despite his current firm grip on power, potential for growing popular discontent, increasing international isolation, and loss of support from traditional allies. Nevertheless, it is crucial not to consider these factors as "objective" indicators of a severely weakened, disoriented, and deeply insecure North Korea that is unable to wage war against the South and is compelled to adopt pragmatic policy prescriptions. In the final analysis, the biggest security challenge does not lie in forging a strategy that will enable North Korea to prevent itself from collapsing, as is commonly perceived. If such a strategy did exist, there would not be a security dilemma on the Korean peninsula. The real challenge lies in thinking and planning for a range of developments that deviate substantially from preferred but unlikely options and outcomes.

SOUTHEAST ASIA

Overview

The Southeast Asia subregion is undergoing a remarkable transformation that includes growing regional prosperity and economic, political, and even social interconnectedness. Foremost among the major forces shaping a nascent Southeast Asian community is economic dynamism, including a rapid expansion in direct foreign investment, burgeoning intraregional trade, technological innovation and flows, and vigorous economic growth. Growing trade and investment links are in turn increasing the incentives for peaceful regional cooperation among Southeast Asian states, as expanding levels of economic interaction create shared interests in managing potential sources of conflict.

Even Southeast Asians' perceptions of themselves are changing. Dynamic growth and expanding levels of economic interaction are contributing to an increasing sense of self-confidence and the formation of a nascent Asian identity. Expanding social linkages stem from closer intraregional communication and travel. Whereas ethnic and religious tensions exist both within and across national boundaries, domestic insurgencies are no longer a major threat to political order in most of Southeast Asia. These developments are positive for the United States in the sense that the likelihood for U.S. involvement in a regional conflict are significantly diminished, but they also portend declining U.S. influence in the subregion at a time when U.S. economic interests in the subregion are rapidly growing. Any dramatic diminution in the stabilizing influence performed by the United States could in turn have negative, long-term implications for regional stability, especially should U.S. influence decline precipitously before meaningful Asian integration is achieved.

Economic prosperity equates to a growing middle class, which is leading to greater pressures for meaningful participation in politics in many developing Southeast Asian states. As a result, the recent democratic transformations of South Korean and Taiwanese politics could be eventually replicated in Southeast Asia, increasing the prospects for extending the zone of peace and prosperity among advanced industrial democracies to include Southeast Asia.

One major reason for the remarkable "econophoria" sweeping the subregion is that the Southeast Asia security complex is no longer the object of great-power territorial ambitions. At the same time, however, the economic stakes of China, Japan, and the United States are rapidly growing in Southeast Asia. As a result, economic rivalry between the major powers over access to Southeast Asia's labor, production, and raw resources remains a potential source of future discord. Nevertheless, while successful management of the triangular balance of power between China, Japan, and the United States remains a long-run challenge, the threat of conflict among the major powers in the Asia-Pacific region has at least temporarily receded. A less threatening regional security environment—as a result of the end of the Cold War, ASEAN's success as a regional forum, lessened regional suspicions of Japan, increasing intra-Asian trade ties, and improved dialogue between China and its neighbors—has led to blustery output from some Southeast Asian elites, who publicly discount the importance of trans-Pacific security ties with the United States.

A relatively benign security environment has allowed Southeast Asian states to focus on economic development not simply for the purpose of building national power, but also for improving living standards and mitigating social pressures that stem from economic development. As a result, prospects should improve for stable political transitions, including more open and participatory regimes. Even more important, economic development will also create a strong and enduring interest among Southeast Asian regimes to maintain economic growth through expanding levels of external economic interactions, thereby furthering the development of a peaceful, regional security complex. As a result, the incentives for regional actors to resort to force to resolve myriad ethnic tensions and territorial disputes throughout the region are diminished.

For a benign and stable Southeast Asia security complex to emerge, security will eventually need to concern "flows of people, ideas, and goods within a context of shared views about how best to organize the participants' economies, societies, and political systems."[56] Such a consensus of views is nowhere yet evident, and the potential resort to military force remains central to an understanding of regional security. Nevertheless, expanding levels of economic interaction are increasing the demand for institutions designed to promote confidence-building measures among potential regional rivals and manage conflicts that could disrupt or even undermine regional economic growth. These institutions include the ASEAN Free Trade Area (AFTA), ARF, ASEAN, and the ASEAN Post-Ministerial Committee (PMC). As a result, the region has witnessed what could be termed "institutional euphoria" after the Cold War, including a strengthening in the scope and membership of existing regional institutions and the creation of embryonic institutions.

Despite such promising regional dynamics, long-term prospects for peaceful regional integration are less than robust. Instead, Southeast Asia's cultural and ethnic diversity, variety of economic and political systems, as well as smoldering historical legacies and rivalries among both subregional actors and extraregional major powers (especially China) could impede the emergence of a benign security environment. Nearly every ASEAN member has conflicting territorial claims with another Southeast Asian state. Similarly, demands for more open and participatory regimes by the region's growing middle class could destabilize certain types of regimes (e.g., Indonesia) and weaken or undermine economic dynamism. Moreover, regional dynamism could erode the influence of the United States, which has historically played an important stabilizing role in terms of supplying both a large and open market for regional exports and a forward-based military presence in East Asia. No other country appears ready (or capable) to replace the United States and assume this role. While increasing financial, technological, and economic interdependence has altered the political calculus of states by both raising the cost of conflict and lowering the incentives to resort to war, many factors—including arms races, differential rates of economic growth, na-

---

[56]Patrick Morgan, "Multilateralism and Security: Prospects in Europe," in John Ruggie (ed.), *Multilateralism Matters,* New York: Columbia University Press, 1993, p. 336.

tionalism, territorial conflicts, and relative gains concerns—could easily undermine future regional cooperation.

Despite a veneer of optimism among Southeast Asian regimes, the above concerns have led to hedging behavior on the part of many Southeast Asian states. Many Southeast Asian states are now increasing their level of military spending, although, as a percentage of GNP, military expenditures are generally declining or remaining constant. While no arms race yet exists, rapid economic growth has allowed many Southeast Asian states to upgrade aging weapons systems and procure the most sophisticated arms available for export (especially from those countries focused primarily upon the economic benefits of arms exports), resulting in increasingly lethal and sophisticated force structures.

The remarkable level of religious and ethnic tolerance in Southeast Asia (compared with other developing regions of the world) could be undermined by future regional developments. These developments could include growing economic disparities between certain ethnic and religious groups, economic recession, trade tensions among Southeast Asian states, and, most significantly, military tensions with those major Asian powers that have a significant diaspora in Southeast Asia (i.e., China and India). Tensions with China could lead to persecution of ethnic Chinese minorities in Indonesia and Malaysia, which could lead to economic stagnation and domestic political instability; conversely, domestic instability and economic recession could lead to the persecution of ethnic Chinese and hence military intervention by China. ASEAN political unity would be undermined by such developments.

Trends

The above discussion suggests the following trends in the Southeast Asia security complex:

Domestic Political

- Key leadership transitions in strategically significant Southeast Asian countries (Indonesia and Malaysia).

- Rising aspirations for more meaningful political participation among Southeast Asia's growing middle class, leading to democratization or civil unrest.

- Growing irrelevance or resolution of domestic insurgencies.

- Growing nationalism, including pan-Asianism, linked to regional development achievements.

Domestic Economic

- Rapid economic growth.

- Economic development strongly influenced by foreign capital investment patterns.

- More-even income distribution, thereby mitigating conflict across ethnic and religious cleavages.

Domestic Military

- Significant military modernization through the acquisition of increasingly lethal and advanced conventional power projection capabilities and force multipliers (including land-based fighters, electronic warfare (EW), helicopter carriers, attack submarines, air refueling, and missiles).

- Strengthening of nuclear nonproliferation regime. However, should a menacing China develop and in the absence of a U.S. nuclear guarantee, a WMD and delivery system capability remains possible.

Regional Security Environment

- Strategic ambiguity. Elements of competition and cooperation coexist uneasily among Southeast Asian states, between ASEAN and China, and between Japan and the United States.

- Region not now an object of major-power competition, although it will likely again become an arena of competition among the major powers unless a benign Asian security environment emerges.

- Important regional power transitions under way: diminution of U.S. influence, growing influence of Japanese economic power;

differential rates of economic growth in China's favor via-à-vis Japan and the United States, creating potential for high salience of relative gains concerns and long-term conflictual relations between China and other Asian powers.

- Uncertainty about long-term U.S. commitment to region.

- Despite high levels of uncertainty, absence of an arms race.

- Expanding levels of institutionalization of Southeast Asian security affairs.

- Expansion in membership of ASEAN to include all Southeast Asian states, strengthening its bargaining position but also likely impeding its ability to act in unison against outside powers.

- Many remaining conflictual territorial and resource claims.

- Hedging behavior toward the major powers and internal efforts by Southeast Asian governments in addressing security dilemmas.

Drivers of Conflict. The above discussion suggests possible drivers or precipitants of conflict involving Southeast Asia that will be critical for rapidly growing U.S. interests in the subregion. These drivers include: (1) the outcome of leadership and social transitions, especially in Indonesia; (2) ethnic and religious cleavages; (3) the long-term sustainability of economic growth, with implications not only for domestic political stability and the resources available for military expenditures, but also for the distribution of regional power (this driver will in turn be strongly affected by the next two drivers); (4) the future course of trade liberalization within AFTA and APEC by Southeast Asian states; (5) the availability of foreign capital for economic development and extraregional export markets; (6) the strength of the U.S. commitment to the region; (7) Chinese/Japanese/Indian calculations with regard to the region; (8) the acquisition of advanced weapons systems; (9) the long-term strength and durability of ASEAN, AFTA, and other subregional institutions critical to mitigating subregional economic and security conflict, as well as the strength of ASEAN's bargaining position vis-à-vis larger Asian powers; and (10) the level of adherence to the Non-Proliferation Treaty (NPT) and other arms control and confidence-building measures among Southeast Asian states.

The long-term emergence of a stable subregional security environment would require as a minimum the evolution of

- stable leadership and social transitions in key Southeast Asian states,

- long-term sustainability of moderate-to-rapid economic growth, with requisite availability of capital and foreign export markets,

- low disparities in income distribution across social groupings,

- emergence of a free-trade zone in Southeast Asia,

- continued U.S. military presence and strong U.S. commitment to the subregion,

- emergence of a status quo China,

- Japan closely allied to the United States and acting in concert with the United States vis-à-vis the region,

- an understanding among major powers regarding competition over Southeast Asia,

- transparency in arms acquisitions,

- continued adherence to NPT norms by all Southeast Asian states, and

- a strong and durable ASEAN.

Given the likelihood that some of these drivers will fail to evolve in the above manner, a number of conflict scenarios in Southeast Asia become possible, including civil war, intra-ASEAN conflicts, and conflicts with an extraregional power.

SOUTH ASIA

For several millennia, the South Asian region existed more or less in splendid isolation. Separated from the rest of Asia by the Hindukush, the Karakoram, and the Great Himalayan ranges in the north and the Indian Ocean in the south, the Indian subcontinent developed a distinctive civilizational identity and structured relations between the various local political entities as the critical component of "high politics" for much of the region's history. To be sure, the subcontinent was periodically invaded by outside powers, usually land invasions from West and Central Asia. Only in the latter half of the modern period did the subcontinent confront seaborne invasions mounted by various European colonial powers, one of which—Great Britain—eventually triumphed and ruled over the South Asian region for close to two hundred years.

Irrespective of the source of these invasions, however, the dominant patterns of strategic interaction remained the same. The local South Asian states interacted mostly with each other. The invaders either left the subcontinent after ransacking its wealth and riches or they stayed behind, were slowly absorbed into the local civilization, and proceeded to join other regional entities in jostling with one another as had been the case for hundreds of years. This pattern of behavior continued even after the demise of the British *Raj* left behind two new and independent states, India and Pakistan. The conflictual interaction between these two countries has dominated the strategic environment on the Indian subcontinent since 1947. To be sure, there were external interactions, mostly with the United States, the Soviet Union, and China. But these relations were mostly overlays that fed into the primary security competition between India and Pakistan. Despite all external intercourse, the Indian subcontinent thus remained a relatively autonomous enclave in international politics.

This section focuses on explicating the emerging trends that promise to integrate South Asia with the larger Asian arena for the first time in modern history and how the process of integration could lead to conflicts along the way. The first subsection identifies three crucial trends that define the current political-strategic landscape in South Asia. Flowing from these, the second subsection identifies the critical drivers of conflict that will affect war-and-peace outcomes in the region. The third and final subsection highlights the "worst case" scenarios involving deterrence breakdown, scenarios to which U.S. policymakers and strategic planners should be sensitive.

Emerging Regional Trends

The first salient trend is that all South Asian states are increasingly taking their bearings from strategic developments along a wider can-

vas than the local arena alone, and their responses will thus contribute to the elimination of the subcontinent's traditional isolation.

For the first time in memory, the relative strategic isolation of South Asia appears to be on the verge of disappearing as the result of dramatic changes both within and outside the region. The Indo-Pakistani security competition, which was the most familiar feature of local politics, will continue, but it will be increasingly less a bilateral affair than a unilateral one. Pakistan, by virtue of its weakness, fragility, and continued fear of India, will attempt to "compete" with its larger regional neighbor to preserve its security and autonomy. Having lost its traditional Cold War supporter, the United States, Pakistan will increasingly attempt to rely on Chinese protection, weaponry, and technology in its struggles against India.[57] India, in contrast, has changed direction completely. It still seeks the regional hegemony it believes is warranted as heir to an ancient civilization, possessing a large population and an extensive land mass, and having great economic, technological, and military potential. But, in a dramatic departure from its traditional grand strategy which sought hegemony at the price of direct competition with Pakistan, New Delhi's new strategic orientation calls for the "benign neglect" of Islamabad.

Replacing the previous "Pakistan obsession" is a new effort to look beyond the constraining environs of South Asia to pursue the larger great-power capabilities that eluded India throughout the Cold War. This new approach, centered upon both internal economic reforms and concerted political attempts at making new friends—particularly among its neighbors in South Asia, with the "tigers" in East Asia and, of course, the United States—does not entail abjuring the quest for hegemony within the Indian subcontinent. Rather, this approach implies that the requisites for local hegemony will be treated as a "lesser included capability," which automatically derives from India's capacity to stand shoulder-to-shoulder with the great powers in Asia and beyond.

This reorientation in perspective is driven primarily not by an Indian desire to "beat" Pakistan this time around by an "indirect approach,"

---

[57]"President Leghari Addresses Defense College on National, Regional Security," *FBIS-NES-96-138*, July 17, 1996, pp. 67–71.

but by fears of increasing dangers in the regional environment and by a recognition that continuing underdevelopment will make India only more insecure than before. The rise of China to the north is viewed with anxiety and apprehension because of what enhanced Chinese capabilities imply for the outstanding border disputes as well as for Sino-Indian political competition more generally. China's transfers of nuclear and missile technologies to Pakistan and its gradual penetration of Myanmar are already perceived as a covert— long-range—effort at outflanking India. Coupled with the looming uncertainties in the trans-Caucasus, Central Asia, and the Persian Gulf—when Indian energy dependence promises only to increase— New Delhi's fears of a deteriorating regional environment become more manifest at a time when old friends such as Russia seem to be truly enervated and new friends such as the United States have yet to live up to their expected promise.

All these factors taken together have forced a perception that the strategic isolation traditionally enjoyed by South Asia is steadily disappearing, and hence India has to pull itself up by its bootstraps to accommodate a much more extensive range of threats than previously encountered. These threats include the nuclear and missile threats mounted by both China and Pakistan, the theater ballistic missile capabilities resident in the Persian Gulf, as well as the evolving chemical, biological, and long-range conventional attack capabilities steadily proliferating around the Indian subcontinent. Not surprisingly, therefore, all the South Asian states, for different reasons, are increasingly condemned to take their bearings from strategic developments along a wider canvas; and, in the process, the subcontinent's traditional isolation, too, is condemned to finally disappear.

The second salient trend is that there are critical regional power transitions under way in South Asia, transitions that will bequeath India local hegemony while increasing the intensity of Sino-Indian competition down the line.

Precipitated in part by fears of impending changes in the threat environment, all the South Asian states have begun a series of consequential economic reforms aimed at liberating their economic systems from the clutches of bureaucratic regulation and state control. India, Pakistan, and Bangladesh have all joined Sri Lanka (which began first) in embarking on wide-ranging economic reforms. The results thus far have been spectacular. Growth rates have generally exceeded 6 percent per annum throughout the 1990s, and, on the expectation that current trends will continue, most analyses conclude that the South Asian region will be the "new growth pole"[58] in Asia. The power political consequences of these developments are equally critical, implying a coming power transition that will make India, in particular, among the most important actors in Asia.

The studies undertaken at RAND by Charles Wolf et al.[59] suggest that, assuming conservative growth rates of 5.5 percent, the Indian economy will grow from $1.2 trillion in 1994 to $3.7 trillion in 2015, an increase from 46 percent of Japan's 1994 GNP to 82 percent of its GNP in 2015. Similarly, on the heroic assumption that China continues to grow at the present rate of 12 percent plus, India's GNP is expected to increase from 24 percent of China's total to 27 percent by 2015. Because the Chinese economy will in all probability be unable to sustain its present growth rates over the long term, the size of the Indian economy will be larger—relative to China—than these figures suggest—assuming, of course, that India can sustain a growth rate of 5.5 percent over the long haul. Other analyses suggest that this is not improbable. It is in fact estimated that the Indian economy could sustain an average growth rate of at least 8 percent per annum if the present reforms are successfully extended and more attention is paid to increasing investments in power and infrastructure.[60]

Such growth in economic capability leads directly to increased military potential, as is evident from the fact that India's military capital stock similarly shows dramatic improvement. From 79 percent of Japan's 1994 stock, it is estimated to increase to 204 percent of Japan's 2015 stock (assuming Japanese military growth does not exceed 1 percent of GNP). And India's stock is expected to constitute 79 percent of China's military capital stock by 2015 (assuming stable growth in China), and actually exceed China's military capital stock

---

[58]Ernest Stern, "Developing Asia: A New Growth Pole Emerges," *Finance & Development*, Vol. 31, No. 2, June 1994, pp. 18–20.

[59]Charles Wolf, Jr., et al., *Long-Term Economic and Military Trends 1994–2015*, Santa Monica, CA: RAND, 1995, pp. 1–21.

[60]Prabhu Chawla, "Gambling on Growth," *India Today*, March 31, 1997, pp. 35–45; Neelesh Misra, "Chidambaram forecasts 8% growth by the year 2000," *India Abroad*, March 14, 1997, p. 20.

(if disrupted growth in China is assumed).[61] In summary, then, given current trends India will not only attain local hegemony in South Asia but will also become the world's fourth largest economy some time in the first quarter of the next century. While it will remain the weakest of the Asian great powers (including China and Japan), India will nonetheless become the dominant entity along the northern Indian Ocean and will serve to diminish emerging Chinese power by functioning as a potent military threat along Beijing's southern flank, assisting the Southeast Asian states in their efforts to preserve their autonomy against potential Chinese penetration and dominance, and possibly participating in some future U.S.-led containment strategy aimed at restraining China. As a consequence, India will increasingly play an important role in continental geopolitics thanks to fact that it will "emerge as the only Asian power not seriously challenged regionally."[62]

The third salient trend is that internal instability could interact with changing military-technical and power political capabilities to make the incipient power transitions in South Asia relatively unstable.

The coming regional power transitions, like those occurring previously in history, could be accompanied by potentially serious instability. In the South Asian case, this instability could be even more problematic for both technical and political reasons. The technical reasons essentially center on the fact that the general power transitions unfolding in the background are occurring amidst the steady proliferation of weapons of mass destruction and the acquisition of new lethal delivery systems. WMD competition for the most part still centers on nuclear weapons, perhaps the most lethal form of WMD, and engages both the Indo-Pakistani and the Sino-Indian dyads. While the former is presently the most active strategic interchange, the latter will become the increasingly important one over time. This fact notwithstanding, the Indo-Pakistani interaction still promises to be the more dangerous interaction of the two for a variety of reasons. First, there are active political disputes between the two entities that have resulted in three past wars and currently involve an ongoing

---

[61]Wolf et al., 1995.

[62]Sandy Gordon, "South Asia After the Cold War," *Asian Survey*, Vol. 35, No. 10, October 1995, p. 895.

war waged by proxy. Second, the nuclear programs on both sides are currently in a state of precarious evolution; any weapons stockpile is likely to be relatively small and may be unreliable. The level of deterrent efficacy is uncertain, and the newer delivery systems exhibit some of the classic characteristics that could result in crisis instability.

Furthermore, Pakistan may find its own nuclear program inadequate as India begins to respond to the Chinese nuclear arsenal. The latter interaction will, in all probability, be less troublesome. China already possesses a substantial nuclear capability (at least relative to India), and all Indian efforts will be oriented to playing catch-up. The Sino-Indian nuclear interaction is thus unlikely to be violently unstable, as India will probably develop only a relatively small, mobile, deterrent force—either land- or sea-based or both—oriented toward counter-value attacks on a small, fixed, target set. Because the development and deployment of these capabilities will not take place simultaneously or interactively (as seems to be the case now in Indo-Pakistani interactions), and because India and China are both large land powers with less asymmetricality in their power relations (compared once again to the Indo-Pakistani case), the worst effects of a future Sino-Indian nuclear competition can arguably be escaped.

Because this optimistic expectation will be tested only over the long term, the problems associated with the current Indo-Pakistani nuclear transition will remain. These technical problems are complicated by the internal political transformations currently working themselves out on the subcontinent. The dominant political trends in India are threefold. First, the country is experiencing the slow demise of the Congress Party, which not only brought India to independence but also functioned traditionally as the critical mediator between the institutions of state and civil society. Second, the gradual demise of the "big tent," represented by the Congress Party, has resulted in the rise of new regional, class-, and caste-based parties, spearheaded by a new generation of leaders who lack the stature of India's founding fathers, are comparatively less catholic and cosmopolitan in outlook, and do not possess the support of a vibrant nationwide political base. Third, the old ideologies of secularism and class conciliation are increasingly under attack from a new set of political interests, represented, for example, by the Bharatiya Janata Party (BJP) and the Bahujan Samajwadi Party (BSP), which promise to make Indian politics a much more chaotic environment. Logrolling over ideational and distributional issues will increasingly take place in the open as opposed to the closed confines of intraparty politics (as was the case when the Congress Party was still intact). These changes do not necessarily bode ill for India, but they do increase the levels of uncertainty in both domestic politics and international relations and may create opportunities for miscalculation on the part of India's competitors, thereby increasing the possibility of inadvertent conflict.

Pakistan, just like India, is also undergoing a domestic transformation, but the challenges facing it are immeasurably greater. The polity as a whole is struggling to come out from under the shadow of overt military rule, but its efforts thus far have been dogged by mixed success. This outcome is primarily the result of four factors.

First, the presence of feeble political parties, ineffectual civilian leaders, and weak democratic institutions has resulted in the dominance of patronage rather than issue-based politics; pervasive corruption at all levels of government and state; and infirmities in the legislature, the judiciary, and the institutions of civil society. Moreover, the preeminence of a few charismatic personalities who not only are beholden to a narrow ethnic and social base but also despise one another has resulted in all engaging in competitive efforts at wooing the military to intervene on their behalf.

Second, strong provincial centers and particularist loyalties reinforce either feudal social organization or ethnic affiliation over the demands of the national interest, as manifested by the episodic regional uprisings that occurred throughout Pakistan's history as an independent state and led to the 1971 war.

Third, a strong bureaucracy, both military and civil, stands behind the curtains of Pakistani politics. These bureaucracies, dominated by Punjabis and to a lesser degree Pathans, continue to possess disproportionate power in Pakistan's political life, especially in relation to elected institutions such as the National Assembly. While this power balance will hopefully change in the future, it is as yet unclear how the historically entrenched bureaucracies will respond to possible losses of power. The present leadership of the Pakistan army, however, represents a dramatic exception to the historical norm: Not only has it welcomed a restoration of the proper balance between the civilian and military arms of the state, it has also scrupulously stayed out of active politics to focus on its professional obligations and commitments and, in general, has been an exemplary voice of moderation and restraint.

Fourth, radical Islamist parties participate in the episodic political manipulation of Islam in political life in an effort to acquire and maintain their legitimacy. It is in fact ironic that these groupings, though poorly represented in elected institutions, often wield more street power than established political parties do and have established tentacles in all institutions ranging from the armed services to the universities, thereby possessing the unique ability to constrain the political center in more ways than pure electoral representation would suggest.

The internal weaknesses of the Pakistani state are thus problematic because severe economic vulnerability could interact with the structural fissures and tempt other states, such as India or Iran, to exploit Pakistan's weaknesses. Or, even more likely, certain segments of the Pakistani polity—especially weak civilian leaders— might be tempted to control domestic discord by embarking on diversionary brinksmanship with India.

Drivers of Conflict

The multiple trends identified above could give rise to problematic possibilities that could result in armed conflict between the regional states. These drivers include at least five specific factors that could determine the prospects for war or peace.

The first driver is Indian, Pakistani, and Chinese decisions with respect to supporting insurgencies in each other's territory. Clearly, the dyadic competition between the first two states is often what receives most public attention, in part because their low-intensity conflicts are highly visible, have occasionally threatened to lead to high-risk escalation, and take place under the shadow of relatively weak nuclear capabilities. Despite these considerations, however, it is important to recognize that low-intensity conflicts have occurred in the Sino-Indian case as well. China has supported insurgencies in the Indian northeast off and on for more than four decades, and

India, historically, has assisted the Tibetan insurgents in their struggles against Beijing.[63] This pattern of interactions will become more significant over time, in part because geographic limitations constrain—but certainly do not eliminate—more conventional forms of military competition. Moreover, both India and China have relatively less-well-integrated, but nonetheless strategic, border areas that lend themselves as arenas for low-intensity war. In the near-to-medium term, however, Sino-Indian competition is likely to be muted as both states attempt to secure breathing space to complete their internal economic and political transformations.

It is in this time frame, however, that Indo-Pakistani decisions about low-intensity warfare will be crucial. In particular, two sets of decisions are pivotal. The first relates to the choices Pakistan makes with respect to the present insurgency in Kashmir. The Kashmiri rebellion has for all practical purposes reached the limits of its success. Whether Pakistan chooses to escalate by altering either the quantity or the quality of support offered to the insurgents will make an important difference to the future of Indo-Pakistani security competition in the near term. The second set of choices relates to the decisions made by the present government and its successors in New Delhi. Whether they choose to continue the Narasimha Rao regime's strategy of forbearance or shift to a more aggressive strategy of playing "tit-for-tat" will also determine the future of security competition. Both Indian and Pakistani decisions are in some sense interdependent and, therefore, immediate Pakistani choices with respect to Kashmir will determine both the prospects for Indian conventional retaliation as well as the prospects for future Indian support for insurgencies in Pakistan.

The second driver is Indian, Pakistani, and Chinese decisions with respect to conventional and nuclear modernization. It is not an exaggeration to assert that deterrence stability on the Indian continent today is simply a function of the Indian, Pakistani, and Chinese inability to prosecute and win major conventional wars. As research elsewhere has demonstrated, India's gross numerical superiorities

---

[63]This problem might reassert itself, or may even arise outside of New Delhi's control, as a younger generation of more restive Tibetan émigrés in India takes over the leadership of the exiled Tibetan community in India after the passing of the Dalai Lama.

vis-à-vis Pakistan are misleading and do not enable it to win a major war within a short period.[64] The Sino-Indian balance along the Himalayas is similarly stable for now, because the Chinese do not have the logistics capability to sustain any major conventional conflict in support of their territorial claims, whereas the strong and refurbished Indian land defenses, coupled with their superiority in air power, enable New Delhi to defend its existing positions but not to sustain large-scale acquisition of new territory. Consequently, deterrence stability exists along this frontier as well.

What could change this status quo, however, are Indian and Chinese innovations in the realm of technology, organization, or warfighting doctrine. Such change becomes possible as China and India grow rapidly in economic terms. The resulting increases in prosperity will lead to increases in power as the state, availing itself of more resources than it had previously, acquires new military capabilities that, in turn, increase the range of feasible political choices, including war. Chinese improvements in logistics, air power (both defensive and offensive), communications, and the capacity to unleash accurate deep fires could tilt the balance toward deterrence instability along the Himalayas. Similarly, Indian improvements in the realm of combined-arms maneuver warfare, especially involving organization and warfighting doctrine and in the arena of strategic applications of air power, could tilt the current stand-off on the western battlefields toward India's favor, thereby making deterrence unstable if these military trends are not controlled by larger political considerations.

A similar set of transitions in the nuclear realm could drive instability. Most of these transitions will occur in the Indo-Pakistani case rather than in the Sino-Indian case for reasons explored earlier, and most of them will in fact occur even before the potential transformations in the conventional arena come about. The principal changes in question here center mostly on the kinds of nuclear weapons, the kinds of delivery systems, and kinds of deterrence doctrines that may be developed by both states. The issue of stability becomes particularly urgent, because both India and Pakistan are in the process of acquiring relatively short-ranged theater ballistic missile

---

[64]Ashley J. Tellis, *Stability in South Asia,* Santa Monica: RAND, DB-185-A, 1997, pp. 12–33.

systems, some of which may not be survivable but may nonetheless be armed with (or, at any rate, be perceived as being armed with) nuclear warheads. The instabilities caused by such deployments were in many ways a staple of Cold War concerns but oftentimes do not appear to be publicly understood or discussed in South Asia. Mutual deterrence in the Sino-Indian case is today an oxymoron, but even when that changes, the transition is likely to be less trouble-some than the Indo-Pakistani case.

The third driver is the future character of political regimes in India, Pakistan, and China. In the first two instances, the issue of the political regime essentially hinges on the survival and flourishing of moderate centrist parties in domestic Indian and Pakistani politics. In India, the centrist Congress Party has been battered to the point where non-Congress alternatives will probably continue to govern the country in the future. The key question, however, is which alter-native. It is still uncertain whether strongly nationalist parties like the BJP have in fact peaked. Even if they have peaked, there is still a possibility that they could come to power as part of a coalition of re-gional parties that care less than the BJP does for international and security-related problems, and essentially give the latter a free hand in these issue areas. If this includes the pursuit of more radical agendas—both internally and externally—the stage could be set for greater regional confrontation than heretofore, although this is unlikely because the BJP would have to discover the virtues of moderation if it is to secure power and hold onto it. In Pakistan, it is unlikely that radical Islamist parties would come to power in the near term, but their ability to constrain the fragile centrist civilian regimes into following otherwise undesirable policies cannot be underesti-mated. There is a troublesome possibility of diversionary efforts at domestic mobilization, especially with respect to issues like Kashmir, which could lead to self-reinforcing spirals of escalation and conflict. Of perhaps greater concern is the structural viability of Pakistan as a state. Contrary to much popular commentary on the subject, however, it is important to recognize that Pakistan is *not* a "failed state" and is highly unlikely to become one. The real challenge facing Pakistan is not state failure but enervating stagnation—an end-product of severe macroeconomic imbalances coupled with simmering ethnic tensions, both of which could be exploited by external actors with deleterious consequences for stability. Both these challenges can be successfully surmounted by Pakistan and, it is hoped, probably will be.

As far as China is concerned, the news is less reassuring. The best available analyses suggest that whether China has an authoritarian or a democratic government in the future, it is likely to pursue its agenda of "national reunification" without letting up. The specific character of this pursuit will vary in details, but the broad orientation seems clear: China seems intent on recovering those territorial areas it deems itself to have lost through weakness. Because substantial portions of Indian territory in the northwest and northeast are currently claimed by China, it appears that some form of territorial contest between these two Asian giants is inevitable down the line. The implications for regional stability are obvious.

The fourth driver is Indian, Pakistani, and Chinese responses to the power transitions around them. Power transitions occur as a result of the uneven growth in capabilities between states. Two such transitions may be imminent in the greater South Asian region: a dramatic, highly visible, and perhaps unstoppable increase in Chinese power; and a more muted, perhaps more precarious, increase in Indian economic strength. These twin developments will define the future structural environment in South Asia. The growth in Beijing's capability, especially in military power, will result in an increased Chinese capacity for coercion that will affect Sino-Indian political relations, including the outstanding disputes between the two states. Growing Chinese capabilities will in all likelihood compel India to modernize and expand its effective military capabilities as a deterrent to potential coercion by Beijing. Such an increase in the level of direct Sino-Indian competition itself would also threaten to alter the prevailing balance between India and Pakistan—an outcome that could also occur if India chose to expand its military power simply as an autonomous consequence of its increased economic strength. These developments could lead to a variety of unpalatable possibilities that, though remote now, merit continual observation: increased Pakistani resistance toward India in the face of vanishing windows of opportunity; increased Indian truculence as a result of its growing strength; increased Sino-Pakistani collusion as a consequence of converging fears about a rising India; and increased Sino-Indian political-military competition along their common border and elsewhere in Asia. While domestic political developments in each of these states will have a critical bearing on the outcome, the power transitions themselves—if improperly handled—could provide abundant structural incentives for continued conflict.

The fifth driver is Indian, Pakistani, and Chinese perceptions of the role of extraregional powers in any future conflict. Although extraregional powers such as the United States will remain critical and influential actors in South Asia, the nature of their presence and the way their influence is exercised will remain important factors for stability in South Asia. The United States, in particular, contributes to stability insofar as it can creatively use both its regional policy and its antiproliferation strategies to influence the forms of security competition on the subcontinent, the shape and evolution of Indian and Pakistani nuclear programs, and the general patterns of political interaction between India and Pakistan. The nominally extraregional power, China, also plays a critical role here both because of its presumed competition with India and because Beijing has evolved into a vital supplier of conventional and nuclear technologies to Pakistan.

The role of those states—and others such as Russia and Japan—and also *the perceptions of that role* thus become important for stability. If Pakistan, for example, comes to view American and Chinese interest in the region as providing an opportunity to settle old scores with India—on the expectation that one or both states would rush to its assistance in the context of a major war—the stage could be set for deterrence instability on the subcontinent. A similar logic applies to India. If India, for example, comes to view a deepening relationship with the United States as an opportunity to settle old scores with Pakistan—on the expectation that the United States would not penalize India for initiating conflict because of larger geopolitical reasons related to managing China—the stage could be set, similarly, for deterrence breakdown. Comparable concerns apply to China. If Beijing's ascendancy creates expectations that the other major powers would increasingly defer to Chinese preferences, at least as far as its territorial and precedential claims were concerned, such expectations could lead to a more uncompromising Chinese stance with respect to political disputes with New Delhi and could, by implication, lead to an increased potential for conflict. Because Indian, Pakistani, and Chinese perceptions of the role of extraregional powers are thus critical, though in different ways, for future decisions relating to the initiation of war, it is important that all extraregional powers—especially critical actors with a disproportionate impact on Asia such as the United States, Russia, and Japan—pay careful attention to the nature of the political signals transmitted to New Delhi, Islamabad, and Beijing in the context of their bilateral relationships with the greater South Asian states. In this context, it is equally important that all extraregional powers pay particular attention to their policies insofar as they relate to arms transfers and territorial disputes. To the degree that such policies suggest a willingness to countenance dramatic changes in the regional balances of power or encourage territorial revisionism through coercion or force, the stage would be set for serious discord among India, Pakistan, and China.

Anticipating Conflict in South Asia. Based on the general trends in the region and the specific drivers identified previously, it is possible to envisage the following conflicts in South Asia. These outcomes represent only remote possibilities, at least when viewed at the present time. Indo-Pakistani competition leading to deliberate major war is increasingly unlikely, because the political objectives that could be secured by war are rapidly disappearing. As the economic and political transformations in both states work themselves out, it is in fact likely that these South Asian neighbors will be forced to accommodate one another even if the outstanding issues between them are not resolved in their legal detail. This is because Pakistan, the weaker state, will be increasingly unable to resort to territorial revisionism through force of arms, while India, the stronger state, preoccupied with asserting its larger claims to continental and global recognition, will increasingly choose not to resort to force within the subcontinent. The future of Sino-Indian competition, however, is a different matter and it is as yet unclear what the forms of competition, or their intensity, might eventually turn out to be. These contingencies, being more significant, warrant close scrutiny by regional analysts.

With all these considerations, it is possible to map out the incidence of "worst-case" contingencies in South Asia in the following way.

Short Term. In this time period, extending from the current year to 2005, Indo-Pakistani border unrest will continue to be the dominant form of conflict, because neither state will possess the capabilities required to pursue other more decisive forms of combat. Both could continue to support insurgencies in each other's territory while relying on their opaque nuclear programs to prevent such provocations from mutating into full-blown challenges directed at one another. Unless moderated by internal actions or external constraints, South Asia will experience continued "ugly stability"—low-grade violence episodically interrupted by bouts of inadvertent escalation (as occurred during the onset of the 1990s' crisis); efforts at deliberate retaliation (as embodied by Operation Brass Tacks in 1987); and more-or-less serious forms of nuclear brandishing (which also occurred in 1990). The Sino-Indian arena will be generally quiescent during this period.

Medium Term. In this time period, extending from 2005 to 2015, there are three possible kinds of Indo-Pakistani conflicts and one possibly emerging from a Sino-Indian conflict. The first kind in the former category is a premeditated conventional war launched by India if it begins to perform at a less-than-desirable rate economically and is faced with persistent, and ever more costly, Pakistani-supported internal insurgencies. The second kind is a war of desperation launched by Pakistan if India's economic expansion implies the increasing neglect of Pakistan's outstanding territorial claims by the international community (and especially by the United States). The third kind is war launched by Pakistan in the context of state breakdown as a result of relatively successful insurgencies within Pakistan. The only kind of contingency imaginable in the Sino-Indian category is a renewal of Chinese-supported low-intensity conflict in the Indian northeast and similar Indian-supported efforts in Tibet and Xinjiang.

Long Term. In this time period, extending from 2015 to 2025, Indo-Pakistani conflicts would continue to resemble those in the previous time frame, whereas the possibilities of direct Sino-Indian conflicts would probably grow. These could include either direct Sino-Indian border clashes along the Himalayan fronts or perhaps naval clashes (or "incidents at sea") in the Andaman Sea or Southeast Asia as Chinese and Indian naval operations intersect more often in the northern Indian Ocean. None of these scenarios is by any means foreordained; they depend on the evolution of the Sino-Indian political relationship, the political and economic changes taking place in each country, and the nature of the relationships enjoyed by each of these actors with third countries, especially the United States, Russia, and Japan.

REGIONAL CONCLUSIONS AND IMPLICATIONS FOR THE UNITED STATES AIR FORCE

This subsection attempts to synthesize some of the key operational implications distilled from the analyses relating to the rise of Asia and the potential for conflict in each of its constituent regions.

The first key implication derived from the analysis of trends in Asia suggests that *American air and space power will continue to remain critical for conventional and unconventional deterrence in Asia.* This argument is justified by the fact that several subregions of the continent still harbor the potential for full-scale conventional war. This potential is most conspicuous on the Korean peninsula and, to a lesser degree, in South Asia, the Persian Gulf, and the South China Sea. In some of these areas, such as Korea and the Persian Gulf, the United States has clear treaty obligations and, therefore, has pre-planned the use of air power should contingencies arise. U.S. Air Force assets could also be called upon for operations in some of these other areas.

In almost all these cases, U.S. air power would be at the forefront of an American politico-military response because (a) of the vast distances on the Asian continent; (b) the diverse range of operational platforms available to the U.S. Air Force, a capability unmatched by any other country or service; (c) the possible unavailability of naval assets in close proximity, particularly in the context of surprise contingencies; and (d) the heavy payload that can be carried by U.S. Air Force platforms. These platforms can exploit speed, reach, and high operating tempos to sustain continual operations until the political objectives are secured.

The entire range of warfighting capability—fighters, bombers, electronic warfare (EW), suppression of enemy air defense (SEAD), combat support platforms such as AWACS and J-STARS, and tankers—are relevant in the Asia-Pacific region, because many of the regional contingencies will involve armed operations against large, fairly modern, conventional forces, most of which are built around large land armies, as is the case in Korea, China-Taiwan, India-Pakistan, and the Persian Gulf.

In addition to conventional combat, the demands of unconventional deterrence will increasingly confront the U.S. Air Force in Asia. The Korean peninsula, China, and the Indian subcontinent are already arenas of WMD proliferation. While emergent nuclear capabilities continue to receive the most public attention, chemical and biological warfare threats will progressively become future problems. The delivery systems in the region are increasing in range and diversity. China already targets the continental United States with ballistic missiles. North Korea can threaten northeast Asia with existing Scud-class theater ballistic missiles. India will acquire the capability to produce ICBM-class delivery vehicles, and both China and India will acquire long-range cruise missiles during the time frames examined in this report.

The second key implication derived from the analysis of trends in Asia suggests that *air and space power will function as a vital rapid reaction force in a breaking crisis.* Current guidance tasks the Air Force to prepare for two major regional conflicts that could break out in the Persian Gulf and on the Korean peninsula. In other areas of Asia, however, such as the Indian subcontinent, the South China Sea, Southeast Asia, and Myanmar, the United States has no treaty obligations requiring it to commit the use of its military forces. But as past experience has shown, American policymakers have regularly displayed the disconcerting habit of discovering strategic interests in parts of the world previously neglected *after conflicts have already broken out.* Mindful of this trend, it would behoove U.S. Air Force planners to prudently plan for regional contingencies in non-traditional areas of interest, because naval and air power will of necessity be the primary instruments constituting the American response.

Such responses would be necessitated by three general classes of contingencies. The first involves the politico-military collapse of a key regional actor, as might occur in the case of North Korea, Myanmar, Indonesia, or Pakistan. The second involves acute political-military crises that have a potential for rapid escalation, as may occur in the Taiwan Strait, the Spratlys, the Indian subcontinent, or on the Korean peninsula. The third involves cases of prolonged domestic instability that may have either spillover or contagion effects, as in China, Indonesia, Myanmar, or North Korea.

In each of these cases, U.S. responses may vary from simply being a concerned onlooker to prosecuting the whole range of military operations to providing post-conflict assistance in a permissive environment. Depending on the political choices made, Air Force contributions would obviously vary. If the first response is selected, contributions would consist predominantly of vital, specialized, air-breathing platforms such as AWACS, JSTARS, and Rivet Joint—in tandem with controlled space assets—that would be necessary for assessment of political crises erupting in the region. The second response, in contrast, would burden the entire range of U.S. Air Force capabilities, in the manner witnessed in Operation Desert Storm. The third response, like the first, would call for specialized capabilities, mostly in the areas of strategic lift and airborne tanker support.

The third key implication derived from the analysis of trends in Asia suggests that *despite increasing regional air capabilities, U.S. Air Force assets will be required to fill gaps in critical warfighting areas.* The capabilities of the Asian states, including those of U.S. allies and neutral states, have been steadily increasing in the last two decades. These increases have occurred largely through the acquisition of late-generation, advanced combat aircraft such as the MiG-29, and the F-15, F-16, and F/A-18 together with short-range infrared and medium-range semi-active air-to-air missiles. Despite such acquisitions, however, the states that possess these aircraft have not become truly effective users of air power, in part because acquiring advanced combat aircraft and their associated technologies is a small part of ensuring overall proficiency in the exploitation of air power. The latter includes incorporating effective training regimes, maintaining large and diverse logistics networks, developing an indigenous industrial infrastructure capable of supporting the variegated air assets, and integrating specific subspecialties such as air-to-air refueling, electronic warfare, suppression of enemy air defenses, airspace surveillance and battle management capabilities in a hostile environment, and night and adverse weather operations.

Most of the Asian air forces lack full air-power capabilities of the sort described above. The Japanese and South Korean air forces are, as a rule, optimized mostly for air defense operations. Both air forces are generally proficient in all-weather defensive counterair operations, and they possess relatively modest day ground-attack capabilities as well. Because of their specific operating environments, however, the Japanese air force is particularly proficient in maritime air operations, whereas the South Korean air force has some close air support (CAS) experience as well. The Chinese air force (People's Liberation Army Air Force, [PLAAF]) is still a predominantly daylight defensive counterair force with limited daylight attack capabilities, as are most of the Southeast Asian air forces, but the PLAAF has recently demonstrated an impressive ability to integrate its new weapon systems (e.g., the Su-27) much faster than most observers expected. The air forces of the Indian subcontinent have somewhat greater capabilities. Most squadrons of the Indian and Pakistani air forces are capable of daylight defensive counterair, a few are capable of all-weather defensive counterair, and several Indian units are capable of battlefield air interdiction and deep penetration-interdiction strike.

None of these air forces, however, is particularly proficient at night and all-weather ground attack, especially at operational ranges. They lack advanced munitions, especially in the air-to-surface regime. With the exception of Japan and Singapore, they lack battle management command, control and communications (BMC^3) platforms as well as the logistics and training levels required for successful, extended, high-tempo operations.

The brittle quality of Asian air forces implies that U.S. Air Force assets will be required to fill critical gaps in allied air capabilities as well as to counter both the growing capabilities of potential adversaries such as China and the new nontraditional threats emerging in the form of ballistic and cruise missiles, information warfare, WMD, and possibly even the revolution in military affairs.

The fourth key implication derived from the analysis of trends in Asia suggests that *there will be increasing political constraints on en-route and in-theater access.* Problems of basing for en-route and in-theater access will become of concern as the Asian states grow in confidence and capability. For the moment, however, such problems have been held in check because of the continuing threats on the Korean peninsula and recent revitalization of the U.S.-Japanese security treaty. But these developments constitute only a reprieve, not an enduring solution. The availability of the Korean bases after unification is an open question. Even if these and the Japanese bases continue to be available, their use will be increasingly restricted by the host countries for routine training operations and especially for nontraditional out-of-area operations. The recent difficulties caused by the refusal of the Gulf states to permit U.S. air operations against Saddam Hussein will become the norm in the Asia-Pacific region as well.

There are already some indicators to this effect. For example, constitutional and legal restraints in the form of Article 9 could prevent Japan from providing access, logistical support, and reinforcements in the context of crises in Asia. There is also relatively weak political support for all but the most narrow range of contingencies, as became evident in Japanese, Korean, and Southeast Asian reluctance to support U.S. gunboat diplomacy during the recent (1995–1996) China-Taiwan face-off. Even the Southeast states, which benefit most from U.S. presence and deterrent capabilities in the region, were conspicuously silent—and in some cases even undercut American efforts at restraining Chinese intimidation of Taiwan. Besides these growing political constraints, the fact remains that in some feasible contingencies the U.S. Air Force will have little or no access whatsoever to some regions in Asia. The absence of air bases in Southeast Asia and the northern Indian Ocean, for example, could threaten the execution of contingency plans involving either South Asia or Myanmar. The vast distances in the Asia-Pacific region could come to haunt Air Force operations, because existing facilities at Diego Garcia and in the Persian Gulf are too far away for any but the most minimal operations.

Increasing political constrictions coupled with the sparse number of operating facilities available imply that even such potentially innovative U.S. Air Force solutions as the "air expeditionary force" and "composite air wings" could run into show-stopping impediments beyond U.S. Air Force control. This, in turn, has four consequences. First, American policymakers should investigate the possibility of securing additional air base access in Asia. The most attractive candidate, especially in the context of a rising China, is Cam Ran Bay in Vietnam. Other alternatives, especially for contingencies in the Persian Gulf and the greater South Asian region, could include transit rights in India or Pakistan. Second, U.S. Air Force planners will have to devote relatively greater resources to mobility assets and support platforms such as airborne tankers to keep a smaller combat force capable of long-distance operations. Third, planners must begin to give some thought to novel technologies capable of mitigating the access and staging problem. These technologies can include, at the more radical end, floating air bases of the kind proposed by RAND several decades ago, or at the more conservative technical end, more-efficient engines, longer-range aircraft, and the like. Fourth, U.S. Air Force planners must increasingly think in terms of joint operations not merely at the cosmetic level, as in the cruise missile strikes against Iraq, but in terms of a true division of labor, especially in the early stages of a distant contingency.

The fifth key implication derived from the analysis of trends in Asia suggests that *WMD-shadowed environments will pose new operational challenges to air power.* There is little doubt that the number of states possessing different kinds of WMD will increase during the time frames examined in this report. While Russia, China, North Korea, India, and Pakistan are the only nuclear-capable states in Asia at the moment, several other states likely are virtual nuclear powers (Japan, South Korea, and Taiwan), with Iran and Iraq in the wings. All these states are threatened by nuclear capabilities in some form, and many will be able to mount nuclear threats of their own at some point. Although nuclear capabilities concentrate the mind in a way that few other weapons do, chemical and biological weapons will also come in to their own, and their use for either operations or terror may be even more probable. All three forms of WMD, as well as radiological weapons, could be delivered by either ballistic or cruise missiles, advanced combat aircraft, or unconventional means of delivery. These regional operating environments will thus become more complicated over time.

In this context, the U.S. Air Force will require both new capabilities and new concepts of operations for successful combat in such environments. These new capabilities include better means of localizing WMD holdings at long range; better means of interdicting storage facilities, especially those relying on depth or dispersal for survival; and better means of effectively intercepting WMD carriers if their prelaunch destruction is not possible. New concepts of operations involve devising and using better ways to continue combat operations amidst a WMD environment, new forms of warfare including information warfare to subvert an adversary's combat capability rather than physically destroying it, and, finally, new "nonlethal" weapons to attain results previously attainable by lethal means alone.

Chapter Four

SOURCES OF CONFLICT IN THE GREATER MIDDLE EAST

Ian O. Lesser, Bruce R. Nardulli, and Lory A. Arghavan

INTRODUCTION

An Enduring Area of Engagement

Few would question that the greater Middle East is an area of central geostrategic concern for the United States—a place where U.S. interests are at stake, conflict is frequent, and demands on U.S. military forces are high. Moreover, the evolution of the region over the longer term is likely to have an important influence on global prosperity and stability, affecting a broad range of issues in which the United States as a global power will have an interest. Developments in all of these dimensions will influence the demands and constraints imposed on the use of American military power, including air and space power, in and around the Middle East.

For the purposes of this study, the "greater Middle East" is understood to include the states of North Africa, the Levant (including Turkey and the Palestinian entity), and the Persian Gulf. The discussion extends to areas on the periphery of these states, such as the Caucasus and Central Asia.

From a U.S. perspective alone, looking simply at the period 1979–1996 (to include the Gulf War and its aftermath), the greater Middle East has been the dominant theater for U.S. intervention in both frequency and scale (the 1979 Iran hostage rescue effort, deployments to Lebanon in 1982, the 1986 El Dorado Canyon strikes against Libya, the 1987–1988 reflagging and escort of tankers in the Gulf, the 1990 Gulf War, and continuing operations in northern and southern Iraq in the wake of the defeat of Baghdad. Stretching the definition of the region, one might also include the 1992 peacekeeping operation in Somalia). A recent survey of U.S. intervention policy examines 12 prominent cases from 1979 through 1994, of which seven are Middle Eastern.[1] If the repeated interventions against Iraq are treated as separate cases, the number of Middle Eastern deployments is even more overwhelming. Quite apart from these instances of intervention, the region is of enormous significance from the point of view of peacetime presence and planning. In the Cold War period, the Mediterranean and the Persian Gulf stood out as areas where the U.S. military presence held steady or grew. Under current conditions, forces based elsewhere—in Europe or the Indian Ocean—are most likely to be used for contingencies somewhere in the greater Middle East. One of two canonical major regional contingencies (MRCs) is assumed to be in the Middle East.

What Is the U.S. Interest? What Is at Stake?

In an era in which U.S. interests are being examined more critically, the greater Middle East continues to present high stakes for American policymakers. Taking a longer-term (through 2025) perspective, U.S. key national interests include

- the survival of Israel and completion of the Middle East peace process,

- access to oil,

- forestalling the emergence of a hostile regional hegemon,

- preventing the spread of weapons of mass destruction,

- promoting political and economic reform and through it internal stability, and

- holding terrorism in check.[2]

---

[1]See Richard N. Haass, *Intervention: The Use of American Military Force in the Post–Cold War World,* Washington, DC: Carnegie Endowment, 1994.

[2]U.S. interests are discussed in similar fashion in Commission on America's National Interests, *America's National Interests*, RAND/CSIA/Nixon Center, July 1996, pp. 39–41.

Some of these interests are specific to the region, but most are closely linked to broader, systemic interests in stability, nonproliferation, energy security, and evolutionary versus revolutionary change.

Israel and the Peace Process. The United States has been committed to the security and prosperity of Israel since the founding of the state, and this commitment will almost certainly remain a key interest through the period under discussion. U.S. policy over the next decade will, however, be shaped by the parallel national interest in promoting, reinforcing, and bringing to completion the Middle East peace process. Success in this arena will have a considerable influence over the region's future propensity for conflict and the demands on U.S. strategy and forces. Achievement of a comprehensive peace will very likely bring increased demands for monitoring and security guarantees. Failure will raise more conventional demands for deterrence and reassurance. At the same time, the increasing prosperity and military capability of Israel—and economic realities in the United States—will shape the level of support this enduring interest implies.

Energy Security. Access to Middle Eastern oil in adequate amounts and at reasonable prices will almost certainly remain a vital interest.[3] A large proportion of world petroleum reserves are to be found in the greater Middle East. The Gulf states alone account for 65 percent of proven world oil reserves, and despite changing patterns of demand and consumption over the past two decades, almost 35 percent of the industrialized world's oil supply came from the Gulf in 1994.[4] The five countries with the greatest proven reserves are all in the Middle East. If Caspian oil and gas are included—and they should be, since much of the future production from this region will be exported via the Levant or the Gulf—the region's importance in energy terms is greatly reinforced. Growing energy needs in Eastern Europe and Asia could place greater pressure on demand and further increase the strategic significance of the region's oil resources. Al-

---

[3]It is worth noting that our interests, even in the Persian Gulf, have never been driven solely by oil. See Ian O. Lesser, *Oil, the Persian Gulf, and Grand Strategy: Contemporary Issues in Historical Perspective*, Santa Monica, CA: RAND, R-4072-CENTCOM/JCS, 1991.

[4]G. C. Georgiou, "United States Energy Security Policy and Options for the 1990s," *Energy Policy*, Vol. 21, August 1993, pp. 831–839.

though world oil production continues to grow rapidly, world reserves have grown even faster, and the bulk of these new additions have been in the Middle East.[5] Given our systemic interest in international economic stability, the United States is unlikely to abandon its current role as ultimate guarantor of world access to Middle Eastern oil.[6] Future aggression by Iraq or Iran against the oil-rich Arabian Peninsula would doubtless trigger an American military response on the order of the Desert Storm operation.[7]

Containing Hegemons and Proliferators.   There continues to be a strong consensus within the U.S. strategic community about the need to prevent the emergence of a regional hegemon or, more precisely, a "hostile" regional hegemon (i.e., a power capable of and interested in regional domination).[8] From a strategic planning perspective, this need could be extended to include preventing the emergence of competitors capable of successfully challenging U.S. military power. Such competitors could come from within or outside the region.[9] The United States will also continue to have a closely-related interest in preventing regional powers—and nonstate actors—from acquiring new or additional weapons of mass destruction and the means for their delivery at longer range. These weapons can be classed as a systemic concern for the United States. But the greater Middle East has emerged as a focal point for WMD challenges, with longer-range ballistic missiles poised to change the relationship between the traditional Middle East and adjacent regions in

---

[5]Alan Richards and John Waterbury, *A Political Economy of the Middle East*, Boulder, CO: Westview, 1996, p. 53.

[6]Currently, the United States imports some 10 percent of its oil from the Persian Gulf, and Europe almost 30 percent. For two perspectives on this disparity in the context of overwhelming U.S. involvement in Gulf defense, see Shibley Telhami and Michael O'Hanlon, "Europe's Oil, Our Troops," *New York Times*, December 10, 1995; and Lawrence J. Korb, "Holding the Bag in the Gulf," *New York Times*, September 18, 1996.

[7]*America's National Interests*, p. 40.

[8]For a discussion of the role of the United States in preventing the emergence of such a hegemon, see Zalmay Khalilzad, "The United States and the Persian Gulf: Preventing Regional Hegemony," *Survival*, Vol. 37, No 2, Summer 1995, pp. 95–120.

[9]Potential extraregional peer competitors might include a resurgent Russia, a more assertive European Union, or, at the borderlands of the Middle East, China.

security terms. Indeed, many of today's leading proliferation risks are arrayed along an arc stretching from Algeria to Pakistan.[10]

Promoting Internal Stability. It has become fashionable to refer to the greater Middle East as an arc of crisis. Given the strength of pressures for change within societies across the region, it might be more appropriate to describe the region as an "arc of change." As a status quo power, the United States has a strong systemic interest in avoiding violent change and encouraging behavior in line with accepted international norms. The links between political and economic reforms and stability cannot be taken for granted. There is an emerging Western consensus that movement toward modern economic systems, more representative government, and greater attention to human rights will help forestall radical change in societies under pressure. Broadly speaking, we will continue to have a national interest in preventing violent change and the emergence of radical or revolutionary regimes (such regimes are unlikely to "wish us well").

Dealing with Terrorism. Finally, recent events have reinforced American awareness of terrorism as a security problem. Terrorism is a well-established mode of conflict on the Middle Eastern scene. We will continue to have a keen stake in limiting the threat of terrorism to friendly regimes and Western citizens and assets, as well as preventing the spillover of political violence emanating from the region. A variety of future regional conflict scenarios may stem from terrorist action, and counterterrorism is likely to be a motivating factor in many instances of U.S. and Western military intervention. Terrorism might also emerge as a tactic for regimes bent on more-traditional forms of regional aggression. In the future, U.S. strategy will need to address the problem of terrorism both as a stand-alone threat and as a "fifth column" or "asymmetric" risk in regional conflicts.

Study Objectives and Structure

Our analysis assesses the demands and constraints likely to be imposed on the U.S. Air Force and U.S. strategy more generally as a re-

---

[10]See Ian O. Lesser and Ashley J. Tellis, *Strategic Exposure: Proliferation Around the Mediterranean,* Santa Monica, CA: RAND, MR-742-A, 1996.

sult of developments across the region. We take as our starting point the premise that political-military trends inside the region, as well as on its periphery, will influence the uses of air and space power in defense of the national interests outlined above. This chapter considers likely developments in the near and mid-term (through 2005) and the longer term (through 2025).

The notion of the "greater" Middle East has been adopted to capture one of the key macro trends in the current strategic environment, and one that we believe will be even more significant in the future— that is, the steady erosion of traditional distinctions between "Middle Eastern" security and "European" and "Eurasian" security. This erosion is the result of the growing reach of military systems and the growing economic and political interdependence of regions. Spillovers of different sorts, from transregional terrorism and smuggling to refugee flows and migration, are further contributing to the breakdown of old regional definitions. Although trends and scenarios in Europe and Eurasia are treated elsewhere in this volume, our analysis considers interrelationships and effects beyond the Middle East.

It is also increasingly clear that an understanding of the emerging strategic environment and its implications for defense planning should look beyond the traditional sources of conflict on Israel's borders and in the Persian Gulf. These places will remain essential from the perspective of interests and the likelihood of demands on U.S. military forces. But key flash points exist in other areas and could acquire greater significance for planning purposes over time. Thus, within our greater Middle East framework, we devote considerable attention to North Africa, Turkey and its neighbors, and the problems of Mediterranean security in general.

The following sections discuss regional trends and their consequences, with specific attention to key internal and external drivers; alternative "strategic worlds" and their implications; and overall implications for U.S. policy and Air Force planning.

KEY INTERNAL TRENDS AND THEIR CONSEQUENCES

Societies Under Stress

States across the region are facing threats to stability as a result of internal trends. The most consequential trends in this context include

- demographic change and relentless urbanization,

- problems of economic growth and reform,

- dysfunctional societies and the erosion of state control, and

- crises of political legitimacy and the challenges of Islam and nationalism.

Taken together, these trends have encouraged and will almost certainly continue to support a pervasive sense of insecurity within Middle Eastern societies. When officials and observers within the region itself talk about future security, they will be concerned first and foremost with *internal* security. The key "drivers" identified here will all have consequences for the types of conflict and non-conflict demands and constraints the U.S. military is likely to confront across the region through 2025. The drivers represent deep systemic factors that will be at the forefront of challenges to stability in the region for the next several decades.

Demographic Pressures, Urbanization, and Migration

Although global population growth has slowed considerably, disproving the extremely pessimistic assumptions of the 1970s, population trends in the Middle East have not followed this hopeful pattern. Overall, the Middle Eastern population is expected to double by 2025, with annual growth rates of roughly 3 percent. Over the last ten years, the Gulf states and the countries of the Maghreb, including Egypt, have experienced population growth on the order of 40 percent—with the result that per capita GNP has dropped sharply. The population around the southern and eastern shores of the Mediterranean is likely to reach 350 million not long after the end of the century (by contrast, the total population of the current members of the European Union will not exceed 300 million in the same period). From a social viewpoint, it is perhaps more significant that the proportion of people under 15 years of age in these highest-growth areas will reach 30 percent by 2025.[11]

Demographic change of this kind will have a number of potentially destabilizing consequences. First, it will reinforce long-standing trends toward urbanization across the region as populations move to the cities in search of jobs and social services. Uncontrolled urbanization is already a well-established trend around the southern Mediterranean and the Middle East. Cities such as Cairo and Istanbul, designed for hundreds of thousands, now rank among the most densely populated in the world, with populations approaching 15 million. Indeed, the Middle East has long been dominated by its cities, including provincial cities in the rural hinterland. Cities are and will continue to be the focus for intellectual, economic, and political activity. As a whole, the region is more heavily urbanized than East Asia, South Asia, or Africa.[12] The challenges of housing, feeding, and providing transport and medical care for ever larger and younger populations, evident almost everywhere in the region, are most acute in the cities. The inability of states to adjust to the problems of urbanization is also having political consequences for established regimes. Islamist movements in particular, including Algeria's FIS (Islamic Salvation Front) and Turkey's Refah (Welfare) Party, first made their mark in urban politics where they registered striking electoral successes.

Whereas traditional rural relationships among families, clans, landowners, and peasants once formed the basis for political stability in many Middle Eastern societies, Middle Eastern politics now turn increasingly on economic relationships and new systems of patronage based in the cities. It is in the cities that disparities between the "haves" and "have-nots" are most striking. The future shape of Middle Eastern politics, whether radical or moderate, is likely to center on urban areas, and control of the cities will be a leading measure of state control. Any Western involvement in the region's internal conflicts over the next decades—for example, to defend Gulf

---

[11]An amalgam of World Bank and UN estimates. See *World Economic and Social Survey 1995*, Department for Economic and Social Information and Policy Analysis, United Nations; New York, 1995; and Eduard Bos et al., *World Population Projections 1994–95*, Baltimore, MD: Johns Hopkins University Press, 1994.

[12]Richards and Waterbury, p. 251.

monarchies or to protect Western citizens and assets—will have to account for the likelihood of operations in urban areas, with all the constraints on deployment, mobility, and the use of force this implies.

Population increases are also changing the character of Middle Eastern states and introducing or deepening sources of internal conflict. For example, in the early years of the Turkish republic, the population was perhaps 15–20 million. By the end of this century, Turkey's population will approach 90 million, most residing in urban areas. In this context, it is hardly surprising that Turkey's secular, Westernized elite feels itself under pressure from more traditional, religious, and "Middle Eastern" arrivals from Anatolia. Population growth and urbanization have simply changed the nature of the country. Similar transformations have occurred as a result of migration and population growth elsewhere in the region. In some cases, disparities in population growth along ethnic and religious lines have fundamentally altered political balances and the prospects for stability.[13] Prominent examples include the steady erosion of the Maronite position in Lebanon in the face of a growing Muslim population; the expanding and increasingly assertive Shi'ite population in the smaller Gulf states; the relatively rapid growth of Kurdish communities in Turkey, Iran, and Iraq; and the high birth rates among Palestinians and Israeli Arabs. Demographic changes along these lines will continue to be a source of friction within Middle Eastern societies as old political arrangements and ethnic compacts lose their relevance. For this reason among others, ethnic and separatist conflicts are likely to be a feature on the regional scene over the next decades.

Population size and growth will be a factor in the power and potential of states. In the Middle East, however, large populations can be a source of vulnerability when coupled with low economic growth rates and the pressures noted above. The most stable and powerful states in the future may be those where demographic pressures and economic performance have been brought into line, allowing regimes to devote additional resources to investment, development

---

[13]See discussion of the politics of differential fertility in Richards and Waterbury, pp. 96–100.

of defense industries, and the acquisition of modern military forces without risking domestic chaos. The ability to control corrosive demographic trends is also likely to play a key role in determining the relationship of Middle Eastern states to the "rich" societies on their periphery, above all the European Union (Israel, as a "rich" regional state, is in a special category of its own). The EU, even those members with a keen awareness of the consequences for their own security of instability in the south, will be reluctant or unable to provide aid and investment if the case seems hopeless.

Demographic and economic disparities will be the engine of migration, from rural to urban areas, from poor to rich—or less poor—areas, and from insecure to more-secure states and regions. It has become fashionable to speak of migration and refugee movements as key facets of the post–Cold War security environment worldwide. The Middle East as a whole is a leading source and recipient of the movement of people for economic and political reasons, and is home to the world's largest refugee population.[14] Within the region and worldwide, Iran has the single largest refugee population, composed largely of Afghans, Iraqis, and migrants from adjacent Kurdish regions. The Gulf states have also been large net recipients of migrants from poorer states in the Middle East and Asia. Remittances from migrant workers make a significant contribution to the economies of key countries such as Egypt.

At the same time, the countries of North Africa are large net exporters of labor to Europe. The potential exists for larger-scale movements based on turmoil in North Africa, including the collapse of the Algerian, Libyan, or Moroccan regimes, although there is considerable debate about the likely scale. For the poor and increasingly populous countries of North Africa and the Levant (including Turkey), the migration of workers to Europe has been an important economic and social safety valve.[15] To the extent that the European Union places

---

[14]The refugee population of the Near East and South Asia is almost nine million. See U.S. Department of State, *World Refugee Report, 1993;* cited in William B. Wood, "The Geopolitics of International Migration," in George Demko and William B. Wood (eds.), *Reordering the World: Geopolitical Perspectives on the 21st Century,* Boulder, CO: Westview, 1995; see pp. 191–205.

[15]There are almost two million Turks in Germany alone, perhaps one-third of whom are Kurds.

increasing restrictions on legal immigration and makes illegal migration more difficult, this outlet could decline over the next decades, resulting in increased pressure on already hard-pressed states.

The potential for destabilizing migration is a growing concern for key states within the region. Iran, Syria, and, above all, Turkey will be wary of potentially large movements of Kurdish refugees fleeing instability on their borders. Beyond the problems of absorption and cost, it is feared that such flows could worsen existing separatist violence. The insecurity of a growing Kurdish population is likely to be a permanent operating factor in the stability of the northern Gulf and the Levant for the foreseeable future. A very different example can be seen in the case of Egypt and Sudan. Egyptian observers are increasingly concerned about the implications for Egyptian security and stability of large-scale migration on the country's southern border. Egyptians are also concerned about the way in which migration can interact with other sources of conflict—e.g., Nile waters, terrorism—in their relationship with Sudan. The prospect of refugee movements as a result of ethnic conflict or leadership change in Sudan also imposes some constraints on Egyptian policymakers, who might otherwise see benefits in the destabilization of their southern neighbor.

Migration and refugee issues, both north-south and south-south, could emerge as a leading point for Western diplomatic and military engagement in the region and on its periphery. In the Mediterranean, migration is likely to be largely a European responsibility, although U.S. assistance might be required in monitoring and helping to control disastrous flows. Elsewhere, the U.S. role is likely to be more central, with implications for surveillance and humanitarian assistance capabilities. The situation in northern Iraq that gave rise to Operation Provide Comfort in the wake of the Gulf War is unlikely to be the last of its type in a region where the drivers for such crises are durable.

Dilemmas of Economic Growth and Reform

With some notable exceptions, the countries of the greater Middle East face a troubled economic future, with serious implications for stability and the propensity for conflict. High levels of unemployment, inflation, and external debt are commonplace. For most states in the region, the prospects for significant economic growth are poor given relentless population pressure and the entry of larger numbers of young people into the economy. Unemployment rates are very high by world standards. Algeria, Iran, Lebanon, Yemen, and the Palestinian territories have unemployment rates at or above 30 percent (an extraordinary 45 percent in Gaza). GNP growth across the region has generally been flat or little better than flat over the last decade. Some states, including Afghanistan, Algeria, and the leading oil producers, have experienced a decline in GNP over the last decade, the result of political turmoil and declining oil revenues. Given the importance of oil production to the regional economic environment, it is not surprising that many Middle Eastern economies are "vulnerable, single commodity dependent," with 40 percent or more of revenues hinging on the export of a single product.[16]

Israel and, potentially, Turkey are exceptions to this dismal economic picture. The Israeli economy is not without difficulties, with a history of high inflation and high levels of unemployment by OECD standards. Yet Israel is an increasingly prosperous society with Western levels of economic performance embedded in the Middle East. For a decade prior to the Gulf War, Turkey benefited from the highest rates of economic growth in the OECD. Over the last few years, however, Turkey has returned to the historical pattern of wildly fluctuating economic performance and high inflation (currently nearly 100 percent per year). As in a number of other places in the region (e.g., Morocco), a dynamic private sector has emerged, but little progress has been made in the dismantling of state industries or improved distribution of wealth.

It is widely assumed that economic reform, including privatization and the reduction of government subsidies, will be essential to the emergence of more productive and modern Middle Eastern economies over the next decades. This path will be difficult even for states such as Turkey with relatively good human capital, abundant resources, diversified economies, and well-developed links to West-

____

[16]*Handbook of International Economic Statistics, 1995,* Directorate of Intelligence, Central Intelligence Agency, September 1995.

ern markets. For countries such as Egypt, the political risks of economic reform are daunting.

From a "sources of conflict" perspective, the relationship between prosperity and stability is potentially critical. Yet the link between these elements is unlikely to be as clear or predictable as some observers and policymakers (inside and outside the region) have tended to assume. Significant improvements in economic performance over the longer term are widely thought to be unlikely in the absence of economic reform. The absence of reform continues to be the basis for much U.S., EU, and international financial institution policy toward the region. But real economic reforms are at best unpredictable in their effect on political stability, because they spread the burden of adjustment unevenly and interrupt established patterns of patronage and corruption. Where a highly visible class of new capitalists has emerged—in Turkey, Morocco, Egypt, and pre-revolutionary Iran—problems of inadequate distribution of wealth and unsatisfied rising expectations have made themselves felt on the political scene. Even the issue of the distribution of income is no clear guide to the likelihood of instability. Morocco, often viewed as the most stable society in North Africa, has the worst distribution of income among its neighbors, with a somewhat better situation in Tunisia. Algeria, embroiled in savage political violence, has long had the best distribution of income in the region.

For the region as a whole, the relationship between economic factors and regime stability is likely to remain unpredictable in most scenarios short of economic collapse. Even where economic progress may well contribute to stability, it might prove difficult to reconcile economic time horizons, typically longer term, with immediate political challenges. Even for those states undertaking serious reforms, managing the lengthy transition will be demanding and risky. Success or failure in managing economic reform could also have implications for the likelihood of a durable Arab-Israeli settlement, because instability flowing from economic inequality will weaken the position of regimes essential for the peace process. Sensitivity to the distributional effects of economic reform might even prove "a necessary condition for sustaining a peace negotiated from above."[17]

The pervasive insecurity of Middle Eastern states has bred high levels of spending on security establishments and military equipment. Apart from the strategic implications (examined below), this trend has negative implications for the economic future of a region critically short of investment in other sectors, including education and infrastructure.[18] Taken together with the inability of economic growth to keep pace with expanding populations, the prosperity gap between the greater Middle East as a whole and its rich European and Asian periphery (including Israel) is likely to grow over the next decades. One implication of this is that the issues currently at stake between north and south in economic terms—aid, investment, trade, and migration—are likely to become more prominent and more contentious.

The scale of Middle Eastern requirements for aid and investment will very likely far outstrip available Western resources, especially if the reintegration of Eastern Europe proceeds apace. Some indication of this looming imbalance between needs and resources can already be seen in the context of the EU-Mediterranean Partnership launched in Barcelona in November 1995.[19] At Barcelona, the EU committed itself to a five-year program of assistance for North African and Middle Eastern states of slightly less than $7 billion, much less than the amount of assistance to be devoted to Eastern Europe, and dramatically short of the roughly $70 billion the EU will transfer to its southern European member countries in the same period. Even greater stringencies are likely to apply in the case of U.S. aid through the end of the century and beyond. In Egypt, the leading recipient of U.S. economic assistance, it is increasingly assumed that the aid relationship will decline and perhaps evaporate altogether over the coming years. In this environment, hard-pressed Middle Eastern states are likely to place great emphasis on diversifying their economic rela-

---

[17]Etel Solingen, "Quandaries of the Peace Process," *Journal of Democracy*, July 1996, p. 151.

[18]See Richards and Waterbury, pp. 103–133.

[19]The 12 Mediterranean partner countries are Algeria, Cyprus, Egypt, Israel, Jordan, Lebanon, Malta, Morocco, the Palestine National Authority, Syria, Tunisia, and Turkey.

tionships and on pursuing closer political and security ties where they appear to offer an advantage in the competition for scarce aid and investment.

Insecure Societies and the Erosion of State Control

The pervasive insecurity characteristic of Middle Eastern societies makes itself felt at several levels: at the level of regimes concerned about survival and the external exploitation of internal weakness; at the level of ethnic and religious groups, or classes, concerned about preserving their position or carving out additional autonomy; and at the level of individuals confronting dysfunctional states. The notion of "failed states," common in discussion of sub-Saharan Africa, may also have considerable relevance for the future of the Middle East. States confronting the demographic and economic challenges outlined above may simply prove incapable of adjustment and face collapse over the next decades. Political forces with more radical agendas may emerge to provide new solutions with different social and ideological bases, particularly Islam. Such successor regimes will still have to confront basic challenges, but may succeed in redefining these challenges in ways that defer traditional tests of governance (e.g., management of the economy). In other cases, the alternative to existing regimes may be prolonged chaos—the "coming anarchy" described by Robert Kaplan.[20]

Over the past few years, it has been fashionable to point to the growth—or absence—of civil society as a measure of political development and change in the Middle East.[21] In places where civil society is well developed, it is generally viewed as an indicator of stability and democratization. Pressures for greater transparency and democratization have arguably been growing across the region, evident in states as diverse as Algeria, Egypt, Turkey, and Saudi Arabia.[22] The development of organizations outside the (most often

---

[20]See Robert Kaplan, "The Coming Anarchy," *Atlantic Monthly*, February 1994.

[21]See Jillian Schwedler (ed.), *Toward Civil Society in the Middle East*, Boulder, CO: Lynne Rienner, 1995, in particular the chapter by Augustus Richard Norton, "The Future of Civil Society in the Middle East."

[22]See Ian O. Lesser and Graham E. Fuller, A *Sense of Siege: The Geopolitics of Islam and the West*, Boulder, CO: Westview, 1995, p. 4.

authoritarian) government framework provides a potentially significant force for change over the longer term, suggesting that Middle Eastern societies are likely to become more complex and more diverse as new interest groups and substate actors emerge. This social complexity has potentially significant implications for the way in which states outside the region seek to influence the behavior of regional actors, especially in the context of economic instruments. A related trend, already evident in many places across the region, especially where a dynamic private sector has been accompanied by dysfunctional or chaotic government, has been for individuals increasingly to organize their lives without reference to the state. Ethnic, religious, and other "networks" have been leading beneficiaries of this phenomenon, reinforced by the growing ease of communication within and outside Middle Eastern societies.[23]

Indeed, the information revolution is itself likely to be a leading driver in the political and security future of the greater Middle East. From North Africa to the Persian Gulf, the infrastructure for modern telecommunications is expanding rapidly, providing new opportunities for private enterprises, the independent media (where it exists), and others in "civil society." This infrastructure is also bolstering the effectiveness of opposition movements, both peaceful and violent, including terrorists. Algeria's FIS and Turkey's Islamist Refah Party provide good examples of the way modern information gathering and dissemination can be harnessed to help produce electoral success. Modern telecommunications have emerged as the basis for more effective communication between exiled opposition leaders and their supporters in the Persian Gulf and elsewhere. In the 1970s, Ayatollah Khomeini used smuggled cassettes to spread his message in Iran. Today, Islamists in Saudi Arabia or Tunisia rely on fax machines and the Internet to reach over the barriers to political organization erected by authoritarian regimes.[24] The net result of this trend

---

[23]The rise of networks and their political implications are treated in David Ronfeldt, *Tribes, Institutions, Markets, Networks: A Framework About Societal Evolution,* Santa Monica, CA: RAND, P-7967, 1996.

[24]Currently, Algeria, Egypt, Iran, Israel, Kuwait, Tunisia, Turkey, and the United Arab Emirates have access to the Internet. Saudi Arabia has Bitnet; and Jordan, Lebanon, and Morocco have access to E-mail and are moving toward Internet links. See Brian Nichiporuk and Carl H. Builder, *Information Technologies and the Future of Land Warfare,* Santa Monica, CA: RAND, MR-560-A, 1995.

is likely to be a progressive loss of central control in traditionally authoritarian societies across the greater Middle East. Although this loss by itself is unlikely to result in the collapse of regimes, it will be an important factor in the ability of diverse groups, whether moderate or extreme, to undermine the power and legitimacy of ruling elites.[25]

The information revolution will also reinforce the potential for spillovers of political violence between regional states and between the region and the West. Arms smuggling and terrorist cells established in support of violent Islamist groups in North Africa are already an established phenomenon in Western Europe. Recent terrorist incidents point to the spread of this problem to North America and Asia. The communications-based support for this trend is likely to deepen over the next decades, contributing, along with the movement of peoples and the spread of ballistic missiles, to the declining ability of peripheral regions to insulate themselves from the consequences of instability and conflict within the greater Middle East.

Unresolved Political Futures

From Morocco to the Persian Gulf, leaderships across the region are aging. By 2025, most if not all of the established figures on the regional scene, whether moderate or radical, will have disappeared. Who will replace them? In the near-to-mid term, many states, including key moderate regimes such as Morocco, Jordan, Saudi Arabia, and the smaller Gulf states will face potentially destabilizing successions. More broadly, it is worth considering how durable traditional monarchies and authoritarian leaderships can be in an era of decreasing control, greater transparency, and pressures for reform. The problem of unresolved political futures is already a key driver in the evolution of the strategic environment in the greater Middle East, and one that is likely to acquire even greater significance as the current generation of leaders comes to an end.

The issue of legitimacy is likely to be central to the region's political evolution over the next decades. Regime legitimacy will be under

---

[25]Recent empirical studies suggest a strong correlation between the growth of networked communications and the propensity for democracy.

increasing pressure from many quarters, ranging from the inability to address pressing economic and social problems to crises of identity involving the organization of society as well as interactions with the West. Many of the traditional external moorings for regime legitimacy—anticolonial struggle, Arab nationalism, the Arab-Israeli conflict, "non-alignment"—have disappeared or shown signs of disappearing. At the same time, changing economic and demographic patterns have undermined traditional sources of legitimacy within societies. Even the Moroccan and Saudi monarchies, which have relied on deep religious and clan ties as a basis for legitimacy, are finding it difficult to hold at bay the forces of political change. Secular dictatorships such as Libya, Syria, and Iraq are even more fragile.

Islam and Nationalism

It is likely that the two most powerful forces on the Middle Eastern political scene toward 2025 will be Islam and nationalism. Almost 20 years after the Islamic revolution in Iran, political Islam is far from a spent force in the internal politics of Muslim countries. Indeed, it shows clear signs of vigor in a wide variety of settings in and around the Middle East. The evolution of key states, including Algeria, Egypt, Libya, Turkey, Jordan, and Iran—as well as Bosnia and Chechnya on the periphery—is already being driven by Islamic politics in government or in opposition. Attempts by established regimes to crush radical Islamic opposition—as in Tunisia, Algeria, Egypt, and Saudi Arabia—regardless of their success in the near term, are unlikely to be fully successful. These movements reflect deep-seated political, economic, and social problems. Repressed and driven underground, Islamic movements tend to be viewed by much of the Muslim public as the only legitimate answer to their societies' predicaments and to a deepening identity crisis. "Under these circumstances . . . Islamist movements are acquiring a monopoly by default as the only serious opposition to failing regimes."[26] The pressures giving rise to the Islamist phenomenon are long term, and the phenomenon itself is likely to prove durable.

---

[26]Lesser and Fuller, p. 165.

It would be a mistake, however, to conclude that the pervasiveness of the problems encouraging Islamic opposition suggests a uniform path for Islamist movements and regimes. On the contrary, existing regimes and the West are likely to confront a variety of movements, ranging from the most radical (on the pattern of Algeria's Armed Islamic Group) to well-organized parties capable of gaining power through conventional political means (as in Turkey and Jordan). In overall terms, however, the power of Islam as a religious, cultural, and political force is likely to be another "permanently operating factor" across the greater Middle East. Indeed, it is very likely that the region will see the advent of at least one and possibly several more Islamic regimes between the end of the century and 2025.

The growth of Islamist movements and the possible rise of new Islamic regimes will have potentially important implications for conflict within and among Middle Eastern societies, as well as between the Muslim world and the West. Where violent Islamist movements exist but cannot easily triumph, as in Algeria, the stage may be set for prolonged strife affecting regional balances and the ability of states to clash or cooperate with the West. Moderate movements in power may establish an acceptable modus vivendi with the West. Others may adopt an uncompromisingly revolutionary and anti-Western stance. In security terms, the Western debate about Islamic "fundamentalism" has turned on the potential for the emergence of a concerted Islamic bloc poised for a "clash of civilizations" with the West.[27] Our analysis suggests that powerful cleavages within the Muslim Middle East, and equally pronounced differences of approach in the West, make the prospects for a broad civilizational clash remote. Moreover, it is worth noting that while Islamic movements in general may not "wish us well," their principal targets are internal, and their agendas, even in power, are likely to be overwhelmingly domestic.

In the fashionable focus on Islam as a force in Middle Eastern futures, it is easy to forget the powerful role of nationalism as a driver in the evolution of the region. In leading countries such as Algeria, Egypt, and Turkey, the experience of throwing off the old regime and constructing a modern state remains a powerful image in contempo-

---

[27]See Samuel Huntington, "The Clash of Civilizations?" *Foreign Affairs*, Summer 1993.

rary politics. Some observers have described the current Algerian turmoil as the second half of an unfinished nationalist revolution. Turkey's Islamists rely heavily on nationalistic images and rhetoric. Nationalism can arguably be seen as the leading force behind the recent behavior of states as diverse as Egypt, Syria, Iraq, and Iran. Many of the same forces that helped bolster the legitimacy of regimes across the region also helped to foster identities (e.g., Arab nationalism, rejection of Israel) transcending individual states. In the more fluid environment already emerging on the post–Cold War scene, a renationalization of perceptions and policies is likely. In this respect, trends in the Middle East are very much part of a broader tendency toward more assertive nationalism evident in Europe, Asia, and elsewhere. Islam and nationalism can also interact in ways that bolster the legitimacy of regimes and reinforce external orientations, with implications for interactions with the West. For example, the reluctance of regional states to support U.S. actions against Iraq in the wake of the Gulf War—most recently in September 1996—has been couched in terms of Arab and Islamic solidarity at the public level, together with sensitivity about the national sovereignty implications of U.S. presence and operations.

The recent experience of terrorism against U.S. military facilities in Saudi Arabia highlights the question of how a U.S. military presence in the region will affect the perceived legitimacy and stability of friendly regimes. In Saudi Arabia, Bahrain, and elsewhere in the Gulf, the U.S. presence will almost certainly continue to serve as a flash point for Islamist and nationalist groups looking to undermine existing governments. Short of this, U.S. presence and operations, as at Incirlik Air Base in Turkey, can pose dilemmas of sovereignty even for more moderate, Western-oriented elites. Regimes across the region will, of course, want to keep the U.S. presence for purposes of deterrence and reassurance, but will seek to limit its visibility and potentially destabilizing effects on public opinion. From a U.S. perspective, the level and character of presence in the region will need to be more carefully measured in terms of the balance between defense requirements and the desire not to undermine the legitimacy of allied regimes.[28]

Strategic Implications of Internal Trends

The internal trends or "drivers" noted here will have significant implications for the strategic environment that will confront U.S. policymakers and military planners in the near-to-mid term as well as toward 2025. First, the tension between increasing (and younger) populations and low economic growth will increase the pressure on already hard-pressed regimes. Leaderships across the region face wholesale generational change, raising the possibility of very different patterns of governance and regime behavior. Existing regimes face, on the one hand, an erosion of traditional means of control, and on the other, increasingly assertive opposition from ethnic and religious movements. The result is likely to be even more emphasis on the internal dimensions of stability and security and an increasing propensity for conflict arising from domestic power struggles and local anarchy.

Second, relentless urbanization suggests that cities will be the central backdrop for internal conflict of this nature, and will also be increasingly important nodes in the economic, industrial, and information infrastructure. Attacks on highly visible urban targets cannot easily be ignored by regimes, and such attacks will be high on the agendas of terrorist and insurgent groups.[29] Given these trends, the use of force in future regional crises may have more in common with the 1982 Israeli operations in Beirut, or the air war against Baghdad's economic infrastructure, than the desert battles of the Gulf War.

Third, unsettled political futures and the continued power of Islam and nationalism on the regional scene suggest a far less predictable and less congenial environment from the perspective of security cooperation. Key moderate regimes, from Morocco to Egypt and Saudi

---

[28]The reticence of friendly Arab states with regard to NATO's Mediterranean Initiative is explained, in large measure, by the wariness of public opinion and questions of sovereignty and legitimacy.

[29]Mary Morris, *The Post-Peace Agenda for the Middle East: Coping With Demographic Stresses*, Santa Monica, CA: RAND, P-7895, 1994, p. 11.

Arabia, are vulnerable and will measure their relationships, in particular with the United States, against public opinion and the dictates of national sovereignty and perceived legitimacy. In the worst case, friendly regimes might collapse and be replaced by more-or-less revolutionary states. The result could be a substantial erosion of U.S. military presence, of direct security cooperation, and of access. The leaderships of today's "rogue states" are similarly vulnerable to the erosion of state control and the pressures of Islam and political change more broadly. The chances of the current trio of "rogue" regimes—Libya, Iraq, and Iran (and one might reasonably add Syria)—remaining unchanged in direction and behavior over the next 25–30 years are slight. The essential point is that current assumptions about the nature of regimes are likely to be challenged, if not overturned, by inevitable political change. The impressive U.S. forward structure of bases and relationships characteristic of the 1990s could be profoundly shaken by instability and leadership change across the region.[30] Pressures for democratization, evident across the region, may produce a more stable environment over the long term. But democratization might be achieved only at the cost of considerable instability and nearer-term risks to Western interests in the status quo. The process of democratization in previously authoritarian states might even imply an increased risk of regional conflict, as one well-known study suggests.[31]

Finally, the internal evolution of Middle Eastern states may well bring to power movements disposed toward confrontation with the West, although it is most unlikely to take the form of a sweeping ideological or religious confrontation between civilizations. Interests and stakes in relations with the West vary greatly across the region, and as the discussion below suggests, intraregional cleavages are unlikely to diminish and may well deepen. While new regional alignments are possible, even likely, the prospects for broad-based combinations of "Islamic" or "Arab" power and potential for the purpose of confronting the United States as a peer competitor in regional terms are strictly limited.

---

[30]We are grateful to Dr. Geoffrey Kemp of the Nixon Center for Peace and Freedom for his comments on this point at a June 1996 seminar at RAND, Santa Monica.

[31]See Edward Mansfield and Jack Snyder, "The Dangers of Democratization," *International Security*, Summer 1995.

KEY REGIONAL AND GLOBAL TRENDS AND THEIR CONSEQUENCES

As the preceding discussion suggests, trends within Middle Eastern societies will have a substantial influence on the future shape of the region as a whole. At the same time, a number of key trends on the regional and global level will also drive the nature of conflict and the strategic environment toward the year 2025. These key drivers include

- the search for strategic weight through new military technologies and strategies,

- growing economic dimensions of security and regional geo-politics,

- the erosion of traditional distinctions between the Middle Eastern and adjacent security environments as a result of "reach" and spillovers,

- unresolved regional frictions and threats to the territorial status quo,

- new security geometries (alignments), and

- the role of extraregional powers—above all the United States.

The Search for Strategic Weight

A leading characteristic of the future environment in the greater Middle East is likely to be the continuing search for strategic "weight" on the part of ambitious regional actors. The search for greater weight in regional and international affairs can take many forms, including active diplomacy, new geopolitical alignments, buildups of conventional military forces, and, most significantly, the acquisition of weapons of mass destruction and the means for their delivery at longer range. The desire to be "taken seriously" by Middle Eastern neighbors, the United States, and the West as a whole will be a key driver in the policies of rogue regimes as well as more moderate regimes in pursuit of prestige and influence.

The end of Soviet patronage and the declining utility of "non-alignment" as a means of leverage in international politics have had a profound influence on Algeria, Libya, Syria, and Iraq. Arms and advisers from the Eastern bloc contributed to the power and potential of Middle Eastern states within the Soviet orbit, including Egypt through 1973 and technically non-aligned states such as Algeria. Far more important, however, was the strategic weight that Soviet patronage represented in relations with Israel and the West. The prospect of Soviet backing in crises and the potential for superpower escalation made it more difficult to bring pressure to bear on these regimes and lowered their costs of limited regional adventures (e.g., Algerian intervention in the Western Sahara, Egyptian involvement in Yemen and Oman). Nonetheless, the Soviet connection and the risks of superpower involvement also implied certain limitations on the freedom of action of regional actors. The Iraqi invasion of Kuwait probably would not have been possible under Cold War conditions: Moscow simply would not have permitted such provocative and potentially escalatory behavior by a key client state. In the current environment, superpower constraints of this sort are largely absent, with negative implications for regional stability. This condition is likely to persist and acquire more troublesome outlines as friendly status quo actors as well as revolutionary states seek to augment their regional weight.[32]

Proliferation Dynamics. With the exception of North Korea, the world's leading WMD proliferators are arrayed along an arc from North Africa to South Asia, making the greater Middle East a focal point for America's systemic concern about the spread of unconventional weapons. Substantial WMD capabilities, including missiles and longer-range aircraft capable of reaching within and beyond the region, are already present in North Africa, the Levant, and the Gulf. In assessing current and future WMD capabilities, it is useful to divide regional proliferators into three categories.[33] The first category consists of states that do not now possess WMD systems and have shown no inclination to acquire them. States in this category include Morocco, Lebanon, Jordan, and the smaller Gulf sheikdoms. It is

---

[32]Proliferation trends beyond the rogue states are beginning to attract wider attention. See, for example, Amy Dockser Marcus, "U.S. Drive to Curb Doomsday Weapons in Mideast Is Faltering: Not Only Rogue Countries but America's Own Allies Try to Expand Capability," *Wall Street Journal*, September 6, 1996, p. 1.

[33]See Lesser and Tellis, pp. 36–37.

most unlikely that such states will find it useful or practical to develop any such capabilities over the next decades. The second category consists of states that either possess or have demonstrated an interest in acquiring WMD and associated delivery systems (including WMD-capable aircraft) but are not capable of developing such capabilities on their own. External sources of weapons, equipment, and expertise are essential to proliferators in this category. Algeria, Libya, and Saudi Arabia follow this pattern.

States in the third category have or are proceeding to acquire WMD and delivery capabilities, and also possess the expertise, resources, and defense industrial base to permit substantial indigenous development of WMD. These internal capabilities may also be enhanced through a network of external supply relationships. States currently in this category include Egypt, Iraq, and Iran, and, of course, Israel. Turkey, as a NATO member, has remained largely outside the debate about proliferation in the Middle East. But given the character of proliferation risks on its borders and growing uncertainty about the future of Turkey's security relationship with the West, the question of Turkey's capabilities and WMD potential is not irrelevant for the future.

There is some potential for states now in the second category moving toward the category of indigenous capability, but this movement is likely to be limited by broader structural and economic factors. The essential point is that there already exists a core of WMD-capable states within the region. This core will remain and perhaps grow. More significantly, the core may deepen to the extent that states with indigenous capabilities—or the financial wherewithal—acquire nuclear weapons and the means for their delivery at longer range. Definitive judgments about the likelihood of the current proliferators with nuclear ambitions actually acquiring workable systems between now and the year 2025 are beyond the scope of this discussion. Iran and Iraq, have this possibility within the decade. Libya, Syria, Algeria, Egypt, and even Saudi Arabia could all become nuclear powers by 2025 if they are sufficiently motivated and the international environment is permissive enough. Chemical, biological, and radiological capabilities are sufficiently well established in the region today to suggest that they will be a feature of the strategic environment toward the year 2025, quite apart from the issue of their use in conflict.

The range of delivery systems, whether aircraft or cruise and ballistic missiles, is increasing. Several states are on the threshold of acquiring systems of 1000–2000 km range. Israel and Saudi Arabia already possess such systems. It is very likely that by the year 2000 or shortly thereafter, ballistic missiles of transregional range will be in the arsenals of most if not all of the leading regional powers, complicating traditional notions of the operational rear and increasing the potential for political blackmail within and beyond the region in times of crisis. In addition to the potential delivery of WMD, these systems also will provide opportunities for increasing the effectiveness of conventional forces when armed with smart and increasingly accurate submunitions.

The motives of regional states for acquiring WMD are already pronounced and are unlikely to change substantially over the next decades under most likely conditions. In purely military terms, WMD offer a low-cost alternative relative to the expense and difficulty of deploying advanced conventional technology. Past use in the region and the active pursuit of such capabilities by a number of powers is creating its own spiral of increasing demand, both as a tool of intimidation and as a deterrent.

Israel's nuclear deterrent combined with her conventional superiority remains a major issue for her neighbors, further stimulating efforts to achieve some form of strategic parity through WMD. Even a comprehensive settlement of the Arab-Israeli dispute would not eliminate the drive for strategic weight—although it might well dampen the prospects for nuclear proliferation. The potential for Western intervention will remain, and targets of intervention will likely continue to view WMD as a useful trump. The generalized quest for regional influence and international prestige appears durable and ironically could even be given a boost by an Arab-Israeli détente, because the confrontation with Israel has been a leading sphere for Arab activism in the past. Finally, the bureaucratic motives for launching and sustaining WMD programs also appear durable.[34]

---

[34]At least one analysis also suggests a correlation between liberal economic and political behavior and the willingness to compromise on WMD, particularly nuclear, options. In this context, and with some exceptions, the Middle Eastern outlook is not

Certain proliferation "wild cards" are worth noting: a serious deterioration in Arab-Israeli relations, complete Iranian or Iraqi breakout from existing control regimes, the rise of new revolutionary states with WMD ambitions (Saudi Arabia, maybe Algeria), a sharp reduction in the taboo against WMD use as a result of a regional crisis in which WMD are effectively employed; even more active participation of Russia and China as supplier; or large-scale cooperation among regional proliferators (an "Islamic bomb" à la Samuel Huntington).[35] All would serve as spurs to proliferation. Some wild cards might serve to dampen proliferation, including disastrous consequences of WMD use in a regional crisis, effective global or regional disarmament regimes, and preemptive Western (or Israeli) action that dramatically raises the perceived cost of proceeding with WMD programs.[36] The deployment of more-effective ballistic missile defenses might also influence the propensity to acquire certain types of systems, but will leave many WMD options unaffected.

Growing Conventional Capabilities. Beyond the WMD issue, the future strategic environment in the region is likely to be characterized by continued high levels of conventional armament and the growing sophistication of weapons systems. The Middle East continues to be the largest arms market in the developing world, accounting for roughly 50–60 percent of the total value of all transfers between 1988 and 1995 (excluding Turkey—if Turkish acquisitions are included, the figures would be substantially higher). Saudi Arabia alone accounted for some 30 percent of all developing world arms transfers in this period. It is worth noting, however, that the Middle

---

encouraging. See Etel Solingen, "The Political Economy of Nuclear Restraint," *International Security*, Fall 1994.

[35]Potential WMD collaborators under current conditions include Syria-Iran and Iran-Pakistan. During the Gulf War, there was some speculation about Algerian cooperation in hiding Iraqi nuclear material. Changing regimes and geopolitics could well lead to cooperation along other axes toward 2025.

[36]Decisive progress on the bilateral track of the Middle East peace process—with Syria—is a necessary but not a sufficient condition for progress in regional security and arms control arrangements. The collapse of the Arms Control and Regional Security (ACRS) process in 1994, with Egypt in the vanguard, points to the entrenched character of regional suspicions. On the prospects for regional arms control and disarmament, see Gerald M. Steinberg, "Non-Proliferation: Time for Regional Approaches?" *Orbis*, Summer 1994; and Shai Feldman (ed.), *Confidence Building and Verification: Prospects in the Middle East*, Tel Aviv: Jaffee Center for Strategic Studies, 1994.

Eastern market is not the fastest growing; this distinction belongs to Asia.[37] The United States has been the dominant supplier.

A number of the regional drivers previously discussed will directly contribute to the demand for large conventional military forces throughout the region. Egypt, Turkey, Israel, Syria, Iraq, and Iran all can be expected to retain major conventional forces well into the next century. Several factors contribute to this projection, including enduring sources of state-to-state conflict that could result in major wars; growing competition over resources; and enduring territorial and cross-border ethnic disputes. Ideological competition and terrorism could also result in major state-to-state conflicts. The ability to defend national territory from invasion, as well as the ability to seize and hold territory, will remain the key driver of core conventional capabilities among the major regional states.

Internal political factors will continue to shape regional military forces. For many regimes, national military power will remain a symbol of legitimacy and state power as well as an instrument of internal security and deterrence against domestic sources of opposition. Large military establishments carry with them their own political weight. As with general economic reforms, serious risks may be associated with restructuring and reducing armed forces. Aside from challenging the vested interests of senior military officers who may be part of the ruling elite, the reduction of standing forces is likely to increase unemployment and social discontent. For many of the economically strained countries of the region, the military serves as a jobs program and safety valve.

The increasingly sophisticated way of war will also influence conventional forces in the Middle East. While less-developed states throughout the region will meet specific armaments needs through imports, their ability to develop the complex organizations and expertise required to extract anything approaching maximum capability from this weaponry will remain limited. Consequently, regional states will be reluctant to trade away potentially useful mass. Future force structures are therefore likely to consist of large traditional forces interlaced with sizable inventories of advanced weaponry.

---

[37]Richard F. Grimmett, *Conventional Arms Transfers to Developing Nations, 1988–1995*, Washington, DC: Congressional Research Service, August 1996.

The sheer size and sophistication of arsenals being acquired in the region could have an effect on regional balances for some time to come, even if arms transfers to the region begin to slow over time as a result of favorable regime changes. achievement of a comprehensive Arab-Israeli settlement, or economic stringency (including a likely decline in U.S. security assistance to Israel and Egypt). The combination of growing arsenals and insecure regimes, with considerable potential for changes of orientation in key friendly states over the next decades, introduces another disturbing variable. The dilemma posed by current defense needs in the Gulf and elsewhere and the possibility of sophisticated arms falling into the wrong hands will be difficult to resolve. Few supplier states will be willing to signal their declining confidence in the stability of friendly regimes by curtailing arms sales, quite apart from the economic stakes.

The effects of the military buildup in the Middle East will also have implications on the periphery. New Turkish systems and improvements in the capacity of Turkish forces for power projection have already begun to affect perceptions in the Aegean, the Balkans, and in Russia. Weapons acquired by Egypt, Syria, or Saudi Arabia largely for prestige and "weight" within the Arab and Muslim world could also begin to affect security perceptions in Europe if "civilizational" relations deteriorate. It is worth observing, however, that the most likely first victims of new conventional and unconventional weapons being acquired in the region will be neighboring Middle Eastern states.

Arms for Oil? Over the longer term, it is possible that shifts in the oil market could affect transfers of weapons and militarily useful technologies. Arms-for-oil policies were a noteworthy outcome of the first oil crisis, as European oil consumers sought to ensure themselves adequate oil supplies. Tightening of the oil market as a result of economic trends or a political crisis could encourage a return to this practice (whether the region could absorb transfers much in excess of current levels is an open question). Less sophisticated, but also less expensive sources of arms and technology are likely to expand, on the pattern of current Russian and Chinese transfers. More assertive regional policies in Moscow and Beijing—already evident— could hasten this development. Finally, new sources of arms and technology will develop within the region or nearby. Turkey, Egypt, Pakistan, and Iran are all likely to emerge as more important suppliers with increasingly capable defense industries. These "third tier" suppliers may also be the least amenable to participation in any new regimes aimed at controlling conventional arms transfers to the region.[38]

Peer Competitors or Niche Competitors? Of principal concern to U.S. security over the longer term would be the emergence of military "peer" or "niche" competitors. In the case of the former, it is difficult to envision a true peer military competitor arising, even by 2025. Given the many systemic problems facing all of the major states, none will realistically be able to challenge core U.S. military power in anything approaching peer status. The emergence of a niche competitor, in this case a state or alliance of states sufficiently powerful militarily to dominate the local balance of power in ways detrimental to the United States, is more plausible. There are a variety of alternative futures in which the United States could find itself facing such niche competitors. Two paths are most plausible. First, a major outside power could invest heavily in building up one or more regional clients. Candidates for such a role include a resurgent Russia or a much more actively engaged China. Second, a niche competitor could emerge from the collapse of key friendly regimes. The rapid loss of major regional partners, combined with substantial military capabilities possessed by U.S. opponents, could yield a sharp shift in military balances and present a demanding "niche" challenge.

Niche competitors as well as less-potent adversaries are also likely to employ "asymmetric strategies" against the United States—that is, strategies designed to exploit U.S. vulnerabilities while avoiding U.S. military strengths. The threat of WMD is most frequently invoked in this regard, as are selective "high-leverage" uses of advanced conventional technologies (e.g., in the Gulf region, combining a surprise attack with use of advanced mines and missiles to impede initial U.S. access, or cleverly penetrating and collapsing information systems linking U.S. forces). The posited "endgame" of such strategies is to present the United States with options so unattractive that Washington is deterred from mounting an effective response. Although long-

---

[38]For a discussion of the potential for new control arrangements, see Kenneth Watman, Marcy Agmon, and Charles Wolf, Jr., *Controlling Conventional Arms Transfers: A New Approach with Application to the Persian Gulf*, Santa Monica, CA: RAND, MR-369-USDP, 1994.

standing adversaries will plan and equip for a confrontation with the United States, for most states the United States will be a secondary planning factor. The demands and challenges presented by immediate neighbors will remain the dominant drivers of military strategies. Therefore, while states can be expected to seek ways to exploit asymmetric strategies that could offer leverage in dealing with the American way of war, they must first address more immediate challenges. To the extent that these two demands are in tension, the ability of regional states to mount truly high-leverage asymmetric strategies against U.S. military forces may be constrained.

Niche competitors could also employ asymmetric military strategies aimed at the political vulnerabilities of their neighbors as a means to offset superior U.S. military capabilities. For example, a state with aggressive intent could choose to inflict widespread countervalue damage against neighboring societies. Targets could range from population centers to high-value infrastructure such as desalination plants, hydroelectric facilities, dams, and critical energy facilities. Such threats could provide an effective form of political blackmail against weak governments. Similar threats could also be used to deter regional states from granting access and support to U.S. forces. Under these circumstances, more traditional military instruments could then be used to take advantage of delays or denials.

Finally, niche competitors could use terrorism—directly or through proxies—in parallel with more-conventional operations, hoping to throw U.S. strategy off balance and erode political support for intervention. This tactic was feared during the Gulf War, but never materialized. It could easily figure in future regional contingencies.

The Growing Economic Dimensions of Security

The economic aspects of Middle Eastern geopolitics have always received considerable attention as a result of the region's energy resources. Over the next decades, it is likely that new energy, water, and infrastructure issues will substantially alter the strategic environment facing regional and extraregional powers.

Energy and Energy Routes. The continuing significance of the region for world energy supply has already been noted. This significance could well expand over the next decades as a result of increased demand and the exploitation of large, newly proven reserves in North Africa, the Gulf, and, above all, Central Asia. Proven and potential oil reserves in the Caspian Sea basin are estimated at some 200 billion barrels, roughly equivalent to Iraqi reserves. Caspian natural gas reserves could be on a par with those of the United States and Mexico combined.[39] The exploitation and transport of these resources over the next decades will be a dramatic new element in regional geopolitics. A variety of alternative routes have been under consideration for the shipment of "early" and long-term oil—pipelines across Russia to the Black Sea, routes through the Caucasus and Turkey to the Mediterranean, shipment through Iran to the Gulf, pipelines to Pakistan and China, as well as combinations of these schemes. On a cost basis alone, it is quite possible that a substantial portion of future production from the region will go through Iran, despite U.S. opposition (will Iran still be seen as an adversary in 20 years?). This route will have important strategic consequences, because an Iranian route for Caspian oil will further increase world reliance on unimpeded navigation in the Gulf and the Strait of Hormuz. A route through Turkey—more likely in the case of "early oil"—would have the contrasting effect of diversifying the lines of communication (LOCs) for oil, but would be hostage to stability in the Caucasus and the Kurdish regions within and outside Turkish borders.

The broader point is that new energy production and LOCs will change long-standing assumptions about choke points and economic interdependence. Major new producers will not have the luxury of shipping oil directly from their own territory. They will be dependent on stability within and stable relations with neighboring states. Another example of this phenomenon is emerging in the Mediterranean, where high-capacity pipelines for gas are being built. The new trans-Maghreb pipeline links Algerian fields with growing energy markets in southern Europe via Morocco and Spain. Expansion of the existing trans-Mediterranean pipeline will allow increased energy shipments from Libya to Europe via Sicily. The net result is likely to be a more complex set of geopolitical relationships based on energy infrastructure. The implications of this trend could vary sub-

---

[39]Rosemarie Forsythe, *The Politics of Oil in the Caucasus and Central Asia*, Adelphi Paper No. 300, London: IISS, 1996, p. 6.

stantially depending upon the overall stability of the Middle East and its subregions. New vulnerabilities and opportunities for leverage in conflict will emerge. On the other hand, more diverse energy routes could also reinforce economic interdependence and help to dampen the potential for conflict where energy revenues and pipeline fees are at stake.

The Revival of Overland Links.   Overland transportation in the Middle East has not fared well over the last century. Transportation infrastructure within states has remained relatively underdeveloped. More significantly, political obstacles have impeded the growth of transregional links. The lack of such links is striking given the potential that was recognized in the early years of the 20th century, when rail links across the Balkans to the Levant and the Gulf were viewed as a natural extension of land communications in Europe (the "Berlin-Baghdad railway").[40] After nearly a century of stagnation, new links are beginning to emerge, with potentially important implications for regional geopolitics. The recently opened rail lines between Iran, Georgia, and Turkmenistan open the possibility of overland shipment of oil from Central Asia (or China) via Iranian or Turkish ports, or onward overland to Europe—while bypassing Russia. This trend will almost certainly reinforce the importance of the greater Middle East in economic terms, and could be critical to the independence of the new republics of the former Soviet Union should Russian policy take a more assertive course over the next decades. Similarly, a comprehensive settlement of the Arab-Israeli dispute would open up the possibility of direct overland trade between Israel and its neighbors and the European Union. This trade could be an important aspect of a broader movement toward regional economic integration as a result of Arab-Israeli peace.

Economic Infrastructure. Another key trend in the economic security of the region is likely to be the continuing concentration of high-value and potentially vulnerable economic infrastructure, especially around the Persian Gulf. A complex and apparently vulnerable oil

---

[40]The strategic implications of the Berlin-Baghdad railway scheme for German and British positions in the Middle East and the Indian Ocean were a subject of great concern at the time. The railway—never completed—threatened to outflank British maritime access to Mesopotamia and the Gulf. See E. M. Earle, *Turkey, the Great Powers and the Baghdad Railway,* New York: Macmillan, 1924.

production and transport infrastructure has long been a feature of the Gulf and North Africa. Although this infrastructure has been targeted in regional conflicts and insurgencies, including the Iran-Iraq war and the invasion of Kuwait (although at considerable economic cost in the latter case), it has proven surprisingly resilient. In Algeria, terrorist groups have not made the gas infrastructure a serious target, perhaps in anticipation of its utility to a successor regime, or perhaps as a result of tough security measures.

In the future, the key targets for regional aggressors may be the increasingly modern and highly concentrated infrastructure for power generation, desalinization, industrial production, telecommunications, and the services needed to support urban life. States or groups bent on regional intimidation will very likely seek the ability to attack such targets. This strategy in turn will raise new problems of defense for local states and their extraregional security guarantors, above all the United States. Simply put, as Middle Eastern societies become more urban, more highly industrialized, and more "modern," they will steadily acquire new economic vulnerabilities. The growth of an indigenous defense industrial sector will also offer new targets for attack and problems for defense across the region over the longer term.

Water Fears, Water Rivalries. Competition over water resources is widely seen as a key source of conflict in the region over the next decades. By 2010, virtually all of the region's countries and territories are projected to be "water stressed."[41]   Water is already an increasingly prominent issue in the security perceptions of regional states (as in other instances of resource "vulnerability," perceptions can be as important as reality in driving the actions of states). Leading water-related flash points will include Iraq, Syria, and Turkey (a key water-surplus state) over the Tigris, Euphrates, and Orontes waters; Iran and Afghanistan over the Helmand river; Egypt, Ethiopia, and Sudan over the Nile; and Israel, Jordan, Syria, and Lebanon over the Jordan, Yarmuk, and Litani Rivers and the West Bank Aquifer. Of these, the dispute between Syria and Turkey is probably the most dangerous.

---

[41]That is, having available fewer than 1,000 cubic meters per person per day, a level below which water scarcity begins to affect agriculture and industry. Lester R. Brown et al., *State of the World 1993*, A Worldwatch Institute Report on Progress Toward a Sustainable Society, New York: W. W. Norton, 1993.

But observers around the region are increasingly inclined to cite water as a likely source of future conflicts.[42]   Here, as in several other cases, friction over water can interact with territorial and political disputes to produce a volatile geopolitical mixture.

The persistence of water dependence and, above all, perceived vulnerabilities will make control over downstream water supply a source of leverage in crises and conflicts. Turkey would be in a position to exercise such leverage over Syria and Iraq, and is already doing so in a veiled manner in an effort to end Syrian support for PKK (Kurdish Workers Party) terrorism in Turkey. Sudan might similarly threaten Egypt over the Nile waters in a future crisis. In reality, tampering with the downstream flow is not easily accomplished without environmental and political costs to the upstream states, suggesting that instances of large-scale strategic interference with water supply might be a rarity. But the effect of perceived water vulnerability on regional behavior, including the possibility of preemptive action to secure water supplies, should not be dismissed.

Where the general evolution of relations is positive, cooperation over increasingly valuable water resources could spur the peaceful resolution of disputes. This cooperation has already been evident in the normalization of Jordanian-Israeli relations. The prospects for a wider settlement will require more serious treatment of water issues, especially in the Golan Heights and in the West Bank and Gaza. Under these conditions, Turkish water resources will be a key asset for encouraging and consolidating Middle East peace, and a variety of water-shipment schemes have already been suggested by Ankara and others.[43]

Economic Warfare. From the perspective of relations between regional states and the international community as a whole, the economic dimension will be critical, and not simply because of energy and nonenergy trade. Use of economic sanctions has become a

---

[42]Boutros Ghali, Egypt's Foreign Minister, is reported to have commented that the next conflict in Egypt's region would be over the Nile waters.

[43]Turkey plans to ship water by tanker to Israel and Gaza, and might build pipelines to ship water to Jordan and the Gulf. Chris Cragg, "Water Resources in the Middle East and North Africa," in *The Middle East and North Africa 1996*, 42nd edition, London: Europa Publications Limited, 1995, pp. 162–165.

regular feature of U.S. and United Nations policy in dealing with "rogue states," many of which are Middle Eastern. The factors identified earlier in this discussion suggest that the region will continue to produce more than its share of rogue states over the next decades. The fashion for sanctions may vary over time, especially as multilateral regimes prove difficult to launch and sustain. To the extent that sanctions continue to be applied in a Middle Eastern context, however, the United States will need to address the implications of an increasingly diverse and interdependent economic scene across the region. The proliferation of lines of communication for energy and other trade will complicate monitoring and enforcement. The industrialization and urbanization of Middle Eastern societies will change the conditions for economic warfare generally, including the effectiveness of blockades and the attack of economic targets in periods of conflict. Targets will be more varied, and new nodes and bottlenecks will present themselves, but the capacity for substitution and adjustment may also increase. Overall, however, the economic dimension of future regional crises and conflicts is likely to be more prominent rather than less.

The Erosion of Distinctions Between Regions in Security Terms

Western strategists have become accustomed to thinking about security in terms of discrete theaters—"European security," "Middle Eastern security"—with relatively little interdependence across regions (a notable exception to this tendency could be seen early and late in the Cold War, when protracted conventional conflict between East and West seemed possible, and "theater interdependence" and "horizontal" strategies became fashionable notions). In the future, such compartmentalized thinking will be less useful as developments across the greater Middle East raise the prospect of more direct effects on the security of Europe, Eurasia, and even Asia, with important implications for U.S. freedom of action in future contingencies.

By the end of the century, it is possible that every European capital will be within range of ballistic missiles based across the Mediterranean, in the Levant, or in the Gulf. This, taken together with the potential for refugee flows and spillovers of political violence from crises on Europe's Mediterranean and Middle Eastern periphery, makes it clear that future strategies will have to pay attention to Europe's growing exposure to the retaliatory and spillover consequences of Western action anywhere in the Middle East. Some awareness of this issue could be seen during the Gulf War, with (ultimately overstated) concerns about terrorism, ballistic missile risks to southern Europe, and threats to Western assets in North Africa and elsewhere.[44] A future conflict in the Gulf, under conditions of greater European exposure, could have very different consequences, including greater European and Turkish reluctance to offer access to facilities, overflight, and military forces if this means placing their own territory at risk. Cooperation might ultimately be forthcoming if the stakes are high and clear enough, but the calculus of cooperation and its price could be very different. In the context of the ballistic missile risk, more effective and rapidly deployable defenses may be part of the answer to improving the prospects for en-route (as well as in-theater) access and cooperation. The reality, and the perception, of other spillover risks may be more difficult to address.

Developments in the greater Middle East will also have a potentially important role in security within Russia and its "near abroad." There will be numerous points of interaction, from the character of Islamic activism on Russia's southern flank and its effect on separatist movements and on the political evolution of the Caucasus and Central Asia, to Russia's own WMD and ballistic missile exposure. The evolution of Eurasia in security terms will be directly affected by the prospects for stability in Afghanistan, Iran, or Turkey. The prospects for the reassertion of Russian control over Central Asia and the Caucasus will be constrained to the extent that land communications between the new republics and the Middle East expand. A more assertive Turkey could also find itself in overt competition with Russia for influence in the Turkic republics. In the worst case, political vacuums and separatist movements in the Caucasus could pull Moscow and Ankara into conflict, directly or through proxies.

---

[44]Spain had a more specific concern about the security of the Spanish enclaves of Ceuta and Melilla on the Moroccan coast in the heated pro-Saddam atmosphere prevailing in Moroccan opinion. The Spanish military garrison was substantially reinforced during the crisis.

The Asia-Pacific region may also be increasingly, although less directly, exposed to the consequences of developments within the Middle East. Energy security is a long-standing point of interaction for Japan and could become an important stake for China. Beyond economic interests, there is a demonstrated potential for Muslim and Turkic identity and separatist pressures to affect the stability of western China. Pakistan could be drawn into closer strategic relationships with Muslim states to its west, with arms and technology transfer implications noted earlier.

Threats to Borders

The future strategic environment in the Middle East will almost certainly feature the threat of weapons of mass destruction and terrorism as permanently operating factors in military operations. Problems of regime support amidst internal conflict, of humanitarian and evacuation operations, and of other low-intensity or nonconflict contingencies will also be key elements in planning for the region. Against this background, it is essential to consider that many of the most likely and militarily stressful demands on U.S. involvement in the region over the next decades will continue to arise from the conventional defense of borders against large-scale aggression.

The Control of Territory and the Control of People

The scenarios considered for this study reveal the persistence of serious geopolitical rivalries, often reinforced by resource or stability concerns, in which attempts to overturn the territorial status quo are possible.[45] Three Arab-Israeli conflicts, two Gulf wars, and numerous lesser crises highlight the centrality of the conventional attack and defense of territory in regional conflict. The often artificial character of borders established by colonial competition and arrangement from the Maghreb to the Gulf will continue to encourage irredentism. Boundaries will continue to be essential to the exercise of

---

[45]Some of the more prominent scenarios along these lines include potential conflicts between Morocco and Algeria, Tunisia and Libya, Egypt and Libya, Egypt and Sudan, Israel and Syria, Syria and Turkey, Iraq and Iran, Iran or Iraq and the Gulf sheikdoms or Saudi Arabia. Over the longer term, Saudi Arabia itself could develop territorial ambitions on the Arabian peninsula, beyond existing territorial disputes with Yemen.

power within the nation-state system, which, despite rising competition from nonstate actors and networks, is likely to remain a cornerstone of the regional order over the next decades. There will, however, be a growing tension between the control of territory and the control of people. The latter has been an historically important feature of Middle Eastern geopolitics, central to the management of the Ottoman Empire and a powerful feature of the contemporary scene.[46] The most recent crisis and realignments in the Kurdish region of northern Iraq illustrate this point superbly. As in the post–Cold War Balkans, the temptation to bring territorial arrangements into line with the control of people—to consolidate the national "space"—could be a highly destabilizing feature of the Middle East in the 21st century. This impulse could also spell the fragmentation of key states, including Algeria, Turkey, Iraq, and Iran, where ethnic separatism is already a threat to the unitary character of the state.

It is arguable that the buildup of conventional military forces across the region, apart from the issue of "strategic weight" discussed earlier, is also a leading symptom of the perceived insecurity of borders. Today's friendly regimes are among the leading consumers of sophisticated conventional arms transfers. But with the exception of Israel and perhaps Egypt, few if any of our current allies are likely to be capable of defending their borders alone against a determined aggressor (e.g., Tunisia against Libya, Kuwait against Iraq). As a result, a serious U.S. commitment to Middle Eastern security and the defense of key allies implies a continuing requirement for deterrence and defense against large-scale aggression.[47] This requirement suggests a key task for the presence and projection of air and space power to the region through the end of the century and beyond.

Renewed Arab-Israeli conflict, perhaps with a threat of direct aggression on the Golan Heights, would raise the stakes in terms of territorial defense. By contrast, a comprehensive Arab-Israeli peace would reduce (but not eliminate) the net risk to the territorial status

---

[46]Bradford L. Thomas, "International Boundaries: Lines in the Sand (and the Sea)," in George J. Demko and William B. Wood (eds.), *Reordering the World: Geopolitical Perspectives on the 21st Century*, Boulder, CO: Westview 1994, p. 92.

[47]The parameters of deterrence in the region are explored in Aharon Klieman and Ariel Levite (eds.), *Deterrence in the Middle East: Where Theory and Practice Converge*, Tel Aviv: Jaffee Center for Strategic Studies, 1993.

quo. The development of *effective* regional or subregional (Mediterranean, Gulf) collective security mechanisms would presumably be aimed at guaranteeing existing borders; the emergence of such mechanisms is a remote possibility.

New Security Geometries

Geopolitical theorists like to describe the Middle East as a "shatterbelt"—a strategically oriented region that is a politically fragmented area of competition, classically between the continental and maritime realms.[48] The Middle East's six regional powers—Egypt, Iran, Iraq, Syria, Israel, and Turkey (Algeria has the potential to serve as a seventh)—cast their shadow over their smaller neighbors and groups within neighboring states. With the end of the Cold War and with movement, however inconclusive, on the Middle East peace process, the alliances among these states and their subordinates are increasingly fluid.[49]

Even the partial, tenuous reintegration of Israel as a valid partner for Arab and Muslim states has opened new avenues for cooperation and friction. Turkey has launched an overt strategic relationship with Israel, involving intelligence sharing, training, Israeli access to Turkish airspace and, above all, joint pressure on Syria. Jordan has a strong interest in Israeli cooperation in regional stability and the containment of risks from various quarters, including Iraq and the Palestinians. Strategic cooperation among Turkey, Israel, and Jordan suggests the possibility of a formidable new alignment with U.S. backing. This potential has not gone unnoticed in the region, and has produced considerable anxiety in Syria and Egypt, the former concerned about strategic encirclement and the latter seeing in these moves tangible confirmation of its declining influence in regional affairs. Possible counters to a Turkish-Jordanian-Israeli alignment could include closer Syrian-Iranian and/or Syrian-Egyptian cooperation. Examples of shifting alignments can also be found elsewhere in the region, from the reluctance of some former members of

---

[48]Mahan, Fairgrieve, Mackinder, and Spykman are the exemplars. See Saul B. Cohen, "Geopolitics in the New World Era: A New Perspective on an Old Discipline," in Demko and Wood, pp. 2–35.

[49]See Cohen, p. 34.

the Gulf coalition to confront Iraq, in part because of growing concerns about Iranian power, to the off-again, on-again character of Algerian backing for the Polisario movement in the Western Sahara. Smaller Arab states in the Gulf as well as the Maghreb have used the multilateral track of the Middle East peace process, including the arms control and regional security (ACRS) talks, to press their subregional agendas and to assert their discomfort with Egyptian leadership.

Narrow, national self-interest will be the driver for many types of realignment. Turkey will be interested in closer relations with Iran as a means of satisfying the country's growing demand for energy. The proposed natural gas deal between Ankara and Iran should be seen in this context. Similarly, Turkey will not hesitate to open a new economic relationship with Iraq, the country's largest trading partner before the Gulf War—or even, under certain conditions, to cooperate with Baghdad in facilitating the reassertion of Iraqi sovereignty in northern Iraq. The fact that Turkish policymakers are willing to envision normal relations with Iraq and Iran, despite the consequences for relations with the United States, is a measure of the strength of Turkish national interest in the region.

The conditions that have given rise to these shifting geometries could change many times over between now and the end of the century and beyond. Radical changes in regimes or the emergence of new relationships along ideological lines could produce even more striking alignments. The advent of additional Islamic regimes could yield an axis based on Iranian, Sudanese, Algerian, Libyan, or even Turkish and Egyptian ties. In this extreme setting, a secular Syria might make strategic common cause with the West and pursue a rapid disengagement with Israel. Hardly any of these potential combinations are too far-fetched. But it is worth considering the limitations to some potential alignments, even in the face of ideological and tactical interests. For example, Arab suspicion of (mostly Persian) Iran and Turkey will not be easily overcome, and nationalism is likely to remain a potent force in determining how far regional actors are willing to compromise on sovereignty issues. The essential point is that the future regional scene is likely to be characterized by more diverse and more rapidly shifting security geometries.

In some cases, security relationships long taken for granted in U.S. planning will be foreclosed. Would a successor regime in Cairo—even a familiar regime facing public criticism of Egyptian ties to the West—allow the United States to use the Suez Canal in a future Gulf contingency? If the Suez route is not available, this could have serious implications for the pace and character of U.S. power projection, with the potential for far greater burdens on airlift. In other cases, new alignments will open new possibilities for coalition strategies, presence, and power projection (e.g., the expanding defense relationship with Jordan). Flexibility and the recognition of inevitable change will be essential to maintaining freedom of action over the longer term.

Role of Extraregional Powers

The potential for shifting security geometries will not be limited to the region itself. As our analysis suggests, extraregional powers will have a continuing stake in the evolution of the greater Middle East and a growing exposure to the consequences of conflict and cooperation within the region and on its periphery. The roles of Russia, the European Union, and the United States will be central.

Russia is likely to remain extremely sensitive to the strategic orientation of areas on its southern periphery, above all Turkey and Iran. Moscow cannot be expected to remain quiescent if an anti-Russian Islamic coalition emerges in the northern Middle East. A more nationalist and assertive Russia might also seek to keep the United States off balance in the Gulf or the Levant through revived military ties to Iraq, Iran, Syria, or Libya. These ties could also imply more active transfers of WMD technology, not simply leakage of expertise and materials. A more assertive and confrontational China could play much the same role as a supplier of equipment and technology aimed at making U.S. intervention more costly and unpredictable. In general terms, however, it is difficult to envision a return to more sweeping Russian presence and engagement in the region. In places such as the Mediterranean, Russian military presence is unlikely to return in the period under discussion.[50] Similarly, the prospects for

---

[50]Although Turkish policymakers are inclined to see Russia's prospective transfer of surface-to-air missiles to Cyprus in just these terms.

Russian designs on the resources of and maritime access to the Gulf, a perennial concern of the Cold War years, are probably nil.

If the Middle East peace process cannot be revived, or if oil markets tighten, European involvement is likely to accelerate. Even without these negative developments, the future environment is likely to be characterized by a greater degree of multipolarity, with significant European involvement on the political and economic fronts. The European Union and NATO Europe are increasingly attuned to their stakes in stability in the Middle East and the Mediterranean, and are beginning to develop new initiatives along these lines, a trend that is likely to continue. If the economic dimensions of the peace process are to move ahead, European aid, investment, and markets will be essential. In many ways, the European Union is a much more logical co-sponsor of Middle East peace efforts than Russia, whose involvement is an artifact of the immediate post–Cold War period and may not survive the next few years. At a minimum, the EU, led by France, will press for a more active political role in Arab-Israeli and Gulf security matters.

At the same time, Middle Eastern states (and the Palestinians) have already begun to look to the EU as a means of diversifying their security ties. On the economic front, it has long been evident that the future prosperity of the Middle East and North Africa will be dependent on freer access to European markets, as well as European investment and finance. The search for new security geometries that might offer opportunities to address pressing challenges (including violent internal opposition to existing regimes) has also encouraged tentative interest in security ties with the Western European Union and NATO.[51] For Israel, in particular, these ties have special value, because it is arguable that the country may have more to gain from being part of the European security system than from any future Middle Eastern architecture. For the Arab partners in NATO's emerging Mediterranean dialogue, long-standing popular (and to some extent elite) distrust of NATO will make deeper cooperation difficult. Moreover, as NATO focuses more seriously on security

---

[51]NATO's Mediterranean Initiative currently includes Morocco, Tunisia, Mauritania, Egypt, Israel, and Jordan.

problems in the south, it may prove difficult to reconcile partnership with a growing perception of threat.

An important variable for the future will be the extent to which NATO adopts a more active out-of-area posture and the extent to which the transatlantic relationship more broadly comes to grips with common challenges outside the European area. While the notion of greater burden-sharing in the Gulf and elsewhere is engendering heated debate on both sides of the Atlantic, lack of progress in developing a genuine European capability for power projection beyond Europe—indeed within Europe—and continuing disputes over containment versus engagement (of Iran, Iraq, and Libya) suggest little progress in this area in the near-to-mid term. Europe will be a more independent and assertive actor across the region, but is unlikely to be a more capable one in military terms.

Finally, the most important extraregional variable for the future of regional security will be the United States itself. Our analysis highlights the enduring nature of U.S. interests in the Middle East. The level and character of our engagement and presence, and our capacity for power projection in times of crisis, will be dominant elements in the regional security equation for the foreseeable future. The influence of the United States on the strategic environment across the region under current conditions cannot be overemphasized. American withdrawal—the end of America's role as preeminent security guarantor—could transform the security picture in profound terms and could affect the propensity for conflict and cooperation far beyond the region, as other extraregional actors move to fill the strategic vacuum. One of the many potentially disastrous consequences of U.S. withdrawal might be the much more rapid spread of weapons of mass destruction as regional powers strive to substitute for American deterrence or capitalize on their newfound freedom of action.

Even assuming continued American willingness to remain actively involved in the region, and the availability of money to sustain this involvement, the U.S. ability to serve as security arbiter and guarantor across the region will face new challenges as a result of the trends identified in our analysis. It is most unlikely that the United States will face any serious peer competitor in military terms, inside or outside the region, in the period under discussion. Nonetheless, the region is likely to witness types of conflict and upheaval in which

American military power will be highly constrained. In scenarios featuring internal conflicts and regional chaos where vital interests are not at stake, the United States may be reluctant to intervene at all. Indeed, in certain future strategic worlds in which patterns of conflict and regional risks are quite different from those prevailing today, the U.S. role may be an important variable, with consequent implications for strategy and the use of military force.

Strategic Implications of Regional and External Trends

The trends and drivers identified above will have important implications for U.S. strategy and Air Force planning. First, the search for strategic "weight" will provide a continuing incentive for the proliferation of conventional and unconventional arsenals. Middle Eastern rivals will be the first and most likely victims of WMD use, but the existence of such weapons and the means for their delivery at longer range will place heavy demands on surveillance and counterproliferation operations. The growing reach of systems—potentially WMD-armed—deployed in the region will also result in the growing exposure of regional and European allies to the retaliatory consequences of U.S. action in the Middle East. Together with other types of spillovers, from terrorism to refugee flows, this growing exposure will make access, overflight, and other forms of cooperation much more difficult to negotiate with potential coalition partners.

Second, the changing economic and resource aspects of security will offer new possibilities for the attack and defense of economic targets, as well as new sources of conflict and cooperation across the region. The maturing of the region's economies and infrastructure will change the way in which sanctions are likely to be used in dealing with rogue regimes, with implications for monitoring and economic warfare. In general, the significance of economic and infrastructure factors in strategic planning for the region could increase markedly.

Third, the existence of threats on the "low" and "high" ends should not obscure the reality that large-scale conventional threats to borders will persist and perhaps drive requirements for force structure in the region. The likelihood that many friendly regimes, to whose territorial integrity we are committed, will be unable to mount an effective defense of their borders unaided reinforces the importance of this observation for future planning.

Fourth, just as regime changes are inevitable over the next decades, regional alignments will experience significant, possibly extraordinary, flux, creating problems as well as opportunities for coalition strategy, presence, and access. The ability to move forces (e.g., from the Mediterranean to the Gulf) will be less predictable, with the potential for significant changes in the mix of airlift and sealift for Middle Eastern deployments. Such an environment will place a premium on flexibility and "hedging" or on portfolio approaches to regional power projection. Current alignments cannot be taken for granted. Today's unthinkable coalitions may not be unthinkable in 20 years' time.

Fifth, the persistence of a wide range of regional frictions and the possibility of settlements with accompanying international guarantees (Israel-Syria is the most prominent example, but it is not the only one) suggests that the monitoring of regional disengagements and assistance with confidence-building regimes could be an important part of U.S. involvement in the region over the next decades. Security guarantees associated with the settlement of disputes, above all in an Arab-Israeli context, could significantly shape requirements. In more pessimistic scenarios, a reinvigorated Arab-Israeli dispute could also place substantial demands on U.S. power, while further complicating the outlook for regional support in the Gulf and elsewhere.

ALTERNATIVE STRATEGIC WORLDS AND THEIR IMPLICATIONS

The internal, regional, and external trends or "drivers" we have identified could yield a wide range of outcomes and could interact to produce very different strategic worlds. We next trace four alternative net outcomes for the region. Each alternative world will have different meanings for stability; the nature of risks, strategy, and demands; and constraints on military power. The selection of these alternative worlds, while not arbitrary, is meant to be illustrative rather than definitive. We have deliberately modeled these worlds on theories prominent in the current debate on the future of the international system as a whole ("great game," "clash of civilizations," "the coming anarchy," and the "end of history"), with the objective of illuminating the implications in a Middle Eastern setting. See Table

7. It is perfectly possible, even likely, that the evolution of the region toward 2025 will be a "hybrid"—exhibiting traits characteristic of more than one strategic world. We have also identified signposts or indicators that the region might be moving toward one or another world.

The "Great Game"

The thrust of this world is not unlike the current situation, with regional rivalries free of Cold War constraints and the rigidities of traditional Arab-Israeli confrontation. Specific subregional rivalries (Morocco-Algeria, Egypt-Libya, Turkey-Syria, Iran-Iraq, Iran-Turkey-Russia) would likely exist alongside broader struggles for Middle Eastern leadership, with Egypt and Iran in the vanguard. Nationalism will be a leading force in this world, possibly reinforced by religious or ideological themes. But this vision of the future environment posits an essentially secular competition among regional rivals, with considerable potential for the involvement of extraregional powers. The term "great game" is especially appropriate because one of the leading focal points for regional rivalry in this setting will

Table 7

Alternative Strategic Worlds

Parameter	Great Game	Clash of Civilizations	Anarchy	End of History
Driver	Regional rivalry	Islam vs. West	Uncontrolled ethnic/urban conflict	Convergence/ integration
Strategy	Balance	Deterrence	Containment	Reassurance
Focus	Resources/ territory	Borderlands	Internal	LOCs/networks
Risks	Borders	WMD/terror	Spillover	Haves vs. have-nots
Signposts	Shifting alliances	Rise of blocs	Failed states	Successful reform

be the northern Middle East—the Caucasus and Central Asia—with Russia, China, and Pakistan as potentially important actors along with Iran and Turkey.[52] This world would constitute something of a geopolitical free-for-all, with heightened risks to the territorial status quo, heightened perceptions of vulnerability with regard to vital resources (oil, water), and attempts by unsatisfied states and groups to undermine the stability of rivals. Areas of vacuum, such as the western Sahara, Lebanon, or northern Iraq, will be focal points for conflict.

A variation on this world might see the rise of a new, modified Cold War—perhaps between the United States and China—with the Middle East as a theater for renewed strategic competition. In the worst case, the region could see new proxy wars, with the additional ingredient of weapons of mass destruction.

In this world, stability can be achieved by a balance of power or by regional hegemony. The former implies considerable flux in alignments and constant attention to the behavior of neighboring states. The latter implies an extraregional security arbiter with overwhelming military power that can be brought to bear (historically, "Pax Britannica"; currently, "Pax Americana"), or in the absence of such a power, the emergence of a regional state bent on playing the role of hegemon. The development of nuclear weapons could be an essential factor in the ability of regional states to aspire to this role over the longer term. The leading military risks under "great game" conditions will flow from the conventional threat to borders and the potential use of WMD, acquired by regional powers as part of the general quest for strategic weight and by smaller powers as a hedge against aggression.

Key indicators of movement toward this world would include a shifting pattern of regional alignments, more intensive competition over scarce resources, and more aggressive interventions by regional powers in security vacuums. Recent experience offers several of these signposts.

---

[52]The "great game" refers to the 19th century rivalry between Russia and Britain over the control of Central Asia. See Peter Hopkirk, *The Great Game: The Struggle for Empire in Central Asia*, New York: Kodansha, 1990.

"The Clash of Civilizations"

Samuel Huntington's widely debated *Foreign Affairs* article (and recent book) bearing this title suggests that after the competition between communist East and capitalist West, the next great global confrontation will be along civilizational lines ("the West against the rest"). In this schema, the most prominent and dangerous cleavage will be between Islam and the West. Our analysis of the strength of political Islam across the Middle East suggests that such a bloc-to-bloc confrontation is unlikely.[53] But the Huntingtonian thesis is worth mentioning as a stark alternative to other possible worlds. Preconditions for a clash of civilizations would include the advent of several new Islamic regimes (virtually all Middle Eastern states are candidates, not simply Algeria, Egypt, and Turkey, as often noted), and the emergence of broad-based cooperation among Islamic states, including security cooperation. WMD-related cooperation (an "Islamic bomb") could be a feature of this environment. An Islamic bloc, incorporating earlier arrivals to Islamic politics such as Iran and Sudan, could move beyond distaste for Western power and culture to embrace active confrontation with the West. Nationalist impulses would be set aside in the service of ideological aims.

Under these conditions, a new "Iron Curtain" could emerge along north-south lines and along the borderlands between Islam and the West. The Mediterranean would serve as the focal point for confrontation. Given the extent of Russian nationalist concern about the "Islamic threat," Russia might well form part of the Western bloc in this world, with Russia's southern flank forming an additional line of confrontation. In many respects, this possible, but rather unlikely, world would represent a return to the thousand-year confrontation between Islam and Christianity centered in the Mediterranean and the Balkans.[54] Indeed, Spanish observers first coined the term *guerra fria*—cold war—to describe the competition between Spain and the Ottoman Empire.[55] This strategic world would mark a return to the

---

[53]See the discussion of this question in Lesser and Fuller; see also John L. Esposito, *The Islamic Threat: Myth or Reality,* New York: Oxford University Press, 1992.

[54]See Bernard Lewis, *The Muslim Discovery of Europe,* New York: W. W. Norton, 1982.

[55]See Ada B. Bozeman, *Strategic Intelligence and Statecraft: Selected Essays,* Washington, DC: Brassey's, 1992, pp. 235–255.

first cold war, but possibly with many of the trappings of the more familiar Cold War, including ballistic missiles and nuclear weapons. In a generalized clash of civilizations, Israel's strategic position as an outpost of the West would become much more precarious, reinforcing the significance of Israel's nuclear arsenal and perhaps encouraging more concrete, formal strategic cooperation with the United States and NATO (if the latter exists in its current form through the year 2025).

In this world, the thrust of U.S. strategy toward the region will be deterrence, over-the-horizon presence (except in the Mediterranean— few if any regional states will want a U.S. military presence on their territory), and counter-terrorism. A variation on this world might include threatened cutoffs of oil from Islamic producers, and disastrous price increases. Operations aimed at seizing readily accessible oil resources in the Gulf or North Africa might be a part of this environment (the feasibility of such operations was widely debated in the mid-to-late 1970s).

Relevant signposts for this world would include the rise of new Islamic regimes, the emergence of overt "civilizational" blocs, and the adoption of declaratory strategies in the West aimed at countering an "Islamic threat"—all most unlikely, with the exception of new Islamic states.

"The Coming Anarchy"

This alternative world springs directly from the observations offered earlier in relation to rapid population growth and uncontrolled urbanization across the greater Middle East. The notion that these trends, evident throughout much of the Third World, are leading to the breakdown of societies and the "failure of states" was popularized by Robert Kaplan in a 1994 article entitled "The Coming Anarchy," as well as in a recent book.[56] The hallmarks of this world are growing economic disparity between "haves" and "have-nots," political chaos, rampant urban violence, and new risks to stability in

---

[56]See Robert D. Kaplan, "The Coming Anarchy," *The Atlantic Monthly*, February 1994; and Robert D. Kaplan, *The Ends of the Earth: A Journey at the Dawn of the 21st Century*, New York: Random House, 1996.

the form of environmental degradation and epidemics. Large-scale ethnic conflict, migration, and refugee flows are also leading features of this world.

In this environment, the leading sources of conflict are domestic, and the strategic imperative for regional states and extraregional powers alike will be the containment of chaos and associated spillovers, from terrorism and organized crime to refugee movements and disease. Ethnic, tribal, and religious cleavages could also be expected to thrive in these chaotic conditions, and the containment of these problems will become the focus of extraregional actors as well as more-capable regional powers. Some degree of regional exploitation of these conditions can also be expected. The situation in the Sudan provides perhaps the best glimpse into this type of future. More dramatic examples are to be found in sub-Saharan Africa (Rwanda and Liberia are the archetypes). The "coming anarchy" model predicts similar breakdowns of society in Egypt, Algeria, and even Turkey. Intervention for peacekeeping or humanitarian purposes in such an environment will be extraordinarily challenging, and the scope of the chaos envisioned in this regional world may discourage Western attempts to intervene at all. Containment rather than intervention may be the longer-term policy focus for the United States and Europe.

The most important indicator that the region may be heading in the direction of anarchy would be increasing examples of "failed states" in which the economic, political, and social order has broken down. Egypt will be a key bellwether over the next decade.

"The End of History"

Notwithstanding these pessimistic scenarios, it is also possible that the Middle East—at least parts of it—will evolve along much more positive lines in economic, political, and security terms over the next decades. Francis Fukuyama's notion of the "end of history" referred directly to the triumph of Western liberalism over its ideological competitors as a means of organizing society, with positive implications for the international system.[57]

With some interpretive license and *pace* Frank Fukuyama, the broad outlines of this world in Middle Eastern terms would include a comprehensive and durable settlement of the Arab-Israeli dispute, successful political and economic reforms and peaceful transitions from authoritarian rule, and movement toward regional integration and effective security architectures. Population growth will be brought under control. Secularism, democracy, and free-market economies will flourish in key states (e.g., Turkey, Egypt) where future paths now are uncertain, and will eventually become characteristic of changing societies across the region, including the republics of the Caucasus and Central Asia. Human rights performance will improve and will be accompanied by wider adherence to international norms of internal and external behavior, all of which will contribute to regional security and stability. In addition to economic integration within the region, the Middle East and North Africa will develop a closer economic and political relationship with Europe. Over the longer term, the more dynamic Middle Eastern economies will begin to converge with (a much enlarged) Europe in terms of prosperity. Under these conditions, Turkey might even become a full member of the EU. The combination of relatively full access to European markets and greatly improved infrastructure will contribute to growth from the Maghreb to Central Asia.

In short, this world envisions a transformation of the region from high levels of insecurity and a high propensity for conflict to an environment in which security is a second- or third-order concern. U.S. and Western strategy toward the region in this setting would more nearly approximate strategy for Europe: reassurance against residual risks. These risks will flow from transitions gone awry and from the resentment and social tensions that economic reforms will doubtless produce. The character of likely risks in this very optimistic scenario suggests that military requirements could be satisfied without large-scale extraregional presence. The settlement of basic disputes may also encourage the emergence of genuinely effective regional secu-

----

[57]See Francis Fukuyama, *The End of History and the Last Man,* New York: The Free Press, 1992.

rity and arms control arrangements for the Middle East, including the limitation of weapons of mass destruction.

The leading indicators of movement toward this (perhaps unreasonably) optimistic scenario would be evidence of successful political and economic reform in key states, successful conclusion of the Middle East peace process, and the withering of revolutionary and radical religious movements and regimes. These developments are possible for the region over the next decades; the difficulty will be getting from here to there and the considerable risks to stability arising from the transitions.

Military Demands and Constraints in Alternative Worlds

The alternative worlds discussed above have distinctive implications for the demands and constraints on the use of air and space power and other military instruments. The "great game" is perhaps closest to the environment facing military planners today, with high demand arising from diverse risks and potentially stressful contingencies. Regional rivalry places a premium on the defense of borders and the protection of resources. A significant regional presence is a necessity for purposes of reassurance and rapid response. On the other hand, constraints are relatively light. The desire for balance and reassurance allows for a considerable degree of regional cooperation and host-country support. We have adversaries, but we also have allies. The aggressive nature of potential adversaries allows scope for the use of force in response. Potential contingencies are, for the most part, amenable to the application of conventional air power.

A "clash of civilizations" would pose very different challenges for U.S. strategy and power projection. The emergence of an Islamic bloc with conventional and unconventional military capabilities and the capacity, by virtue of geography, for pursuing horizontal strategies, will be highly demanding. The borderlands between Islam and the West would become a new front line for European security. Israeli security would become much more tenuous and could impose additional requirements on the United States. WMD risks and delivery systems of longer range would take on new meaning if Western—perhaps U.S.—territory emerged as a primary target. At the same time, much of this demanding agenda for deterrence and defense would have to be met from over the horizon—few if any regional states would tolerate a U.S. military presence, and the maintenance of substantial forces offshore (e.g., in the Gulf) might become untenable. A broad-based confrontation between Islam and the West therefore implies high demands and high constraints.

"Anarchy" would imply a very different strategic environment for the use of force, including air power, with a proliferation of internal conflicts and murky clashes among nonstate actors. Humanitarian and environmental crises will also be a prominent feature in this world, and urban settings will figure prominently. Successful intervention in these situations will require specialized forces and coalition arrangements. Restrictive rules of engagement and general limitations on the use of forces will be the norm. Overall, constraints will be high. But demand may also be low, as few contingencies will be major in character, and the national taste for intervention in this environment may be limited.

Finally, the "end of history" implies fewer and lesser conflicts across the region, and thus far lower demand (and even this may be met by regional or near-regional powers). In those rare instances in which the use of U.S. military force is required, constraints will be moderate or low. Limitations on the use of force will exist, especially in the context of peacekeeping operations, but regional consensus for action is likely, increasing the prospects for access and cooperation. Relevant models from a different setting might be NATO land and air operations in Bosnia. A summary is shown in Figure 3.

REGIONAL CONCLUSIONS AND IMPLICATIONS

Overall Observations

To the extent that the United States remains actively engaged in global security, crises and conflicts in the Middle East will remain a leading source of demands on U.S. military power, including air and space power. At the same time, the definition and character of the region in security terms are likely to change substantially over the next decades. Indeed, many of the trends driving these changes are already observable on the regional scene.

- *Future sources of conflict will be more diverse; old centers of gravity are changing.* The long-standing U.S. focus on the Persian

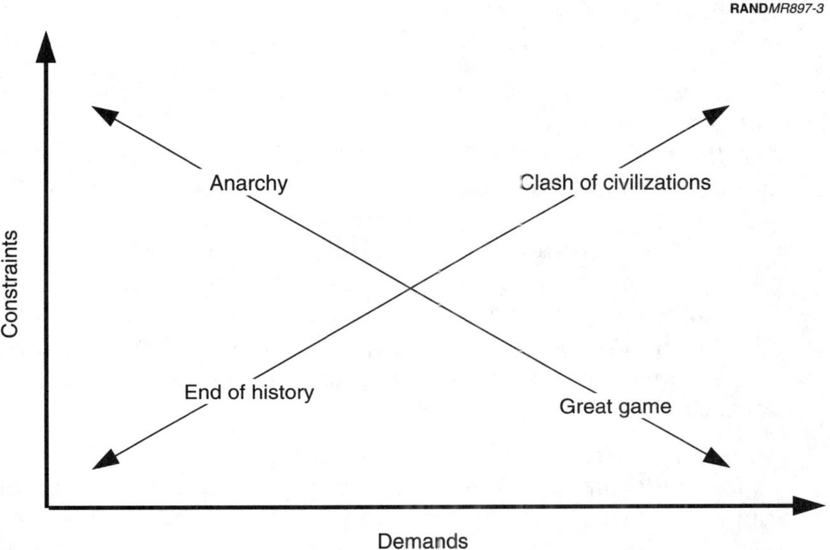

Figure 3—U.S. Military Demands and Constraints in Alternative Worlds

Gulf and the Arab-Israeli confrontation in the Levant will remain, but demanding future contingencies are just as likely to arise from instability in North Africa, on Turkey's borders, and in the Caucasus and Central Asia—formerly peripheral areas on the borderlands of the Middle East. Air Force planning for the next decades must anticipate a far broader range of scenarios and missions, functionally and geographically.

- *Many of the leading sources of conflict in the region will be internal, and for most regional states security will be, above all, a question of internal security.* Aging leaderships and a steady erosion of the legitimacy and capacity for control of economically hard-pressed regimes suggest that the political constellation of the region may change significantly over the next decades. Few, if any, of today's regimes—from U.S. allies to rogue states—are assured of survival toward the year 2025. Our capacity to influence the internal evolution of regional states is likely to be limited, and thus our strategy and planning for the region must incorporate a significant hedging component, with consideration of alternative means of deterrence and power projection.

- *Islam and nationalism will be key drivers in the evolution of societies and policies across the greater Middle East.* It is very likely that the region will see the rise of additional Islamist regimes, although this need not necessarily imply radical shifts in foreign and security policy orientation. Even where Islam is a powerful political force, rising nationalism is likely to have a strong effect on regional behavior. At a minimum, the future environment is likely to be more unpredictable and difficult from the perspective of risks and prospects for security cooperation. There is a high probability of the loss of major security partners over the next decades.

- *Traditional distinctions between the Middle East and adjacent regions will continue to erode in security terms.* The spread of longer-range weapons systems and the continued challenge of spillovers, from terrorism to refugee flows and energy vulnerabilities, will mean ever-greater interdependence between the Middle Eastern, European, and Eurasian environments. At its most extreme, this interdependence could imply growing problems of homeland defense (e.g., in relation to ballistic missiles and terrorism) emanating from the Middle East.

- *There is little prospect that the United States will face any true "peer competitors" in military terms from within the region, but more capable "niche competitors" may well emerge.* Future regional adversaries will be tempted to pursue asymmetric strategies, making use of terrorist and WMD threats, perhaps in combination with conventional warfare. Given the growing range of ballistic missiles deployed in the region and the capacity of terrorist networks, such threats are just as likely to emerge in distant rear areas (e.g., the Mediterranean or Egypt in the case of operations in the Gulf). Broader frictions between Islam and the West along civilizational lines—however unlikely—will increase the potential for regional cooperation among potential adversaries, especially with regard to WMD and terrorism. More-assertive extraregional powers, including Russia and China, could encourage the rise of niche competitors within the region.

Demands and Constraints on Air and Space Power

The key internal, regional, and external trends shaping the geopolitics of the greater Middle East toward the year 2025 will impose specific demands and constraints on air and space power in the context of regional contingencies.

- *The conventional defense of territory will continue to be a key factor shaping requirements for deterrence, presence, and power projection.* The combination of persistent regional frictions, concerns over the control of resources (oil, water), large conventional arsenals, and the limited capacity for self-defense of key allied states suggests that the defense of borders will be a key task for American air power in the region. Attention to "low" and "high" end threats—terrorism and weapons of mass destruction—should not obscure the continuing challenge of large-scale conventional aggression. To the extent that the Middle East peace process stalls or goes into reverse, demands on military power from this quarter will increase further.

- *The application of air power in urban settings will be a leading feature of the future Middle Eastern security environment.* Crucial political struggles affecting the future of regimes and Western interests will be played out in the region's cities. Critical economic and defense-industrial infrastructures will be concentrated in urban areas. Cities will be a focal point for terrorism risks, both to regimes and to Western citizens and assets, and will be key strategic prizes in regional conflicts. Combined with the likelihood of humanitarian operations in densely populated areas, the demands and constraints associated with the use of force in urban settings will be an increasingly important feature of the environment for air power. Beirut in 1982 might be just as important a model for the future as the desert war in the Gulf.

- *There will be growing demand for air power in the attack and defense of economic targets and for economic warfare generally.* The modernization of Middle Eastern economies is resulting in more concentrated and vulnerable economic infrastructures outside the energy sector. The expansion of indigenous defense industries is another factor in this equation. The defense of economic infrastructure is likely to become a more important issue in the defense of friendly regimes given the growing capacity of regional aggressors to place targets of economic value at risk. At the same time, U.S. air power will be central to the economic dimensions of strategy in major contingencies, and as a means of monitoring and enforcing economic blockades against rogue regimes.

- *The Air Force is likely to face high demands for surveillance and reconnaissance across a broader and rapidly changing region.* Several aspects of the emerging strategic environment will drive this demand, including the prominence of the mobile target problem arising from the intense proliferation pressures in the region; the popularity of economic sanctions as a means of containing aggressive states and the associated monitoring requirements; likely U.S. roles in monitoring any agreements arising from the Middle East peace process (e.g., on the Golan Heights); and cooperation in implementing regional confidence-building measures. Humanitarian, environmental, and refugee crises arising from a more anarchic Middle East will add to this demand. Even if European and regional allies take on more of the security burden over the next decades, they will still look to the United States to provide intelligence and surveillance support in crises (even in cases where our allies act alone).

- *The United States will face a mounting tension between continued demands for regional presence, especially in the Persian Gulf and the eastern Mediterranean, and increasingly contentious and constrained relationships with host countries.* Enduring military imbalances and the need for rapid reaction and visible deterrence, in addition to likely peacetime monitoring requirements, argue for a substantial and continuing presence. Yet this presence will be increasingly difficult to manage. Beyond the exposure of U.S. forces to WMD and terrorism risks, political acceptance problems and the prospect of political instability and economic stringency in friendly regimes will limit host country support and tolerance for the use of air power against neighbors, except in defense of their own borders. Closer attention to sovereignty concerns and more-diverse approaches to regional security among traditional allies will reinforce this trend. The most stressful situation would arise from confrontation with a bloc of revolutionary states, in which the issue of U.S. presence appears in stark "West against the rest" terms. In this case, the demands for deterrence will be high, but few regional states will be inclined to host a U.S. air presence, and new arrangements for over-the-horizon presence will be required.

- Finally, the United States will face greater uncertainty of en route and in-theater access in crises, with implications for regional strategy and Air Force operations. From western Europe to Turkey and the Gulf sheikdoms, traditional allies will be increasingly exposed to the retaliatory consequences of U.S. action anywhere in the Middle East. Even where a basic political consensus exists, cooperation in future crises may have more in common with the October 1973 (Yom Kippur War) or September 1996 (Palestinian-Israeli clashes) experiences than the extraordinarily benign atmosphere of Desert Shield and Desert Storm. Predictable access to air bases and overflight rights cannot be taken for granted today, and certainly not over the longer term. To the extent that traditional allies are still inclined to help, the "price" of cooperation—political, economic, and defensive (e.g., against ballistic missile threats)—is likely to be far higher than in the past. The Air Force will also be affected by the broader prospects for cooperation. If Egypt refuses to allow the use of the Suez Canal for moving forces and materiel to the Gulf in a future crisis, the burden on airlift may increase substantially. Uncertain prospects for Turkish support in regional contingencies—apart from the defense of Turkish territory—could make Incirlik Air Base irrelevant to power projection in the Levant and the northern Gulf, increasing the value of Jordanian and Israeli alternatives.

Chapter Five

SOURCES OF CONFLICT IN EUROPE AND THE FORMER SOVIET UNION

John Van Oudenaren

INTRODUCTION

This chapter assesses the demands and constraints that are likely to be imposed on the U.S. Air Force as a result of developments across the European region, viewed in near-, mid-, and long-term perspective.

The first section provides an overview of U.S. interests in Europe, reviews the near- and medium-term threats or potential threats that could have near-term implications for the Air Force, and provides a brief, foreshadowing discussion of the alternative strategic "worlds" that might begin to emerge in Europe.

The second section analyzes short-, medium-, and long-term trends—economic, demographic, political, and other—in the European region and its main subregions. We identify and examine the key "drivers" that will determine the shape of the region in the next century and the different emerging strategic worlds that could give rise to potential conflicts and requirements for the use of force. The section relies on both qualitative social and political analysis and quantitative forecasts and models, many of which are taken "off the shelf" from government and international organizations and private-sector sources.

The third section develops six alternative strategic worlds that result from the long-term trends identified in the previous section and their interaction with each other. As will be seen, these alternative worlds are the result of the drivers interacting with each other, with the decisive factor judged to be the degree of political, economic, and defense cohesion achieved in different parts of Europe. The section then discusses the implications of these alternative worlds for the strategic environment, for sources of conflict, for conflict scenarios, and for specific planning, and the operational implications for the U.S. Air Force.

The fourth section deals with radical shifts and breaks—with plausible but not predicted departures from the trends discussed in the second section—departures that could result in the emergence of entirely different strategic worlds. Such radical shifts and breaks include war between Russia and China, the rise of a new ideology, the establishment of a global collective security system, a new Great Depression, or an environmental catastrophe. Such possibilities are not discussed in detail, but they are flagged as a way of pointing up the potential limitations of the methodology. Finally, the last section draws overall observations and conclusions, including general findings and specific implications for the U.S. Air Force.

The European Region and U.S. Interests

Security from a Hostile Hegemon. The most fundamental U.S. security interest in Europe is to prevent the emergence of a hostile hegemon or would-be hegemon that could pose a direct threat to U.S. security, as did Nazi Germany and Soviet Russia.[1] Germany—following defeat in two world wars, democratizing internal reforms, and integration with other democratic countries in NATO and the European Union (EU)—does not pose such a threat, even though its position in Europe is one of great relative strength. The other potential threat in Europe is Russia. Following the collapse of Communism and the breakup of the Soviet Union, Russia's ability (and possible willingness) to pose such a threat is much diminished, but the reemergence of Russia as a serious "peer competitor" cannot be ruled out. Russia alone might pose such a threat, but it would be

---

[1]See Zalmay M. Khalilzad, *From Containment to Global Leadership? America and the World After the Cold War*, Santa Monica, CA: RAND, MR-525-AF, 1995; and Commission on America's National Interests, *America's National Interests*, RAND/CSIA/Nixon Center, July 1996.

more likely to arise in the form of a Commonwealth of Independent States (CIS) or other grouping that reassembled much of the former Soviet Union (FSU). However, as will be argued below, no Russian-led state or coalition is likely ever again to achieve the global power position or pose the same threat to the United States that the Soviet Union did in 1945–1990.

Russia also remains a strategic nuclear power, with several thousand nuclear weapons that could be targeted against the United States. Proliferation to Belarus, Kazakhstan, and Ukraine was headed off by U.S. policy initiatives in the early 1990s, and nuclear proliferation in the European region in general is less of a challenge than in many other parts of the world. Nonetheless, proliferation cannot be altogether ruled out, given the persistence of historic rivalries and the high level of economic and technological capabilities throughout the region. Proliferation of nuclear, chemical, biological, and even sophisticated conventional weapons from the region—chiefly from Russia but from other countries as well—to other parts of the world constitutes a potential and to some extent actual threat.

The United States has an interest in countering conflict and instability in Europe that may not necessarily involve Russia, in the form of either domestic conflicts within states or wars between small and medium powers. It is hard to argue that such conflicts in themselves could pose a direct threat to U.S. security, but the fact that the United States bases its position in Europe on the NATO alliance creates legal and political obligations, the fulfillment of which constitutes an important interest. Enlargement of NATO to Central and Eastern Europe will increase this interest and the U.S. stake in defending it.

Finally, the rapid economic and geopolitical shifts that are under way throughout the world and the globalization of security in a multipolar world raise the possibility, over the long term, of the United States' coming to define its security interests in Europe partly or largely as a function of geopolitical developments elsewhere in the world. For much of the first part of the 20th century the United States was concerned with supporting a weak Russia in the Far East against an ambitious Japan. U.S. support for Russia against an aggressive China or other Asian power cannot be ruled out and follows from the overriding U.S. interest in preventing the emergence of a dominant and hostile power in *either* Europe or Asia.

Support for Democratic, Free-Market Allies. Apart from these concrete security interests, the United States has a general interest in supporting and enlarging the community of like-minded countries with democratic political systems and free-market economies. After World War II, this interest became a major determinant of U.S. policy toward Western Europe. With the collapse of Communism, the United States has an important, if not necessarily vital, interest in enlarging this community of states by supporting the post-Communist transitions in Central and Eastern Europe and the FSU.

The instruments used in pursuit of this interest are not primarily military, but the U.S. security presence in Europe is widely seen as helping to support favorable economic and political developments—much the way the Atlantic Alliance helped to promote stability and prosperity in Western Europe in the 1950s. In addition, certain missions performed directly by the U.S. defense establishment, such as the Partnership for Peace (PfP) and Cooperative Threat Reduction (CTR) programs, contribute to the success of these transitions.

Support for U.S. Objectives in Other Regions. This interest relates both to the presence of U.S. forces in Europe and the possible engagement of European forces in support of U.S. objectives outside Europe. The U.S. security presence in Europe is justified primarily in terms of the defense of Europe itself, but it also contributes to the U.S. ability to project power to other regions, notably Africa and the Middle East. This ability was demonstrated on a grand scale in the Persian Gulf War, as well as in smaller, more recent peacekeeping and humanitarian missions in Somalia, Rwanda, and elsewhere. The North Atlantic Council has agreed on far-reaching policy changes and institutional innovations that provide a basis for possible future "out of area" activities on a cooperative basis with European allies. As will be seen below, more-ambitious schemes have been advanced in the United States to promote U.S.-West European "partnership" in other regions. While these schemes are problematic for a variety of reasons, the fact that they are advanced underscores the U.S. interest in attempting to secure European support in pursuit of shared objectives in third areas.

Economic Interests. Although Europe's relative economic importance for the United States has declined in recent years owing to the rise of East Asia and other emerging markets, the United States retains an enormous stake in Western Europe and has growing economic interests in Central and Eastern Europe and the FSU. The EU is the United States' largest single trading partner, accounting for 22.8 percent of exports and 19.7 percent of imports. Whereas the United States runs large trade deficits with China, Japan, and other countries, trade with Europe is more balanced, and was in substantial surplus for much of the 1990s. Transatlantic trade in services is about two-thirds the level of merchandise trade and continues to grow more rapidly than trade in goods. Western Europe is also the largest source and destination of U.S. foreign direct investment. U.S. investments in Central and Eastern Europe and the FSU also are increasing rapidly and are primary elements of the global strategies of U.S. firms in such industries as energy, automobiles, and consumer goods. In addition to these direct economic stakes in Europe, the United States has an interest in working with European countries in such bodies as the G-8, G-10, and the Organization for Economic Cooperation and Development (OECD) to manage the global economy. The U.S. security presence in Europe through NATO is not indispensable to the maintenance of such cooperation, but a case can be made that security cooperation facilitates links in these other bodies.

Near-Term Trends and Sources of Conflict

Prospects for conflict in or involving the subregions of Europe over the next five years vary widely and are subject to different degrees of uncertainty. In general, uncertainty and instability increase as one moves from west to east, as do the prospects for conflict. At the same time, the very notion of a sharp divide between east and west is becoming increasingly difficult to define, as countries in transition identify with and seek to join the West. U.S. interests throughout the region also are not uniform. Conflict in parts of the former Soviet Union is highly probable, but most likely would not involve U.S. forces. Conflict in Western and Central Europe is much less likely to occur, but is more likely to engage U.S. interests and forces if it does.

Western Europe has serious economic problems and is encountering difficulties in pushing forward with the latest stages of integration, but the region remains one of the most stable and prosperous in the world. Western Europe is concerned about threats from outside, from both the east and the south, and is likely to become even more concerned about such threats as the concept of "Western Europe" itself changes with the admission of new members to the EU, NATO, and the Western European Union (WEU). Prospect for large-scale war involving any of the West European countries is low, however; there are no major disputes among these countries or among countries in adjacent regions. Greece is an exception to the general pattern, as it could become involved at any time in a war with Turkey over Cyprus or the Aegean.

Central, Eastern, and Southeastern Europe make up a more diverse and unstable region, with considerably greater potential for conflict over the near term. Virtually all of the countries in the region aspire, at least rhetorically, to become part of Western Europe and the broader Atlantic community. But the process of joining the West is not uniform or even unidirectional, and the next few years are likely to see growing divergences among the countries in the region. Those countries that border directly on the EU are, for the most part, politically stable and relatively well developed economically. Several can be expected to join NATO and to make substantial progress toward joining the Union. At the other extreme, Albania and the former Yugoslavia remain highly unstable, and the revival of large-scale fighting involving Bosnia, Croatia, and Serbia is a possibility. Bulgaria, Romania, and perhaps Slovakia are intermediate cases: under favorable political and economic circumstances, they could join Slovenia and the countries of Central Europe on the path to rapid integration with the West, but they also could be drawn into the rivalries and economic difficulties of the more unstable east and southeast. The Baltic countries present special problems, owing to their status as former republics of the USSR and their difficult relations with Russia.

Finally, conditions in Russia and the other Newly Independent States (NIS) are much less stable than in the rest of Europe. All countries in the FSU face severe economic, environmental, and social problems that create possibilities for internal and external conflict. Many international borders are disputed, and the presence of Russian and other minorities in most countries constitutes a flash point. Russia also continues to view itself as a major European and world power, and could come into conflict with countries along its vast periphery over a range of issues.

Against this background, several threat and political conflict situations would appear to have near-term implications for U.S. defense planners and the U.S. Air Force.

Russia and the NIS

- The "canonical" threat posed by Russia (or another major power) to NATO territory is not likely for the remainder of this century and probably beyond. However, current defense policies are in part shaped by a perceived need to hedge against such a possibility over the longer term. These policies include the German commitment to continental defense and the determination of the French and the British to maintain independent nuclear deterrent forces.

- Russia also is unlikely to pose a direct threat to countries in Central and Eastern Europe over the next several years. The Russian armed forces are too weak to mount a serious threat to countries in Central and Eastern Europe (the Baltic countries excepted). A serious effort by Russia to reconstitute its forces directed against Central Europe would cause concern in the countries of the region and could have negative internal political and economic effects in these countries. Over the longer term, the shadow of a revived Russian army looms large and explains in part the desire of these countries to join NATO.

- Russia poses more of a near-term military threat to the Baltic countries. Russia borders directly on Estonia and Latvia and has disputes with both over territory and the rights of ethnic Russians. Belarus and Russia's Kaliningrad region border on Lithuania, and instability or change in the status of either Belarus or Kaliningrad could spill over into conflict with Lithuania. Russian spokesmen also have warned that Russia might take action against the Baltic countries in response to NATO enlargement.

- The one NATO member with which Russia might clash in the next several years could be Turkey. Conflict could be sparked by any number of economic, political, and security disputes. Actions by Turkish citizens and residents of Caucasian origin who are sympathetic to the struggle of the Chechens and other peoples against Russian rule could be especially provocative from Moscow's perspective.

- Russia could use levers short of military intervention to destabilize and expand its influence in some of the countries of Central and Eastern Europe. These levers might include economic dependence, espionage, exploitation of contacts and relationships left over from the Soviet period, and military intimidation through deployments and exercises. Russian stresses of this sort may not necessarily lead to overt conflict but could intensify pressures on the United States and its allies to extend security arrangements and guarantees to countries within what traditionally has been Russia's sphere of influence.

- Russia still poses a major nuclear threat. Analysts and political leaders have raised the possibility of an extremist government coming to power that would control these weapons. Accidental launch and the devolution of nuclear assets and control to competing domestic factions in the context of an internal conflict are also possibilities. Disorganization and criminality in Russia and other NIS pose the threat of nuclear smuggling and possible assistance to rogue states seeking to acquire nuclear weapons.

- There is considerable potential for internal conflict in Russia, as was demonstrated by the war in Chechnya. Such conflicts are disastrous from a humanitarian perspective and weaken democracy and economic reform in Russia. They also raise the risk of terrorist acts, possibly involving nuclear or chemical or biological weapons, committed against targets in Russia or abroad. The danger of rogue armies operating outside of Moscow's central control and posing both conventional and unconventional (criminal) threats to other countries appears to have receded, but has not altogether disappeared.

- Short of military conflict, Russian political and economic weight in the CIS area poses a latent threat to the independence and maneuvering freedom of other states in the former Soviet Union. Reintegration of Belarus into a Russian-controlled union, particularly military reintegration, would pose dangers for Poland, Lithuania, and Ukraine. Ukraine itself could come under growing pressure from Moscow, given its economic, political, and military vulnerabilities along with the apparent reluctance on the part of many in Russia to accept the permanence of Ukraine's separation from Russia.

- Conflicts within and among CIS countries *other than Russia* continue to simmer in many parts of the former Soviet Union. These conflicts pose threats to stability and hinder economic development, as well as provide openings for enhanced Russian leverage in the form of mediation, peacekeeping, the supply of arms, and enhancement of the value of transport and communication routes that run through Russian territory or that Russia controls. China and Iran can also be expected to try to profit from instability in parts of the FSU.

- Environmental disasters could occur that would affect the region as well as other parts of the globe. Of particular concern are the 45 Soviet-built commercial nuclear power reactors still operating in Russia, Ukraine, and Armenia.

Central, Eastern, and Southeastern Europe

- In many parts of Central, Eastern, and Southeastern Europe, the presence of ethic or religious minorities in states dominated by other ethnic or religious groups creates a potential for subnational conflict. Situations in which these minorities also look for protection to an external "homeland" are especially dangerous. Such minorities include the Hungarians in Slovakia, Romania, and Serbia; Serbs in Croatia; Albanians in Serbia (Kosovo); Albanians and Serbs in Macedonia; Turks in Bulgaria; Greeks in Albania; and Turks in Greece.

- The renewal of large-scale fighting in Bosnia, possibly involving Croatia and Serbia, is a possibility.

- Central and Eastern Europe could be affected by major environmental disasters in Russia and the NIS, including accidents at nuclear power plants. Although the environment in the region is improving as a result of local and international efforts, such disasters could emanate from the region itself. Bulgaria, Lithuania, the Czech Republic, Hungary, and Slovakia all operate Soviet-built nuclear power plants, and those in Bulgaria and Slovakia are regarded by independent experts as especially dangerous.

- The countries of Central and Eastern Europe are vulnerable to spillover effects from turmoil in Russia and the other NIS. Such effects include migration and refugees (including possible surges in crisis situations), terrorism, and large-scale cross-border crime.

Instability in Central, Eastern, and Southeastern Europe, including the renewal of large-scale fighting in the former Yugoslavia, in turn could affect Western Europe by causing increased flows of refugees, damaging trade and investments, and providing opportunities for outside powers (Russia, Iran) to establish positions of influence near Western Europe.

Western Europe

- Conflict between Greece and Turkey—over territorial issues in the Aegean, over Cyprus, and over minority issues in Thrace— could erupt. Other European countries automatically would be involved, through Greece's membership in the EU and the membership of both countries in NATO.

- Instability in North Africa or elsewhere in the Middle East could also result in refugee surges, disruption of trade and energy sources, and the export of terrorism to European cities.

- Western Europe faces a proliferation threat to the south. Libya, which has refused to sign the 1993 treaty banning the use, development, and storage of chemical weapons, is reported to be working on a large chemical weapons plant and has obtained Scud missiles from North Korea that could pose a chemical threat to other countries in the region. Six Middle Eastern countries (Egypt, Iran, Iraq, Israel, Libya, and Syria) are reported to have offensive biological warfare capabilities, with Iraq having the most extensive program.

Alternative Strategic Worlds and Their Defense Implications

Although, in the short-to-medium term, Europe is characterized by a range of potential conflict situations, most of them arising from unresolved problems relating to the collapse of Communism and the breakup of the Soviet Union, over the longer term—i.e., to 2025—the threat environment in Europe will be shaped by broad strategic trends in Europe and by the evolution of Europe's interaction with the outside world.

As will be seen below, six alternative strategic worlds can be posited for Europe, each with different strategic implications for the United States:

- *Modified Cold War Order.* This world is based on a strong Russia/CIS and a still relatively weak Western Europe, and entails continued U.S. protection of and engagement in Western Europe and Central Europe, as was the dominant feature of the Cold War era.

- *Atlantic Partnership.* This world is similar to the Modified Cold War Order, in that it is characterized by a U.S.–West European alliance in the context of a strong and potentially threatening Russia. However, it also entails a much closer U.S.-European partnership outside Europe—for example, in joint defense of the Middle East.

- *European Bipolarity.* This order is characterized by a rough political and strategic balance between the Eastern and Western parts of Europe, with the United States relegated to a residual role in European security affairs.

- *West European Dominance.* In this order, Russia and other countries of the former Soviet Union remain weak and fragmented, while Western Europe develops as a major power center.

- *Rivalry and Fragmentation.* In this order, no part of Europe manages successful integration and maintenance of itself as a major global and regional power center.

- *Pan-European Order.* This order is characterized by complete or near-complete transcendence of political rivalries in Europe, and prospective convergence of all parts of the continent, most likely through progressive enlargement of West European institutions to include Russia and other NIS.

Each of these alternative strategic worlds would have different implications for U.S. defense planning over the long term. These implications will be analyzed below along eight dimensions: (1) nuclear deterrence and defense; (2) deterrence and defense against major conventional conflicts; (3) theater ballistic missile defense; (4) Europe as a base for military access to other regions of the world; (5) peacekeeping and related missions; (6) counterproliferation; (7) logistical and other support for allies in major contingencies in which the United States is not directly involved; and (8) defense industry.

In general, the Modified Cold War Order and Atlantic Partnership worlds entail major U.S. defense commitments to Europe, while European Bipolarity, West European Dominance, and Pan-European Order imply less involvement. Rivalry and Fragmentation would have indeterminate implications for U.S. defense planning, and U.S. military involvement in European security affairs could vary considerably according to particular circumstances.

REGIONAL TRENDS

This section examines near-, medium-, and long-term trends in the European region and its main subregions, focusing on the key drivers that are likely to determine the emergence of alternative strategic worlds with different implications for conflict and the potential use of force. The discussion covers five major sets of drivers: demographic and economic, internal political and social, external political, defense and defense industrial, and an "other" category of trends relating to the role of the state and of nonstate actors, the environment, and technology. The basic unit of analysis is the nation-state. "Internal political and social" thus refers to developments within a given country—for example, social cohesion and national unity or fragmentation. "External political" refers to developments external to and among individual countries, notably integration into larger entities such as the EU or the CIS, and foreign policy and defense orientation toward other countries or regions.

Demographic and Economic Trends

In contrast to other parts of the world, where rapid economic growth contributes to instability and uncertainty (such as in East Asia), or where overpopulation and economic collapse are causes of conflict within and between states (e.g., in southern Africa and parts of the Middle East), Europe generally is characterized by demographic and economic stability. Following the collapse of Communism in the early 1990s, major destabilizing shifts within the region are not generally projected, although there will be changes in the relative weight of different states and groups of states that could have strategic implications. The most important trends, both demographic and economic, shaping the strategic outlook in Europe will be a continuation of decline relative to other parts of the world, and relative to the developing countries in particular.

Population: Growth and Composition. Population growth throughout Europe is low by world and Europe's own historic standards. Low population growth will have several effects with long-term political and strategic implications, including a rapid aging of the population in nearly all European countries and the decline of Europe's population relative to other parts of the world. Immigration, which is partly a consequence of these demographic trends, will result in more diverse populations in many countries and is associated with political and social tensions and the rise of extreme-right parties.

Several countries, notably Germany and Italy, are expected to decline in absolute size, whereas others will experience modest growth. Germany's population is projected to fall from 81.1 million in 1995 to 77.7 million in 2015 (and 73.4 million in 2030).[2] Along with the familiar political constraints on Germany, an aging population and smaller draft-age cohorts will help to diminish a perceived or actual German threat to stability on the continent. There also will be a substantial relative shift in population between Russia and its "near abroad." Whereas Russia's population is projected to rise from its current 149 million to 153 million in 2015, a gain of four million, the eight countries of Central Asia and the Caucasus will increase their populations over the same period from 72 million to 96 million, a gain of 24 million.

The population of Europe as a whole will decline relative to the rest of the world and, in particular, relative to adjacent regions in the Middle East and North Africa. Europe currently accounts for 730 million of the world's total population of 5.7 billion, approximately 12.8 percent. By 2015 this share will drop to just over 10 percent, as Europe's population will grow only marginally to 744 million, while world population grows to a projected 7.4 billion. Disparities in rates of growth will sharpen the population gradient between the northern

---

[2]Population data and demographic projections are from the World Bank, reported in Eduard Bos et al., *World Population Projections*, 1994–1995 edition, Baltimore: Johns Hopkins University Press for the World Bank, 1995.

and southern sides of the Mediterranean, and between Russia and its "near abroad." There are now approximately 201 million people in the European countries on the northern side of the Mediterranean, compared with 212 in the southern littoral states. By 2015, the south will have more than 298 million people, compared with 205 million in the north. The increase of 85 million people in the countries of North Africa and the Levant will intensify migration pressures, contribute to unemployment, and could threaten economic and political instability.[3] Russia's demographic decline relative to its "near abroad" will be dwarfed by the shifts relative to other countries to its south and east. Iran's population is projected to grow from 65 million in 1995 to 107 million by 2015. Even though China's rate of population growth has slowed dramatically in recent decades—a trend that is expected to continue—China still will gain nearly 200 million people over the next two decades, more than the entire present population of Russia and fifty times the increase of four million projected for Russia over the same period.

One effect of slow population growth in Europe (coupled with increased life expectancy from improvements in health) is the pronounced aging of the population. By 2025, the number of people in the 15 member states of the current EU aged 60 and above will increase by nearly 50 percent, while those of prime working age (20–59) will fall by 6.4 percent. Rising dependency ratios will place a heavy burden on government finances, particularly in light of the unfunded pension liabilities in most European countries. Small cohorts of draft-age males will mean that European countries, including Russia, will be militarily weaker relative to many non-European countries than the comparison of aggregate population figures alone would suggest.

Migration. Immigration into Western Europe from Central and Eastern Europe and the developing world exploded in 1986–1992 before leveling off and declining in 1993 and thereafter as a result of tightened restrictions on entry and the effects on the labor market of economic recession. Despite the drop-off after 1993, net migration accounted for over 60 percent of the increase in total population in

---

[3]See Russell King, "Labour, Employment and Migration in Southern Europe," in John Van Oudenaren (ed.), *Employment, Economic Development and Migration in Southern Europe and the Maghreb*, RAND, CF-126-EAC, 1996.

Western Europe in the last decade. In some countries, notably Germany and Italy, the natural increase of the population has turned negative, and the increase in overall population has resulted entirely from immigration.[4] As a result, populations in West European countries are becoming more ethnically and religiously diverse.

Western Europe is the primary destination for most immigrants, but the former Communist countries have become targets of immigration as well, partly as a result of free-market conditions that create demand for workers, and as a result of the dismantling of Communist-era controls and the expansion of transportation and business links with other parts of the world. While sending many of their own workers to Western Europe, countries in Central and Eastern Europe that border on the former Soviet Union are absorbing temporary and mostly illegal labor migrants from Russia, Ukraine, and other NIS. Further east, Russia and other NIS also have been affected by immigration—a new trend that these countries find difficult to handle given their economic fragility and legacy of tight controls on the movement of people across their borders, but one that is certain to persist and perhaps intensify as the NIS become more integrated in the world economy.

Apart from these movements of people from outside the FSU, long-term political and strategic developments in Russia and the other NIS will be shaped by the "unmixing of peoples" that is occurring in the wake of the breakup of the Soviet multinational empire.[5] The fate of the ethnic Russians living outside Russia is likely to have particular long-term historical effects, much the way the presence of ethnic Germans living outside of Germany and Austria played an important role in the politics of Central and Eastern Europe before and even, to an extent, after World War II. In the FSU, there are nearly 25 million ethnic Russians living outside the Russian Federation—chiefly in Ukraine and Kazakhstan, but in other NIS as well. Apart from Kazakhstan, the ethnic Russian population in Central Asia and the Caucasus is almost exclusively urban and not deeply rooted. Re-

---

[4]Data in this section are primarily from OECD, *Trends in International Migration: Continuous Reporting System on Migration (SOPEMI)*, Paris,: OECD, various years.

[5]See R. Brubaker, *Aftermaths of Empire and the Unmixing of Peoples: Historical and Comparative Perspective*, Santa Monica, CA: RAND, DRU-563-FF, 1993.

cent migration patterns and surveys of migration intentions suggest that these people are likely to leave over time in response to economic, ethnic, and linguistic pressures. Armed conflicts, such as have occurred in Tajikistan, Georgia, and Azerbaijan, will accelerate the process. The numbers of ethnic Russians in these countries is not large in absolute terms (according to the 1989 Soviet census, 785,000 in the Caucasus; 3,300,000 in Turkmenistan, Uzbekistan, the Kyrgyz Republic, and Tajikistan), but the exodus will have long-term geopolitical effects, lessening an important source of Russian influence and perhaps hastening the reorientation of these countries toward Asia and the Islamic world.

In contrast, northern Kazakhstan, the Crimea, eastern Ukraine, trans-Dniester Moldova, and northeastern Estonia all have substantial and deeply rooted Russian populations that are likely to remain for the foreseeable future and might become a source of conflict between Russia and these countries.[6] Migration of ethnic Russians between these countries and Russia proper will occur, but net outflows to Russia relative to the overall populations involved may not be large. Real or perceived attempts by governments in these countries to accelerate the pace at which Russians leave (or assimilate) could become a source of conflict with Moscow. These attempts might be a particular danger with regard to Kazakhstan, whose government has been walking a fine line between a policy of gradual de-Russification and maintaining good relations with Russia and peace among its ethnic Russian citizenry.

Economic Performance

Western Europe. Economic growth in Western Europe averaged 4.8 percent per year in 1960–1973, fell to just 2.0 percent per year in 1974–1985 following the oil crises and other economic shocks of the 1970s, and then partially recovered to a 3.2 percent annual rate in 1986–1990 in response to falling oil prices and the increased business confidence and higher investment associated with the EC's single market program. Since 1991, economic growth has again lagged, av-

---

[6]See John Van Oudenaren, "Migrations probleme in der ehemaligen Sowjetunion: Eine politische Herausforderung," *Internationale Politik*, No. 11, 1995, pp. 57–64.

eraging less than 1 percent during the 1991–1993 recession before recovering to just under 3 percent in 1994 and 1995.[7]

Economists generally judge the EU's underlying growth potential—based on increases in population and other inputs—to be just over 2 percent per annum. At this level, the EU slowly will lose ground relative to other parts of the world and will have difficulty in dealing with such structural challenges as unemployment and rising dependency ratios. Nonetheless, the EU will remain, along with the United States, a dominant shaper of the international economic order, with a major voice in trade, monetary, and energy matters.

Adjusting to the growth of economic power in other parts of the world will have direct implications for Western Europe's continued high unemployment and downward pressures on wages in low technology industries. Indirectly, the adjustment could mean added political strains or even open rivalry between the United States and its European allies as they, along with Japan, seek to find the right mix of accommodation, cooperation, and competition in their efforts to manage the world economy and the emergence of new power centers. This global shift also will have important implications for Russia, which borders directly on China and which will also be seeking to find its place in the world economic order.

Internally, Western Europe faces structural economic problems that will undercut its ability to play a more influential international role (e.g., through the development of a stronger autonomous defense capability), and that in the extreme case could undermine political and social stability. Total unemployment in the EU stands at more than 18 million, or nearly 11 percent of the workforce. The most worrisome aspect of the unemployment situation in Western Europe has been the steady "ratcheting up" of the base level of unemployment during successive cycles of recession and recovery.

As the costs of maintaining the social safety net have increased and as unemployment has continued to rise, European governments and the European Commission have begun a gradual shift toward what is sometimes called an Anglo-Saxon model that stresses labor market

---

[7]Commission of the European Communities (CEC), *Growth, Competitiveness, Employment*, Luxembourg: CEC, 1993.

flexibility and seeks to expand employment by holding real wage growth below rises in productivity. The effects of this shift have been slow in coming and in any case are difficult to measure—particularly in a macroeconomic environment characterized by slow overall growth. Demographic trends, fiscal realities, and the growing acceptance of flexibility as a new orthodoxy in economic thinking all suggest that in the coming decades Europe may make progress in combating its structural unemployment problems, but that it will continue to do so at the cost of cuts in the social safety net. Many countries thus are likely to be entering long-term situations in which workers are confronted with high albeit declining rates of unemployment, coupled with a cutting back of generous social benefits once taken for granted. Europe may be able to manage this transition without upheaval, but localized or perhaps even more widespread manifestations of political instability, anti-immigrant backlash, and resurgence of worker militancy cannot be ruled out.

Central, Eastern, and Southeastern Europe. Compared with the situation in Western Europe, the long-term economic outlook for Central and Eastern Europe is characterized by greater uncertainty and larger differences among countries and among economic sectors and population groups within countries. All countries in the region suffered sharp falls in output in the early 1990s, but then began to recover as macroeconomic stabilization and microeconomic reforms took hold. Somewhat to the surprise of many observers, Poland has been a star performer, registering five years of rapid growth after the sharp recession and shock therapy of 1990–1991. Growth hit a 7.0 percent annual rate in 1995, and is expected to continue strong over the next several years. At the other extreme, Bulgaria delayed reforms in the early 1990s, and hit a severe economic crisis in mid-1996. Economic growth is projected at a mere 2.1 percent for 1996 and 1.7 percent for 1997. The other countries in the Central and East European Countries (CEEC-10)—those countries that formally are on track to join the EU—range between the Polish and Bulgarian cases, and growth for the region as a whole is projected to average 4–5 percent per year.[8] At these rates of growth, the leading candidate coun-

---

[8]European Commission forecast, reported in Supplement C, "Economic Reform Monitor," *European Economy*, June 1996.

tries for EU membership slowly will close the gap between themselves and the EU average.

A major uncertainty surrounding the economic future of these countries is whether performance increasingly will diverge, leading to an irrevocable split into economic and political subregions, or whether a combination of internal reforms and external assistance by the EU and others will result in convergence. For both economic and political reasons, neither Romania nor Bulgaria is likely to meet the timetable for EU entry—2002–2004—that is widely discussed for the northern tier countries. This delay raises the prospect of a widening and perhaps long-term split between East-Central and Southeastern Europe, particularly if developments in the former Yugoslavia exert a negative influence on these countries. In Albania and the former Yugoslavia, the economic and political outlook is even worse. There is general disappointment with political trends in the region, especially in Croatia and Albania, and a tacit recognition that the Balkan region as a whole is in many respects drifting further from the European mainstream.

Russia and the NIS. Russia presents a mixed and somewhat confusing economic picture. Real GDP fell steadily throughout the early 1990s—by some 40 percent in 1990–1996—before reportedly stabilizing in the second half of 1996.[9] Investment remains low, unemployment is rising, and large segments of the population are living in poverty. Wage arrears—unpaid salaries owed workers by state-owned and private firms—are a major economic and political problem. There are, nonetheless, many bright spots. Official figures understate economic activity by neglecting the output of new private enterprises and of the informal economy. Labor productivity is rising, and in some industries that are especially active on the world market (metallurgy, chemicals, and petrochemicals) production has been increasing since 1995. Most promising is the renewed commitment to economic reform by President Yeltsin following his return to the political stage in March 1997, and the appointment or reappointment to important posts of such prominent reformers as Anatoly Chubais and Boris Nemtsov.

------

[9]IMF, *World Economic Outlook*, May 1996, Table A7.

The most plausible scenario for the next several years is one of continued growth and transformation, although not without setbacks and occasional backtracking and by no means without considerable suffering for those parts of the population that are the main losers in the post-Communist transformation. If this assessment is correct, it will mean a more stable, market-oriented Russia, but also a Russia with growing (although still very small) resources available to devote to national security and international affairs. Russia's growing marketization may also make the country more vulnerable, at least for the transition period, to financial crises and breakdowns. Politically destabilizing financial upheavals cannot be ruled out over the next several years, even if the "real" economy continues to improve.

Apart from the quantitative indicators, the economy continues to evolve into a new variant of distinctly Russian capitalism. Russian industry is restructuring under the leadership of a dozen or so powerful industrial groups, many partially privatized, that have close ties with the Russian government and with individual ministers and political figures. While these firms have no interest in returning to the old command-style economy, they are not necessarily supporters of a liberal economic order in the U.S. and West European sense of the term. Many are suspicious of foreign presence in the Russian economy and essentially protectionist with regard to both trade and foreign direct investment. Crime and corruption have reached alarming proportions and, under some circumstances, could threaten the economic and political underpinnings of the Russian state.

Ukraine's economic and political situation has dramatically improved since the institution of reforms in late 1994 by President Leonid Kuchma. GDP fell by 11.4 percent in 1995, less than half the drop for 1994 as measured in official statistics. Performance was no doubt even better if the greater volume of unmeasured private activity in 1995 is taken into account. The government has managed to reduce the budget deficit and to lower inflation to an annual rate of 140 percent, although it remains unable to control monetary expansion.

By reversing the deep economic and political slide of 1991–1994, Ukraine has demonstrated even to skeptical observers that it is a viable state. Its long-term survival is by no means assured, but there will be no near-term implosion followed by relatively painless reabsorption into Russia, as was expected, feared, or hoped for by many in the first few years of national independence. However, Ukraine may be entering a second phase of vulnerability to Russian pressure, especially in the fuel and energy sector.

In the other NIS, economic performance varies widely, with official statistics telling only part of the story. In the Caucasus, economic performance has been even worse than in the rest of the FSU, partly owing to political chaos and internal and external conflict. Over the longer term, however, these countries face reasonably bright economic prospects, owing to their agricultural assets, to large deposits of oil and gas in Azerbaijan, and to their central location and history of trading links with other countries in the region. A key question will be whether enough political stability can be achieved to allow these economic assets to be exploited in a way that has not happened so far since 1991.

As in the Caucasus, economic revival in Central Asia will depend upon establishing a stable political environment and upon the willingness of neo-Communist elites to undertake genuine reform. The commitment to reform varies considerably across the region, with Kazakhstan, the Kyrgyz Republic, and Tajikistan much further along than Turkmenistan or Uzbekistan. These countries are generally well-endowed with energy and other natural resources, and their integration into global markets through joint ventures with Western and Russian firms will be a major element in their economic development in the coming decades, as well as a potential source of political conflict and realignment.

Energy. Europe is not a cohesive region with respect to energy consumption and supply. Western Europe is a major importer of energy from the Middle East, North Africa, and the FSU, while Russia is a net exporter with great potential for expanded future production. Central and Eastern Europe have some indigenous energy resources, but are on balance energy poor. Several of the NIS are on the verge of becoming major oil and gas producers and exporters.

Four overall trends in the energy sector with potential strategic implications can be identified: (1) increased dependence for many countries on imported sources of supply, although at levels still below those experienced during the two oil crises of 1973–1974 and 1979–1980; (2) increasing integration of the NIS and West-Central European energy systems through investment and the development of transport infrastructure; (3) growing importance of transport, infrastructures, and market volatility (as opposed to sheer shortages of physical supply) as potential sources of economic disruption and political conflict; and (4) a declining role for nuclear power, but persisting and perhaps growing problems associated with nuclear plant safety and waste disposal, especially in Russia, other NIS, and some countries in Central and Eastern Europe.

In Western Europe, the energy crises of the 1970s led to increased domestic production (from North Sea oil, nuclear power, and other sources) and declining use of energy per unit of GDP. Increased domestic supplies coupled with conservation resulted in a significant decrease in dependence on imported sources of supply—from around two-thirds in 1974 to less than half in 1986. Since 1986, EU production has declined and dependence on external sources has increased, although it remains below the levels of 1973–1974 and 1979–1980. Import dependence is highest for oil (78 percent), which is increasingly a transportation-related fuel.[10]

In Eastern Europe and the FSU, little or no net growth in energy consumption is expected in the medium term, as economic reforms in these countries lead to the more rational use of energy. Eastern Europe and the former Soviet Union currently are using less energy than in 1990, and some projections suggest that 1990 levels of consumption will not be reached again until 2005. There is, however, considerable uncertainty surrounding prospects for growth in energy demand in these countries. Economic growth and convergence in living standards to EU levels will put added pressure on world energy supplies, as well as on the environment. The composition of demand will shift from industry to transport, as old factories are closed and private car ownership and use increases. This shift in turn will increase demand for imported oil. There is also great uncertainty on the production side in the former Communist world. Oil production in the former Soviet Union has collapsed in recent years, from 12.5

---

[10]European Commission, *For a European Union Energy Policy: European Commission Green Paper*, Brussels: COM(94) 659 Final, January 1995.

million barrels per day (mbd) in 1988 to just over 7 mbd in 1995.[11] The U.S. Department of Energy projects that oil production in the region will begin rising again to 10.9 mbd by 2010, but this projection is based on the assumption that financial and organizational problems in the Russian oil industry will be overcome and that the foreign investment needed to raise production will materialize. Absent a turnaround in production, world oil markets could tighten and economic recovery in Russia and the NIS could be strained by energy shortages.

Western Europe's dependence on imports of oil and gas and Russia's need for capital and markets create a strong commonality of interest between Russia and the EU with regard to cooperation in the energy field. This commonality was expressed in the signing, in late 1994, of the European Energy Charter Treaty, which is intended to foster pan-European cooperation in the energy sector. Increased trade in energy products between Western Europe and the NIS could lead to growing competition over markets and transit routes, as has already been seen in the competition between Russia and Turkey over pipeline and tanker routes for oil from Central Asia and the Caucasus.

While greater East-West trade in energy may lead to frictions within Europe, its longer-term significance may be to dampen West European interest in the Persian Gulf. World dependence on the Gulf will increase, but as Western Europe's share of world oil consumption decreases and that of other regions increases, and as Russia and other NIS loom larger in West European import figures, the political and economic dimensions of dependence on Persian Gulf oil will take on as much a south-south as a north-south dimension.

Internal Political and Social Trends

Compared with other parts of the world and with Europe's own history prior to World War II, Western Europe since 1945 has enjoyed an unprecedented degree of political and social stability. With few exceptions, governments have been changed by exclusively constitu-

---

[11]Joseph Stanislaw and Daniel Yergin, "Oil: Reopening the Door," *Foreign Affairs*, September/October 1993, pp. 81–93.

tional means, political violence has been limited, and historic nation-states have not fragmented as a result of secessionist movements and civil wars. For much of this period, political and social stability prevailed in Central and Eastern Europe and the Soviet Union, but it was imposed artificially by Communist rule. The collapse of Communism thus resulted in the breakup of three states (the USSR, Czechoslovakia, and Yugoslavia), civil wars in some of their successor states, and widespread social upheaval. Whether relative political and social stability persists in Western Europe and spreads eastward, or whether instability persists in the east, possibly causing or coinciding with renewed instability in the West, is a key question that will shape the future strategic environment. We next examine three sources of political and social instability: movements to break up individual states; ethnic conflicts with cross-border dimensions; and social upheaval not directly linked to ethnic or national factors.

Threats to National Integrity. At the same time that much of Europe is becoming more integrated and transferring sovereignty to supranational bodies, there has been an increasing trend toward regional, ethnic, and religious fragmentation at the national level. Subnational assertiveness has been most apparent in countries that until recently were under Communist rule, but this trend appears to be a general phenomenon with manifestations in Western Europe as well.

The most serious challenges to national integrity in Western Europe are in Belgium, Spain, and Italy. Other countries with active separatist movements are the UK (Scotland and Northern Ireland) and France (Corsica). There are no ethnically based separatist movements in Germany, but the Länder (states) have become increasingly assertive in pressing for a greater voice in national and EU policies. Turkey faces a major threat to its national integrity in the form of the Kurdish insurgency, which in turn affects Turkey's relations with such important neighboring states as Iraq, Iran, Syria, and Russia.

With the breakup of Yugoslavia and Czechoslovakia—both synthetic states created in the Versailles settlement after World War I—national devolution in Central and Eastern Europe appears to have run its course. States in the region either are ethnically homogeneous (Poland, Hungary, the Czech Republic), or have minorities that are more likely to try to secede from one state to join another than to form their own states. Autonomy could be a transitional stage to the movement of borders or the transfer of population, but the creation of entirely new states does not appear likely. Bosnia represents an important exception to this generalization. If the attempt to create the unified multi-ethnic Bosnian state mandated in the 1995 Dayton agreement fails, Bosnia could break up into three ministates: Bosnian and Croat entities formed from the breakup of the existing Bosnian-Croat Federation, and the Serb Republic of Srpska. Most likely, however, the Bosnian Serb Republic and the Croatian Herzeg-Bosnia would be absorbed by Serbia and Croatia, respectively. If this happens, Bosnia would emerge as a new—as well as small and weak—ethnic state in Europe.

The potential for fragmentation is much greater in the former Soviet Union. The Russian Federation's population is approximately 80 percent Russian. By the standards of Russian history, this represents a degree of homogeneity not seen for centuries. Nonetheless, the 20 percent of the population that is not Russian still constitutes some 30 million people, many of whom are Islamic and are concentrated in their own autonomous or semi-autonomous regions.[12] Under the Federation Treaty of 1992, Russia consists of 89 constituent parts having different degrees of autonomy. Many of the non-Russians in Russia live in these autonomous or semi-autonomous regions.

Other states of the FSU also are vulnerable to fragmentation, especially if they are subject to external interference by Russia. Ukraine has a large Russian minority in the east and the Crimea, but it is also vulnerable to a split along cultural and religious lines which could pit Orthodox Ukrainians from the east against Uniate Catholics from the western parts of the country. Other relevant cases include Georgia, which in 1990–1992 was racked by conflict between the government and pro-independence forces in South Ossetia and again in 1993–1995 by a bitter conflict between the government and the secessionist Republic of Abkhazia; and Tajikistan, where a civil war with an ethnic and clan dimension broke out in late 1992.

Ethnic differences and the heightening of ethnic or religious identities are by no means the only factors contributing to the weakening and possible breakup of established states. In Italy, the Lega Lom-

---

[12]See Jack F. Matlock, *Autopsy on an Empire*, New York: Random House, 1995, pp. 727–734, for an overview of minority issues in Russia.

barda does not assert a separate ethnic identity, but rather a different cultural heritage and economic interests from the rest of the country. In Russia, regions dominated by ethnic Russians, particularly in the Russian Far East, have shown a tendency to assert their independence of Moscow to pursue regional economic interests.[13] And to give an example that cuts a different way, the Serbian "nationalist" Milosevic was prepared to abandon his ethnically Serb brothers in Bosnia in order to secure peace and the lifting of sanctions that were crippling Serbia's economy. As these cases all suggest, ostensibly ethnic and national conflicts are closely intertwined with economic and political interests, and in particular with the interests of elites, many of which are struggling to preserve their positions in a world of rapid economic and political change.

Cross-Border Ethnic Conflict. Many mixed ethnic situations could erupt into internal conflicts that might then lead to wars involving neighboring states, as was the case in the former Yugoslavia. Such a development is hard to conceive of in Western Europe, although the activities of Basque terrorists on occasion have led to tensions between France and Spain, and the Irish Republican Army remains a sensitive issue in UK-Irish relations. In Central, Eastern, and Southeastern Europe, the most potentially explosive cross-border ethnic situations are those involving ethnic Hungarians outside of Hungary, the Romanians and Moldovans, and the Albanians of Kosovo and Macedonia.[14] In the FSU, the most serious situations involve ethnic Russians outside Russia and non-Russian peoples living in the Russian Federation, although there are many other situations involving smaller numbers of people that pose a more immediate danger of conflict, as already has been seen in the Caucasus and parts of Central Asia.

---

[13]Yergin and Gustafson develop scenarios for the emergence of three autonomous regions: a northwest region formed around St. Petersburg and including Murmansk and Arkhangel'sk; a South Russian Confederation comprised of Muslim and Russian areas, including Astrakhan', Krasnodar, Stavropol', the Kalmyk Republic, Dagestan, Chechnya, and others; and a Far Eastern region comprised of Sakha (the former Yakutiia), Irkutsk, and the Far Eastern maritime provinces. See Daniel Yergin and Thane Gustafson, *Russia 2010*, New York: Random House, 1993, pp. 144–149.

[14]See, for example, F. S. Larrabee, *East European Security After the Cold War*, Santa Monica, CA: RAND, MR-254-USDP, 1993, pp. 3–4; 9–51.

Ethnic Hungarians living outside of Hungary (in Romania, Slovakia, Serbia, Ukraine, and Slovenia) total some 3.5 million people, or about one quarter of all Hungarians. Hungary reaffirmed its acceptance of its post–World War I borders in the 1947 Paris peace treaty and its respect for the territorial integrity of neighboring states in the Helsinki Final Act of 1975, the Paris charter, and various bilateral agreements, but there is no guarantee that ethnic issues could not become a source of conflict in the future between Hungary and Romania or Hungary and Slovakia.

While Romania is potentially vulnerable to irredentist claims by Hungary, it finds itself in the opposite position with regard to Moldova, the successor state to the Soviet Socialist Republic of Moldavia formed out of territories taken from Romania at the outset of World War II. Following the breakup of the USSR in late 1991 and the establishment of an independent Moldova, leading political figures in Romania joined with colleagues in Moldova to prepare for the eventual merger of the two countries. Unification with Romania proved to have less popular support in Moldova than many expected, however, and further talk of unification was effectively quashed in a March 1994 national referendum on statehood. Nonetheless, it remains possible—particularly if economic performance lags in Moldova but improves in Romania—that the issue of merger will arise again. Change in relations between Romania and Moldova could in turn lead to complications in relations among Romania and Russia and Ukraine, with which Romania has political differences concerning the legal status of the Molotov-Ribbentrop Pact that led to the establishment of the Moldavian Soviet Socialist Republic. Romania also has a specific difference with Ukraine over Zmeinyy (Snake) Island.

Another potential conflict situation with both long- and short-term implications concerns the ethnic Albanians living in the Serbian province of Kosovo, in Macedonia, and to a limited extent in Greece. Kosovo has been the scene of violent clashes between Serbs and ethnic Albanians since the early 1980s. Ethnic Albanians account for 90 percent of the population, but the region has great historic and symbolic importance for Serb nationalists. Riots and uprisings by ethnic Albanians in the late 1980s triggered an exodus of Serbs and Montenegrins, which in turn resulted in a harsh crackdown in the province by the Serb authorities in Belgrade. A worsening of conditions in Kosovo, coupled with the appearance of a more assertive, less patient Albanian leadership in Kosovo could lead to open conflict that might draw in Albania or even sympathetic Islamic states and movements from outside the region.

Macedonia is a weak state that has had highly publicized difficulties with Greece, which refused to recognize the legitimacy of any state calling itself "Macedonia" (a name that to Greece implied revisionist goals vis-à-vis its other northern provinces).[15] Over the longer term, however, Macedonia is more likely to become embroiled with two of its other neighbors—Bulgaria, which does not recognize the existence of a Macedonian language or nationality, and Albania, owing to the 420,000-strong Albanian minority in Macedonia. These people could intensify their efforts to achieve autonomy, perhaps in connection with a broader Balkan or Macedonian crisis, and some Albanian Muslim districts and leaders might even press for incorporation into a Greater Albania.[16] Ethnic issues are also a potential source of conflict between Turkey and Bulgaria. Relations between the two countries were strained in the 1980s over Bulgaria's persecution of its Turkish minority, but improved dramatically since the fall of the hardline Zhivkov regime in late 1990. Sources of conflict remain, however, and could flare up.

In the FSU, the most significant ethnic-related trends are those that concern the nearly 25 million ethnic Russians living outside the Russian Federation. The question of these people is in turn linked to that of borders—internal administrative borders of the USSR that in 1991 became international frontiers. The Crimea in Ukraine and the "virgin lands" of northern Kazakhstan are territories historically thought of as part of Russia and are heavily populated by ethnic Russians. After independence, the Yeltsin government vowed to respect former interrepublican borders as valid international frontiers, but the government has come under domestic political pressure to

---

[15]Greece and the Former Yugoslav Republic of Macedonia (FYROM) finally defused their difference by signing, in September 1995, a UN-brokered agreement normalizing ties between the two countries. On the issue of Macedonia's name, they agreed to disagree, reserving a solution to a possible later date.

[16]James F. Brown, "Turkey: Back to the Balkans?" in Graham E. Fuller and Ian O. Lesser, *Turkey's New Geopolitics: From the Balkans to Western China*, Boulder, CO: Westview, 1993, p. 147.

abandon this approach. Elsewhere in the FSU, potential for cross-border ethnic conflict will also persist. The most violent conflict so far has been the war between Armenia and Azerbaijan over the Nagorno-Karabakh region. There was also fighting in 1992 between Moldovan government forces and separatists from the mainly ethnic Russian and Ukrainian Transdniestria. Substantial Tajik and Kazakh minorities in Uzbekistan and Uzbek minorities in the Kyrgyz Republic, Tajikistan, and Turkmenistan also are potential sources of conflict.

Perhaps the most explosive conflicts in this region are those that could involve ethnic groups that live both in countries of the former Soviet Union and in neighboring countries along the periphery of the FSU. The Moldovans and Romanians, for example, are essentially the same people speaking the same language, and conflict between Slavs and Moldovans in Moldova could in principle involve Romania. Turkey's population includes some 5 million ethnic Caucasians, many of whom have close ties to their compatriots in Russia and elsewhere. Iran has 15 million Azeris living in its northern provinces, while the Kyrgyz Republic, Tajikistan, and Turkmenistan all have co-ethnic groups across their borders with Afghanistan. These cross-border minority situations have the potential to foster conflict between the states of the FSU and countries along its periphery, as well as increase the potential for cross-border crime, terrorism, mass migration, and other spillover effects.

Social and Political Stability. Social and political stability is most threatened in parts of the ex-Communist world, although stability cannot be taken entirely for granted even in affluent and politically stable Western Europe. The source of instability most often identified in Western Europe is unacceptably high unemployment, which interacts with anti-immigrant sentiment and many of the ethnic and regionalist conflicts discussed above. Sources of social instability most often identified in Russia and other countries in transition include mass unemployment, endemic poverty in certain groups, and rampant crime and corruption. These problems often interact with existing ethnic or religious differences.

Throughout the FSU and selectively in other post-Communist transition countries, the incomplete and flawed nature of the political transition from Communism to the establishment of full-fledged democratic systems is an inherent source of political instability. As in large parts of the developing world, governments lack popular legitimacy and thus are vulnerable to domestic upheavals, particularly in connection with elections and other political procedures that may be seen by the electorate as fraudulent.

In addition to the ethnic-based challenge that Turkey faces from its Kurdish population, Turkey faces particular challenges to its social stability—as the term has been understood in Turkey in the postwar period—from rising Islamic fundamentalist sentiment. Elsewhere in Western, Central, and Southeastern Europe, Islamic fundamentalism has limited implications for social stability. Albania and Bosnia are the only other countries with Muslim majorities. Islamic fundamentalist takeovers in former Soviet Central Asia are a possibility, but this danger is widely seen to have been overestimated in the initial aftermath of the breakup of the Soviet Union.

Western Europe's ability to project stability eastward is dependent on the maintenance of stability in Western Europe itself. Although few would argue that this stability is fundamentally threatened as it was in the 1920s, 1930s, and late 1940s, a growing number of observers point to disturbing trends and indications. According to one such analysis, Western Europe is facing "greater social disruption and physical risk than at any time since the early Industrial Revolution."[17] One manifestation of growing instability at the margins has been the rise of radical right-wing parties, which in some scenarios could provide the basis for sharp discontinuities in European politics.

External Political Trends

The strategic transformation in Europe in the course of the last decade was the result of both fragmentation and consolidation. In a culmination of trends long under way if not fully recognized at the time, in 1989–1991 the strained and artificial unity of the east was shattered, even as Western Europe made dramatic progress toward political and economic integration—partly in response to develop-

---

[17]Tony Judt, "Europe: The Grand Illusion," *New York Review of Books*, July 11, 1996, pp. 6–7.

ments in the east. Germany was quickly reunified, and German Chancellor Helmut Kohl and French President Francois Mitterrand immediately pushed for political union as a way of binding a larger and more powerful Germany into the EC.

These parallel and mutually reinforcing processes of fragmentation in the east and consolidation in the west reached their high-water mark in December 1991 when the leaders of the 12 countries of the European Community met in Maastricht, the Netherlands, to finalize the treaty establishing a West European political, economic, and monetary union just a few weeks after the presidents of Belarus, Russia, and Ukraine met in a hunting lodge outside Minsk to sign the agreements breaking up the Soviet Union and laying the basis for the establishment of a much looser Commonwealth of Independent States. Already in 1992–1993 these trends had begun to reverse themselves. In the west, political and economic and monetary union ran into domestic political trouble, beginning with the difficult process of ratifying the Maastricht treaty and continuing with the unexpected problems of the third stage of Economic and Monetary Union (EMU). In the east, the pace of fragmentation began to moderate, as the post-Communist government in Moscow began to lay the groundwork for a reintegration in some form of at least parts of the old Soviet Union.

Western Europe and the FSU continue to be characterized by conflicting and offsetting trends of integration and fragmentation. How these trends evolve in each region and interact with each other over the long term will have major strategic implications. In Western Europe, there is uncertainty surrounding the process of supranational integration within the EU—both its breadth (how many countries of Central, Eastern, and Southeastern Europe will become members of the Union) and its depth (how supranational will the Union be; what functions and responsibilities of national governments will it assume). There is also uncertainty concerning the former Soviet Union and how successful Russia will be in its efforts both to hold itself together by preventing the kind of fragmentation discussed above and, more ambitiously, to fashion a Commonwealth of Independent States that shares characteristics of both the old USSR and the evolving European Union.

The future strategic environment also will be shaped by how the European states or blocs of states—whatever the level of integration that they achieve—orient themselves toward each other and toward non-European powers, including China, Japan, major third world states, and, most important for purposes of this analysis, the United States. Neo-realists such as Kenneth Waltz argue that Western Europe (or a preponderant Germany in a Europe of failed or limited integration) almost inevitably will emerge as an independent power center and a rival to the United States.[18] They do not go so far as to predict war, but they do see a certain degree of conflict as structurally rooted and nearly impossible to avoid. Other analysts stress the close political, economic, and "civilizational" ties between the United States and Western Europe, and argue that conflict and even rivalry among different parts of the same civilization are likely to be increasingly less important in a multipolar world. In this view, "enlargement" and "partnership" rather than geopolitical rivalry are the key policy issues: how far and how fast the core U.S.-West European alliance can be extended, eastward and southward, and how deep and comprehensive U.S.-West European cooperation can become in pursuit of common policy objectives.

A similar range of views exists with regard to Russia. Many policy analysts stress the different cultural and political traditions of Russia and conclude that Russia constitutes a permanent geopolitical challenge to its western neighbors—that "enlargement" of the Western community inevitably will stop at Russia's western border (or, in Samuel P. Huntington's view, at the western edge of the entire Orthodox world). Implicit in this view is an assumption that Russia will have and possibly exercise non-European geopolitical options—for example, alliance with China or with selected Middle Eastern powers against the West. An alternative view stresses Russia's Western roots, its position as a power for which a stable place in Europe can be found, or even as a power that at times has had a close relationship with the United States that has developed independent of the European powers. In this view, Russia and its CIS neighbors are potential members of an "enlarged" Western world, albeit ones whose full in-

---

[18]Kenneth Waltz, "The Emerging Structure of International Politics," *International Security*, Vol. 18, No. 2, 1993, pp. 44–79.

tegration is likely to lag that of Central and Eastern Europe by years or even decades.

As will be seen in the next section, different assumptions about the external orientation of Western Europe and Russia as well as different assumptions about degrees of internal cohesion and integration generate alternative strategic worlds and security and defense implications.

Western Europe. After the optimism of the late 1980s and early 1990s that accompanied the successful completion of the Single European Market, the Maastricht treaty, and the collapse of Communism, Western Europe entered a period of economic and political uncertainty. The difficulties encountered in 1992–1993 in ratifying the Maastricht treaty revealed widespread popular skepticism about a united Europe, and progress toward integration has slowed. Europe's failure to deal with the crisis in the former Yugoslavia has damaged morale at both the elite and the popular levels, as has the persistence of high unemployment. Moreover, the ability of Western Europe to deal with the pressing problems on its agenda has been undermined by weak and unpopular political leadership in many countries. Against this background, the policy agenda of the EU and its member states will be dominated for the next several years by three issues: (1) completing EMU; (2) enlargement to include Central and Eastern Europe; and (3) institutional reform aimed at strengthening the Union's ability to function with a larger and more diverse membership as well as bolstering its external identity and its ability to pursue an effective Common Foreign and Security Policy (CFSP).

Although it is unlikely that a majority of member states will meet all of the Maastricht criteria, the most probable outcome is that EMU will go forward as scheduled. Governments have repeatedly reiterated their commitment to the timetable, and detailed technical preparations are being made by central banks, finance ministries, and the European Monetary Institute—the Frankfurt-based precursor to the European Central Bank. Acceptance of the inevitability of EMU is growing in business and banking circles, and the international bond and foreign exchange markets are increasingly behaving as if EMU will go forward. Despite initial German and Dutch preferences for an EMU with a hard core of six to seven members, France, Italy, and the other Mediterranean countries have lobbied intensively for the inclusion, from the start, of Spain and Italy. Moreover, Italy, Spain, and Portugal have done somewhat better in meeting the convergence criteria than many governmental and private experts predicted in the early 1990s, while Germany has had greater difficulty in doing so than was anticipated. The result of these trends could be a broader and possibly weaker monetary union with as many as 11 initial members. The United Kingdom, Denmark, Sweden, and Greece are not expected to join the single currency when it is launched in 1999, but they will be linked to it through the European Exchange Rate Mechanism (ERM), and may join within a period of several years. While establishment of EMU in 1999 appears to be the most likely outcome, an alternative scenario would see a breakdown of the political will or means to carry through with the project, most likely in France. This would be followed by a shelving of the enterprise, although this in turn would be followed by damage-limiting actions by governments to try to ensure that failure of EMU does not result in the kind of negative spillovers for European integration in general that have been predicted by some of EMU's most ardent proponents.

The second major issue on the agenda of the Union is enlargement. The fundamental question of *whether* to enlarge was resolved at the June 1993 Copenhagen summit, at which the European Council decided that the Union would admit all those "associated countries" from Central and Eastern Europe that were "able to assume the obligations of membership by satisfying the economic and political conditions required."[19] Associated countries were defined as those countries with which the Union had concluded or planned to conclude "Europe Agreements." The current list of such countries includes the CEEC-10, whose economic performance was discussed above. In addition, Cyprus is a candidate to join the Union, having submitted its application in 1990. Given the requirement that accession negotiations can begin only six months after completion of the Intergovernmental Conference (IGC), it is likely that the initial candidates for membership will be selected sometime in the second half of 1997. Accession negotiations could be formally launched in December 1997 and begin in earnest in early 1998. The decisions to

---

[19]Commission of the European Communities, *The European Councils: Conclusions of the Presidency 1992–1994*, Luxembourg: CEC, 1995, p. 86.

begin negotiations and to finalize accession agreements are ultimately political and will require the approval of national governments, parliaments, and the European Parliament; much, therefore, can go wrong. If developments proceed as planned, however, the first new members are likely to join the Union in the 2002–2005 period.

The potential long-term implications of the EU's 1993 decisions regarding enlargement are far-reaching. The Copenhagen decision *in principle* settled a debate about the future architecture of Europe that had simmered in Europe since the fall of the Berlin Wall and throughout the early 1990s. On one side, there were those who preferred little or no widening of the existing EU. In their view, Europe should be organized in a set of concentric circles, with the EU at the core, a grouping of European Free Trade Association (EFTA) and Central European states in a second circle linked to but not part of the Union, and a more distant circle comprised of Russia and the NIS. On the other side, there were those who favored a rapid widening of the EU to include the EFTA countries, Central and Eastern Europe, and perhaps even Russia, Ukraine, and other NIS. The EU would then be a "wider," looser free-trade arrangement, which might avoid drawing sharp lines through any part of Europe that would exclude some countries while including others. The decision to take a middle course—to offer membership to all of the countries of Central, Eastern, and Southeastern Europe (the Baltic states included) but to rule out membership for Russia and the other NIS (and implicitly Turkey)—reflected strong German preferences and will have important strategic implications. In principle, it means that Europe is headed toward a situation in which there will be two main centers of power on the continent—the EU in the west, center, and southeast, and Russia in the east, with Turkey left in a complex position of association with the EU, coexistence with Russia, and historic and religious linkage with the Middle East.

In practice, of course, the strategic landscape in Europe will be determined by the actual pace and character of enlargement as much as by its theoretical possibility. While all of the Associated States of the EU are formally on track for membership, there is no guarantee that all (or indeed any) of the applicants will make it, and there is a very real possibility that membership for some countries could be deferred until well into the next century. If this is the case, the nature of the relationship between the new "ins" and the "outs" (and between the "outs" and Russia and the other NIS) will be an important factor in European and Atlantic politics. EU expansion most likely will be preceded by several years by the expansion of NATO to include Poland, the Czech Republic, and Hungary, followed perhaps by Romania, Slovakia, Slovenia, and other countries. As in the case of the EU, however, NATO is unlikely to expand soon to all of the countries between the current eastern border of the alliance and the western borders of Russia. This limited reach of NATO will leave a "gray zone" in Europe that, depending upon circumstances and developments, could have important implications for U.S. strategy and defense planning as well as for the EU's relations with its eastern periphery.

The third major issue on the EU agenda is institutional reform, the subject of the 1996–1997 IGC. While federalists such as Chancellor Kohl initially approached the 1996 IGC as an opportunity to recoup some of the ground that was not covered at Maastricht—to strengthen the political powers of the Union, to create an effective CFSP, and to overcome the "democratic deficit" by providing for greater direct involvement of the citizens in EU affairs—the hoped-for institutional and constitutional leap forward did not occur at the IGC, given active opposition by Britain and lukewarm support in other member states. The treaty revisions of the June 1997 Amsterdam summit provided for some enhancement of supranational Community competences, particularly in the economic sphere, coupled with a continuing reliance on intergovernmentalism in key areas. Cooperation in justice and home affairs was increased, and there was explicit recognition of the possibility of resorting to "variable geometry" or "reinforced solidarity,"—joint actions, policies, and even institutional arrangements among subsets of EU member-states that wish to proceed faster and further with integration in particular areas than their fellow members.[20]

The near- and medium-term outlook thus is for the European Union to look rather similar to the EU of today, albeit with some important

---

[20] *Intergovernmental Conference 1996: Commission Report for the Reflection Group,* Brussels: European Commission, 1995; *Final Report from the Chairman of the Reflection Group on the 1996 Intergovernmental Conference,* Brussels: European Commission, 1995.

changes. The single European currency will be a reality, shared by as many as 11 member states, but creation of the currency will not in itself lead to major progress in political integration or to a more assertive European Union on the world scene—at least not in this time frame. Politics in Europe will remain somewhat inward oriented as governments seek to ensure that EMU is successful and to deal with other issues on the European agenda. There will be some strengthening of EU institutions and of the WEU, but no decisive breakthrough to a federal Europe. EU enlargement will not have occurred, but it will be on track for Poland, the Czech Republic, and possibly other countries for the 2002–2004 time frame. CFSP will be strengthened somewhat, with an upgrading of selected EU competences and of the role of the WEU, but little progress will have been made on a European "defense identity." Europe will continue to depend on NATO and the United States for its security. Western Europe will have made some progress in dealing with its structural economic problems, but it will remain a relatively weak economic actor in some respects, internally preoccupied with reform of the welfare state, unemployment, and other issues.

Looking further down the road, broad uncertainties arise that make it difficult to determine the ultimate limits of the European enterprise. While federalist sentiment appears to have peaked in the early 1990s, this does not mean that the integrationist impulse will not revive at some point or that Europe will never achieve a decisive breakthrough to political and strategic union. At the same time, leading European officials and commentators have warned against a deep crisis in the Union that could lead to an unraveling of many elements of integration and cooperation that now exist, followed by "renationalization" and a slide into rivalry and conflict reminiscent of the 1930s. In all probability, Western Europe will steer a middle course between these extremes, but the process of integration is uncertain enough to preclude dismissing outcomes at either end of the spectrum: creation of a federal, European superstate, *or* disintegration and renationalization, with the EU becoming little more than a forum for loose intergovernmental cooperation.

In the event that the more pessimistic projections about the EU turn out to be correct and that it either muddles along in its current state or even drifts back toward renationalization, a key question will be whether Germany, as the strongest power in Europe and the one most committed to integration in some form, might take the lead in fashioning an alternative to the current pattern of integration, focusing on a core Europe that might develop under the umbrella of the EU, but that would be held together by close economic, industrial, monetary, and political ties. The economic, political, and cultural center of Europe has shifted northeastward with the reunification of Germany and the accession of Sweden, Finland, and Austria to the EU, and German influence in Europe will be enhanced even further by trends in trade and investment even short of formal enlargement to the east. As German firms seek to improve their global competitiveness, they increasingly will outsource production of components (as well as higher value-added functions) to lower-cost regions along Germany's borders. The European economy thus will be dominated by a powerful trade and production bloc with Germany, the Visegrad countries, Austria, Switzerland, the Benelux countries, eastern France, northern Italy and Slovenia and Croatia at the core; and the rest of southern and eastern Europe, the UK, and Scandinavia at the margins. With its central economic position, Germany would be well placed to exercise political leadership in a faltering Europe.

Apart from the level and nature of integration achieved in Western Europe, the future strategic environment and thus U.S. defense requirements will be shaped by Western Europe's orientation toward external powers. With regard to the United States, the key questions are likely to be the extent to which concepts such as partnership and enlargement are translated into concrete political guidance for defense planning. More specifically, these concepts will be shaped by both the breadth and the depth of the U.S.-European partnership— by how many countries eventually will be part of an Atlantic community and how far east U.S. Article 5 defense obligations will extend, as well as by the quality and scope of the Atlantic relationship and whether the concept of partnership will be limited to defense of Europe narrowly defined (as in Article 5), or will extend to joint military action in third areas such as the Middle East or indeed to cooperative global management in all spheres (economic, political, environmental, and so forth).[21]

---

[21]The outlines of a global partnership already exist in "The New Transatlantic Agenda" and the "Joint U.S.-EU Action Plan" that were signed in Madrid in December 1995, and that include various commitments on promoting peace, stability, and de-

Russia and the CIS. Just as it is necessary to look at the ultimate limits of the West European integration enterprise and their implications for the future geopolitical order, it is important to examine how far trends in the east might go, and specifically how successful Russia, alone or in combination with other states, might be in reestablishing the position of relative geopolitical strength that it enjoyed in the Soviet era. The main determinant of Russia's future weight as a strategic actor is likely to be the course of economic revival in Russia itself. A related factor will be the degree to which Russia manages to create a federation or confederation of states on the territory of the FSU. The latter factor will influence not only the quantity of resources that Russia brings to bear as an international actor, but the quality of Russia's domestic and foreign politics—whether it defines itself exclusively as the Russian nation-state, or whether it retains in some form the old Tsarist and Soviet imperial tradition with its distinctive approaches to international politics. The CIS countries remain heavily dependent on Russia for supplies of energy and other materials. Many, and especially Ukraine, have piled up huge unpaid debts to Russia for these supplies, especially as prices have moved to world market levels. In some cases Russia has suspended deliveries, leading to charges that political pressures are being exerted by Moscow. CIS countries have been allowed to clear up their debts to Russia by ceding controlling stakes in national firms in the energy and other sectors to Russian firms such as Gazprom.

Russian foreign policy continues to concentrate on what Russia officially calls its "near abroad" and is registering some success in achieving reintegration through the CIS. Russian objectives and policy towards the CIS were set forth in a presidential edict signed by Yeltsin in September 1995, "Strategic Policy of Russia Towards CIS Member States."[22] The document stated that the priority in Russian policy given to the CIS is the result of two factors: that vital Russian interests in the economy, defense, security, and protection of the rights of Russians are concentrated on the territory of the CIS; and,

---

velopment around the world and responding to global challenges. But these are political statements of intention rather than legal obligations to joint action.

[22]Presidential Edict No. 940, September 14, 1995; text in *Rossiyskaya Gazeta*, September 23, 1995, in *FBIS-SOV*, September 23, 1995.

significantly, that "effective cooperation with CIS states is a factor which counteracts centrifugal tendencies in Russia itself."

While Russia's official policy treats the CIS as a unit, in practical terms there are great differences among the member-states, and Russian policy can in some respects be seen as one of hub-and-spoke bilateralism, based on special relations with each country under the loose CIS umbrella. The CIS thus can be thought of as a loose set of concentric circles in which integration is proceeding unevenly. The innermost circle consists of Russia and Belarus, which in 1996 concluded a far-reaching economic and political agreement that, if fully implemented, will go quite far in the direction of abolishing Belarus as an independent state. A second circle of integration is comprised of Kazakhstan and the Kyrgyz Republic. In April 1996, these countries, along with Russia and Belarus, concluded an integration treaty that provided for the eventual establishment of a customs union, simplified procedures for the acquisition of citizenship for permanent residents from signatory countries, and harmonization and mutual recognition of legislation and standards. A third circle is made up of Azerbaijan, Armenia, Georgia, Tajikistan, and Uzbekistan. These countries have much looser relations with each other, but along with the four members of the customs union they are all parties to CIS collective security agreements and participate in CIS summits, ministerial meetings, and committees. Finally, there is an outermost circle that includes Ukraine, Moldova, and Turkmenistan. These countries are nominally members of the Commonwealth, but they are most protective of their economic and political independence. Their participation in CIS activities is highly selective. In the case of Ukraine and Moldova, they are also much more oriented toward other parts of Europe and especially the EU than the other CIS states.[23] Although the Russian government seems pleased with the

---

[23]While these four circles reflect different degrees of integration, there are also many exceptions and anomalies. Kazakhstan in particular is following a subtle policy under which it participates in many CIS integration schemes while carefully preserving its sovereignty and freedom of action. It is noteworthy, for example, that Kazakhstan was one of six CIS members—the others being Azerbaijan, Moldova, Turkmenistan, Uzbekistan, and Ukraine—that did not sign the July 1995 CIS external borders treaty, whereas Georgia, Armenia, and Tajikistan did sign. This is clearly an example of the evolving "variable geometry" in the CIS, in which states participate in different integration measures depending upon interest and ability. For the text, see "Treaty on Cooperation in the Protection of the Borders of the Participants in the Commonwealth

progress made in recent years toward closer integration, it does not necessarily follow that these developments presage a weakening of national independence leading to the reconstitution of something like the Soviet Union. The readiness of the Central Asian countries to cooperate more closely with Russia has gone hand-in-hand with the process of state-building in these countries, as increased national self-confidence and capability have made them less wary of working with Moscow on matters that they regard as in their own interest. Over the long term, Russian influence in this region would appear to be a waning asset. The future strategic environment thus is likely to be shaped by the emergence of the Central Asian states as increasingly important and largely independent actors on the European, Asian, and Middle Eastern political stages.

Turning toward the "far abroad," current Russian foreign policy is marked by the great-power assertiveness that was instituted by former Foreign Minister Andrei Kozyrev in response to nationalist pressures and disappointment with the Atlanticist approach. Much of this assertiveness is rhetoric rather than substance, given Russia's weakness and its concentration on the CIS, but some gains have been made. There are two major thrusts to this policy. The first, directed at Europe and the United States, is aimed at blocking, slowing, or otherwise attaching conditions to the expansion of NATO. The second is to reassert Russia's political and economic interests as a world and Asian power, and to strengthen ties with such traditional partners as Iraq, Iran, and India, as well as with long-standing rivals such as China and even Japan.

Apart from these tendencies in relations with particular regions and countries, economic considerations in general loom much larger in Russian foreign policy than was the case in the policies of the Soviet Union, which tended to weight political, military, and ideological considerations more highly than economic gains. On the one hand, a weak Russian economy and certain industries—in particular, armaments, nuclear energy, and space and civil aviation—need to penetrate foreign markets and to earn hard currency in order to survive in the post-Soviet environment. On the other hand, having lost or given up political, ideological, and military levers of influence that

---

of Independent States With States That Are Not Members of the Commonwealth," *Rossiyskaya Gazeta*, July 7, 1995, in *FBIS-SOV*, July 21, 1995.

were available to the Soviet Union, Russia looks to economic instruments in its efforts to maintain or expand its influence in other countries, particularly in the CIS and in Central and Eastern Europe.

Russia's current foreign policy, with its mix of great-power assertiveness and economic opportunism, of reflexive anti-Westernism and preoccupation with NATO expansion, does not add up to a coherent vision of Russia's place in the world. It is thus difficult to predict how Russia's orientation toward such key external actors as the United States, Western Europe, China, Japan, and Iran will evolve. Fundamentally, however, Russia will be compelled to adjust to its drastically reduced power position in the world—although in so doing it may be able to take advantage of certain opportunities that were *not* available to the Kremlin before 1991, owing to its relatively isolated position in world politics. In the future, Russia will be weaker than was the Soviet Union, but it may also be more integrated, economically and politically, into the global system.

The decline and ultimate disintegration of the Soviet Union coincided with and partly made possible a broader set of changes that included the reunification of Germany, the rollback of Russian influence in Central and Eastern Europe, and the enlargement of the European Union to Austria, Finland, and Sweden. These developments were not aimed at weakening Russia's position in Europe; they were more an effect than a cause of Russia's weakness. But having occurred, they will tend to perpetuate and reinforce that weakness. Not only is Russia smaller and weaker than was the former Soviet Union; it also faces an array of middle powers—Germany, Poland, and Turkey—whose relative power has increased with the end of the Cold War and that will constitute a partial counterweight to any revival of Russian power.

Thus, even under the unlikely assumption that all of Ukraine, Belarus, and the Baltic states were again brought under Russian control, Germany would remain united and a member of NATO and, as such, far less vulnerable to Russian pressure than West Germany was in the Cold War. Integration of Poland, the Czech Republic, Hungary, and other Central and Eastern Europe (CEE) states in NATO would further bolster the coalition of states arrayed against a resurgent Russia. At most, Russia could pose the kind of threat to Europe that it posed during periods of ascendancy before World War II, but not the geopolitical preponderance that it had from the end of World War II to the fall of the Berlin Wall.

At the same time, however, Russia has one advantage that the Soviet Union did not have—flexibility and regional diplomatic options. It has smaller capabilities and more modest ambitions, but it has, at least in theory, several broad alternative foreign policy courses that it could choose in the future. One course would be to define Russia in opposition to the West (the United States, Western Europe, and Japan), and to ally itself as closely as possible with Middle Eastern powers and/or with China, all of which have grievances of one sort or another with the West and would like to have more of a say in "writing the rules" that currently are very much the province of such Western-dominated institutions as the G-7,[24] the International Monetary Fund, the international development banks, and the World Trade Organization. An alternative option would be for Russia to reemphasize its European identity, and to seek close relations with Europe, partly as a way of hedging against the rising power of China and against surging instability from countries such as Iran. Even within the European option, Russia would face choices between a German/continental emphasis, and an emphasis on working with the United States in a broader Atlantic structure. These choices of foreign policy orientation, which are likely to play out in the coming years, would be associated with different economic orientations in Russia, and with different paths of development in the world economy.

Defense and Defense Industrial Trends

Western Europe. While European governments are pursuing long-term plans for bilateral, multilateral, and EU/WEU defense cooperation with the aim of making Europe a stronger and more self-sufficient military power, governments everywhere are cutting forces and capabilities in response to the end of the Cold War and the need to meet the Maastricht criteria on debt and deficit reduction. Europe is growing more—not less—dependent on the United States for the

---

[24]At the July 1997 Denver summit, the G-7 was expanded to include Russia. However, Russia was not admitted to the group of Western finance ministers. This arrangement sometimes is referred to as the "G-7-P [political]-8."

conduct of defense missions, particularly those that are "out of area." There is also growing concern about the parlous state of Europe's defense firms and much discussion of what can be done to strengthen their position against intensifying competition from huge U.S. firms that have emerged from the post–Cold War restructuring of U.S. industry. A key question for Europe's future strategic environment is whether these trends are short-term phenomena that will be reversed once EMU is in place, or whether Western Europe will continue to decline as a military factor, thereby increasing dependence on the United States as well as creating an opportunity for even a severely weakened Russia to assert a status as the continent's leading military power.

Defense Capability. Germany, the largest military power in Western Europe, has cut manpower and equipment levels in response to budgetary pressures, the financial burdens associated with German reunification, and the challenge of meeting the EMU convergence criteria. But Germany retains a long-term commitment to continental defense, and is the only country (besides Finland) in Western Europe that does not intend to abolish conscription. Germany also has resolved the paralyzing internal debate over participation in out-of-area missions and is developing modest capabilities for such missions. But Germany is primarily committed to maintaining a large army with mobilizable reserves (a total force of 750,000 is to be available) for continental defense.

France is attempting the same task in the defense realm as Germany: coping with short-term cuts and restructuring its forces to provide more usable and flexible capabilities for the future. In the absence of any immediate threat to its security, France is attempting to position itself for the long term. It intends to reduce its defense forces by 25 percent—from 577,000 to 434,000—by the year 2002. The army will be reorganized, because the French Ministry of Defense intends to have a force that will be capable of dealing simultaneously with two scenarios: the first described as a "major commitment" within the framework of the Atlantic alliance or the WEU, the second for lesser contingencies—not specified but most likely peacekeeping or peace enforcement missions—that would entail the deployment of 35,000 men in one major and one minor theater. The smaller continental countries and the UK all are coping with challenges similar to those facing the French and the Germans: downsizing forces, in some cases eliminating conscription, and restructuring to cope with expected out-of-area missions such as peacekeeping and disaster relief.

Apart from the current restructuring, there is the question of to what extent Western Europe will take part in the "revolution in military affairs" (RMA) that defense analysts and policymakers believe is under way, and whether failure to participate fully in this revolution could further widen the military gap between Western Europe and future military allies or competitors. Many of the reforms in the West European defense sector, such as the move to smaller, more professional forces, modernization of force structure, and increased investment in intelligence-gathering and precision-strike systems, could speed the adaptation to RMA. The European Union and various national governments also have devoted massive attention (albeit so far with mixed results) to fostering leading-edge commercial technologies that are relevant to RMA. On balance, however, Western Europe is just beginning to think about these revolutionary developments, and the near-term outlook is for a continued widening in the gap between U.S. and European capabilities.

The general outlook for the defense sector over the next several years is for continued declines and for an overall increasing level of dependence on the United States. Western Europe's ability to make a meaningful contribution to a major regional contingency (e.g., in the Persian Gulf), will decline, as will even the ability to take on or sustain less-demanding peacemaking or peacekeeping missions. There are influences working in the opposite direction—namely, the restructuring of the French forces and the lifting of constitutional constraints on Germany's ability to deploy outside the NATO area—but these influences will translate only gradually into enhanced capability.

While the near-term outlook in Western Europe is one of continued decline, the political, institutional, and even to an extent the physical elements of a stronger and more independent defense capability are being established. Many European collaborative initiatives are already under way, such as the Eurocorps and EURMARFOR. Headquartered at Strasbourg, the Eurocorps consists of one French and one German division, the Franco-German brigade, and smaller units from Belgium, Spain, and Luxembourg. EURMARFOR is a standing WEU naval force that was activated in October 1995. It consists of units ranging from single ships to naval-air and amphibious task forces from Spain, France, Italy, and Portugal, and is intended for humanitarian assistance, peacekeeping, and crisis response in the Mediterranean area. Over time, these cooperative ventures might result in the establishment of a large and capable European force, such as the 300,000-man force proposed by French Prime Minister Alain Juppé in early 1996, to be based on the contribution of 50,000 troops by each of the major West European states. This force would be integrated into NATO, but it would also be capable of acting on its own in regional contingencies. Juppé's proposal is unlikely to be implemented soon, but it has a logic that could prove attractive in the future, based as it is on intergovernmental cooperation among the major middle powers of Western Europe, all of whom have a long military tradition and who could in principle combine to create an effective force of this size.

Nuclear Deterrence. The next few years are not likely to see major changes in the role of independent nuclear deterrent forces in Europe. Indeed, perhaps the most remarkable feature of the current scene is a level of stability that might not have been expected several years ago, given the geopolitical upheavals that have occurred and the enhanced importance that nuclear weapons might be expected to play in a world characterized by greater multipolarity. An important background development has been the success of efforts, led by the United States, to ensure that following the breakup of the USSR, Ukraine, Belarus, and Kazakhstan transferred "their" nuclear weapons to Russia, which became the sole successor to the Soviet Union as a nuclear power. Another indication as well as a further guarantee of stability was the agreement by all European nonnuclear states, including united Germany, to the indefinite extension of the NPT at the 1995 review conference. On the other hand, France under Chirac has reaffirmed its status as a nuclear power, even though it announced the dismantling of its land-based nuclear missiles and its decision not to build a fifth new nuclear submarine.

Although the current situation is marked by stability, the geopolitical changes in Europe since 1989 and the ongoing process of developing a European defense identity most likely will raise the question, sooner or later, of a European nuclear deterrent. The leading West European powers have always held open the possibility of a European nuclear force, even though this led to considerable strain with the United States in the 1960s, when the NPT was under negotiation. President Chirac has renewed a French offer going back to the 1980s for a "joint deterrent" with Germany and the other EU states in a "joint strategic space."

Concrete steps towards Europeanization might include intensification of the work of the Franco-British Joint Commission on Nuclear Policy and Doctrine that was permanently established in July 1993, or the possible association in some way of Germany with the work of the Commission. Radical change, however, such as German control over nuclear weapons or even Franco-British cooperation going significantly beyond the sharing of information is unlikely in the next several years.

Defense Industry. The defense industry in Western Europe is frequently described as threatened and in crisis. Defense spending, employment, expenditures on R&D, and exports all have fallen since the early 1990s. A number of responses to this situation are being discussed—action at the EU level, multilateral arrangements among selected countries, cross-border mergers, acquisitions, and joint ventures at the firm level. Germany continues its course of the last decade in working to build up a world-class aerospace firm under the wing of Daimler-Benz. In the United Kingdom, British Aerospace and General Electric Corporation (GEC) are market-oriented firms with a strong European and international orientation. So far, however, the development of strong, commercially driven pan-European defense firms has been hindered by state ownership of firms and the reluctance of governments, especially in France and Italy, to privatize and to allow foreign investment in the defense industry.

At the European level, the defense industry was exempted from the Treaty of Rome establishing the European Economic Community (EEC). The European Commission has proposed, in 1990 and again in 1995 in connection with the IGC, that the Union's common external tariff and its rules on competition and procurement be extended to the defense industry sector. Such a move could have important negative implications for transatlantic defense trade, but it is unlikely to happen soon, because it would also limit the ability of member-state governments to favor private or state-owned firms through state subsidies and captive markets. In the absence of a consensus on "communitizing" European defense industrial cooperation, France and Germany agreed to establish a Franco-German armaments agency. The agency became fully operational at the end of 1996, with Britain, Spain, and Italy also joining as charter members. The agency eventually could fall under the umbrella of the WEU or the EU. At the firm level, cross-border mergers and acquisitions in Europe have long been blocked by national considerations and complex ownership arrangements, but industry restructuring is now beginning under market and economic pressures.

Whether a cohesive European industry arises remains to be seen, however. France and Britain have entirely different outlooks and traditions regarding defense production, with Britain relying much more on ties with the United States and open competition, whereas France has systematically favored a "national champion" approach to defense production and now increasingly opts for a "European champion" approach as the most feasible alternative. Germany occupies a position somewhere between France and Britain—more reliant on market forces and cooperation than France, but also open to French arguments regarding the need to create European alternatives. Equally important, low budgets and procurement levels limit the speed at which consolidation and restructuring, irrespective of how they occur, can lead to a stronger and more competitive industry.

Russia and the CIS. Militarily, Russia remains weak and is unlikely in the short-to-medium term to pose an offensive threat to other European countries—with the notable exception of the Baltics. Its armed forces are currently underfunded and understaffed. Draft evasion is rampant, and officers of all ranks are leaving the armed forces in large numbers. Those who remain have suffered a severe drop in status and standard of living and often are reduced to carrying out tasks formerly assigned to enlisted men. Procurement for most categories of weapons has fallen to zero or near-zero levels, and the technological gap between Russia and the advanced Western countries, above all the United States, clearly is widening.[25] The Russian military is attempting to remedy these deficiencies, focusing on

---

[25]See Benjamin S. Lambeth, "Russia's Wounded Military," *Foreign Affairs*, Vol. 74, No. 2, 1995, pp. 86–98.

creating smaller but better and more usable forces, but is severely hampered by low budgets and poor overall economic conditions.

In defense as in foreign policy, Russia draws a distinction between what it calls its "near abroad" and its "far abroad," and at least for now is focusing on the former. Russian national security policy places a heavy emphasis on defense integration in the CIS, even though, as has been seen, several key members do not participate in the CIS's military activities. According to the Russian draft national security policy document issued in early 1996, "the Russian Federation is committed to the idea of creating a collective security system in the CIS unified military-strategic area that is based on the Collective Security Treaty of 15 May 1992 as well as on bilateral agreements with CIS countries."[26] At the February 1995 session of the CIS Council of Heads of State and Government in Almaty, Azerbaijan, Armenia, Belarus, Georgia, Kazakhstan, the Kyrgyz Republic, Tajikistan, Uzbekistan, and Russia adopted two agreements intended to build upon and concretize the obligations contained in the May 1992 treaty. They agreed to joint defense planning and the coordinated control of external borders.[27] They also adopted a three-stage plan for the creation of a full-fledged collective security system.

Much of what has been concluded at CIS meetings on defense can be discounted as rhetoric. Nonetheless, the Russian military presence throughout the CIS is increasing. In 1995, Georgia reversed nearly five years of post-independence policy and informed Russia that it would be willing to allow Russia to base forces on its territory for 25 years in exchange for Russian help in regaining control over the separatist regions of Abkhazia and South Ossetia. Azerbaijan so far has turned down Russian requests for military bases on its territory, but it could change this policy in return for Russian help in regaining at least nominal control over Nagorno-Karabakh, now effectively controlled by Armenia. In the Transcaucasus, Russia has four military bases in Georgia and one in Armenia.

---

[26]See the "Military Policy" section (one of seven), in the draft document on military policy, which appeared in the military supplement to *Nezavisimaya Gazeta*, April 25, 1996, in *FBIS-SOV*, April 26, 1996.

[27]The Tajik-Afghan border is already protected by troops from Kazakhstan, the Kyrgyz Republic, Uzbekistan, Russia, and Tajikistan.

Russian thinking about defense issues as they relate to the "far abroad" is less developed and reflects the dilemmas faced by a country adjusting to loss of global superpower status and not used to defining its security needs in terms of localized, individual threats. The official military doctrine of the Russian Federation no longer identifies particular countries or groups of countries as posing a threat of direct physical attack. The "Basic Provisions of Military Doctrine of the Russian Federation" was signed into law by President Yeltsin in November 1993, one month after he disbanded the Supreme Soviet with the support of the armed forces. This document declared that Russia would "not regard any state as an adversary" and that ensuring Russia's military security and vital interests depends above all on developing close relations with other states and on the further development of a stable international order. This declaration was a shift from the previous defense doctrine, which implicitly singled out the United States and NATO under the label of "some states and coalitions" that wished to dominate the world.[28] The Basic Provisions also formalized the shift in Russian doctrine to an embrace of nuclear deterrence. This shift reflected an assessment, based on Russia's changed geopolitical and economic circumstances, that a highly demanding nuclear warfighting posture as well as reliance on conventional means to meet conventional threats (both of which had been elements of Soviet military doctrine) no longer were viable.

Notwithstanding official doctrine, Russian military planners and political leaders do not exclude the possibility of conflict with the countries of the "far abroad." Border clashes between Russia and Turkey or China cannot be ruled out, and Russian forces operating in Tajikistan may come into conflict with guerrillas operating from Afghanistan in support of the Tajik opposition. Over the long term, Russia could be especially vulnerable to pressure from China.

Operating against a background of severe resource constraints, the Russian military now is trying to build a force for the future. The total Russian military force is projected at approximately 1.5 million men for all forces, including the army, navy, air force, and strategic rocket forces. Russian military planners envision development of a

---

[28]See texts in *Rossiyskaya Gazeta,* May 18, 1996; *ITAR-TASS,* May 16, 1996.

three-tiered military structure, consisting of mobile forces for rapid reaction, ready forces for a major regional contingency, and large, less-ready, but mobilizable forces.[29]

The Russian air force is facing major problems of block obsolescence and has several new aircraft models in development, including the MiG-33 and the Su-35. Despite the heavy emphasis on upgrading quality and technology, it is unlikely that Russia will go forward with the development of a fifth-generation fighter aircraft. The Russian air force has stated that it wants a new fighter and has stressed the growing importance of stealth technology and Russia's need to incorporate this technology into its forces. But competing priorities in the defense establishment as well as the overall shortage of money in the defense budget probably ensure that the Russian forces will not be receiving a new generation of aircraft soon.[30]

The Russian defense industry has fallen on difficult times, as a result of low procurement, shrinking budgets, and the loss of markets in the former Warsaw Pact. The breakup of the Soviet Union also affected the arms production industry—many factories in Russia were dependent upon parts and components from Ukraine and elsewhere. Maintaining these supply relationships has become a focus of cooperation in the CIS.

For the next few years, Russia will continue to look to every possible export market as a way of trying to compensate for these domestic difficulties. But these are stop-gap measures to compensate for collapsing internal demand. Russia's position as a major supplier of the most advanced conventional weaponry has in fact weakened from what it was in the 1970s and 1980s and is destined to weaken further as the technological gap with the West widens.

Moreover, in the near term, Russia lacks the wherewithal to participate in the revolution in military affairs said to be under way. Over the long term, however, Russia is probably better positioned than was the Soviet Union to participate in this revolution because its

---

[29]This discussion is based on Richard Kugler, *Enlarging NATO: The Russia Factor*, Santa Monica, CA: RAND, MR-690-OSD, 1996, pp. 139–156.

[30]For further discussion, see Benjamin Lambeth, *Russia's Air Power at the Crossroads*, Santa Monica, CA: RAND, MR-623-AF, 1996, especially pp. 235–257.

overriding long-term priority is the development of its economy on the commercial side as well as full integration into the broader international economy.

The only other country within the CIS with ambitions to create a sizable military force operating independently of Russia is Ukraine. Kiev appears to be aiming at a total force of some 13 divisions and 500 combat aircraft—about one-third to a quarter of the size of Russia's overall force. With a force of this size (leaving aside the nuclear factor), Ukraine would be far weaker than Russia. However, it would have a much better chance of standing up to one of Russia's mobile forces in the event that Russia needed to deploy forces for other contingencies, perhaps in the Far East, the Baltics, or the Middle East. Conversely, Ukraine's position relative to Russia would weaken were Russia able to mobilize support from other CIS states such as Belarus or Moldova.

Other

In addition to the major drivers discussed in this chapter, developments in several other areas could influence the long-term strategic environment.

The Role of the State and of Nonstate Actors. Many observers of international politics have argued that the role of the nation-state in the international system is changing, and that the rise of nonstate actors such as multinational corporations, international organizations, transnational criminal organizations, and issue-based transnational nongovernmental organizations is challenging the state's traditional dominance in security and international affairs.[31] Long-term trends could shape the strategic environment in Europe and elsewhere, and influence the kind of conflict scenarios that arise and the behavior of actors, including states, in these scenarios.

The Environment. Environmental concerns have been a major political factor in Western Europe since the emergence of the Green parties in the late 1970s. In Central and Eastern Europe and the FSU,

---

[31]For a survey of the relevant arguments, see Stephen J. Del Rosso Jr., "The Insecure State: Reflections on 'the State' and 'Security' in a Changing World," *What Future for the State? Daedalus*, Vol. 124, No. 2, Spring 1995.

the collapse of Communism revealed unexpectedly severe levels of environmental damage, and lent urgency to collective efforts by the West to address environmental problems as part of the overall process of overcoming the division of Europe.

Objectively, environmental factors will have many long-term effects in Europe, but the very slowness of these effects should allow for gradual adjustment. Economic growth is likely to be slower than it might otherwise be as a result of environmental degradation and of efforts to deal with environmental problems by policy, but Western Europe will not be affected by the kinds of ecological disasters that have devastated parts of the Middle East and Africa. In some of the countries of Central Asia, however, economic growth and political stability may be fundamentally undermined by festering environmental problems.

Technology. Identifying long-term technology trends and their social, economic, political, and strategic implications is notoriously difficult. Key trends and developments in this area could include new information technology applications that will increase the already extensive interdependence of European societies (perhaps accelerating the closure of the economic and cultural gap between the eastern and western parts of Europe), but also create new vulnerabilities, as in the possibilities for computer and "cybercash" fraud and information warfare. Developments in energy, such as the widespread introduction of electric cars, could transform large sectors of the European economy. New developments in biotechnology and more advanced medical technologies will contribute to increased life expectancy in European societies. Technological advancements could expedite the continuing revolution in military affairs.

ALTERNATIVE STRATEGIC WORLDS

The Building Blocks

The building blocks of our six alternative strategic worlds, to be discussed later in this section, consist of four alternative scenarios for Western Europe and the EU as well as four alternative scenarios for Russia and the NIS.

Western Europe and the EU. As has been seen earlier in this chapter, the future strategic landscape in Europe will be shaped by a range of interacting economic, demographic, and political trends. Drawing upon the previous analysis, it is possible to develop four alternative scenarios for Western Europe and the EU over the relevant time horizon: (1) Eurofederalist Success, (2) Failed Integration/Renationalization, (3) German Alternative, and (4) Muddling Along.

Eurofederalist Success. This outcome would represent the fulfillment of the federalist aspiration and would be a logical consequence of the integration trends discussed above, provided they were to continue and to cumulate over the course of the next several decades. Europe would have achieved economic and monetary union and would act as a single force in international economic and monetary forums. Another aspect of the Eurofederalist Success would be the development of a common foreign and security/defense policy and the institutions and capabilities to carry it out. A European army would function much as U.S. forces did in earlier periods of U.S. history, with units organized at the state level but available to be "federalized" and placed under the command of the central political authority. European arms production and military R&D would be directed by a single supranational authority analogous to the U.S. Department of Defense and with comparable budgetary authority.

More generally, Europe will have created a powerful set of supranational institutions. The European Parliament would have evolved into a directly elected lower chamber with full legislative powers in the Union and the Council of Ministers into an upper chamber, analogous to the Senate in the early years of the United States. National governments would function in ways similar to U.S. state or Canadian provincial governments, exercising the primary role in such areas as education, welfare, and criminal justice, but leaving macroeconomic affairs, foreign and defense policy, and certain other matters to the "federal" level. Decisionmaking on the federal budget, the use of force overseas, and other issues probably would be cumbersome and time-consuming, but perhaps not significantly more so than in the United States, which even today has difficulty in reaching national consensus on the same issues.

The EU will have been enlarged to include an additional 12 members. Its population is thus approximately 50 percent larger than that of the United States, its GDP some 40 percent larger. Europe in the Eurofederalist Success scenario would still confront problems such as unemployment and rising dependency ratios, but widening and deepening of the European enterprise on this scale presupposes—and in turn would make more feasible—energetic efforts on the part of governments, the EU's central institutions, and the private sector to address many of these internal problems.

Failed Integration. At the other extreme, one could project a "failed Europe" that had not succeeded in carrying any of the integration trends discussed above very far, much less to their logical ends. It will have failed to achieve Economic and Monetary Union. This failure would be accompanied by a renationalization of economic policy and a partial unraveling of the Single European Market. Under Failed Integration, Europe would not have a strong CFSP. Europe's military capabilities would be at a low level, owing to declining budgets and fragmented national efforts. Europe would have failed to reform its institutions to permit coherent and decisive policymaking. Decisionmaking processes would be blocked by the need for unanimity or superqualified majorities. Citizens would identify almost exclusively with their nation-state and little with Europe as a whole, in turn precluding compromise on the basis of appeal to broad European interests.

Europe most likely would not be able to forge the political consensus to tackle internal economic problems. Political deadlocks and fights over resources would preclude extensive enlargement to Central and Eastern Europe. A few countries might make it into the EU, but the Union would decline responsibility for the CEE region as a whole and for the Balkans. The EU thus would be faced with an unstable third region between itself and Russia, which would have enhanced opportunities to expand its role in the region. Western Europe might be more responsive to the United States on some issues than in some of the other scenarios, but Western Europe would be neither a strong rival nor a strong partner on global or regional issues.

German Alternative. An important variable in a "failed Europe" would be the policies and attitudes of key nation-states, especially of Germany. A Germany beset with a weak political leadership, high unemployment, and general problems of competitiveness could drift along in such an order—relying upon American guarantees and Russian weakness for its security, concentrating on domestic economic and other problems, and pursuing friendly but essentially directionless policies toward other European states. Over time, trends in demography and economics would result in Germany's eventual fading away as a major power.

Alternatively, Germany could pursue a dynamic policy, using the weaknesses of a "failed Europe" to pursue national goals and to multiply its own economic, demographic, political, and industrial weight in pursuit of domestic objectives or of economic or strategic competition with other powers and in the overall global economy. In the German Alternative to Failed Integration, Germany would organize a tight economic and political bloc in Central Europe with Germany at its core. Political management of such a bloc would be intergovernmental or even informal, but would depend upon Berlin having a strong voice in the policies of all of the countries on its periphery. Economically, the region would be tightly integrated through extensive transportation and communication linkages, and networks of investment and subcontracting in which German firms are the major players. Bolstered by its position in Central Europe, Germany would deal on an equal basis, either as a partner or a rival, with Russia, and would have extensive economic interests in Ukraine and other NIS.

Muddling Along. A final possible building block—the more likely the shorter the time horizon—would be characterized by continued temporizing and muddling along. The EU would not have moved decisively toward either federalism or renationalization, but would continue to operate with a complex mix of intergovernmental and supranational mechanisms. "Success" or "failure" in meeting Europe's most ambitious agenda items—EMU, enlargement, creation of an effective CFSP entailing an autonomous defense capability—would be blurred either through temporizing (pushing some of these goals into the future with processes in place to give at least an impression of progress toward meeting them) or through subregional arrangements (shifting subgroups of countries that would work together in particular areas—for example, defense or monetary union—in accordance with the concepts of flexibility and variable geometry, without significantly strengthening the Union as such).

Germany would be a major player in the Muddling Along scenario, but bargaining among the major European states rather than decisive leadership from any quarter (Berlin or Brussels) would be the norm.

Russia and the NIS. For Russia and the NIS, depending upon how the various trends discussed above play out, four alternative orders also are possible: (1) Reconstituted Union, (2) Muddling Along, (3) Dynamic Russia, and (4) Sick Man of Eurasia.

Reconstituted Union. Reconstitution of the Soviet Union is improbable but is part of the program of a number of political groups in Russia. Reconstruction could come about only as a result of major upheavals in Ukraine and other European countries. A "Soviet" entity would probably have poor relations with the rest of Europe, as it would constitute a threat to Poland and other states on its western border. The existence of a prosperous Western Europe would exert a pull on Ukraine and elsewhere and would promote instability. Internally, such a union would almost certainly be authoritarian, although a totalitarian ideology such as Leninism would not need to be restored. Economically, such an entity could be stronger and more dynamic than was the Soviet Union, particularly if it were based upon a combination of free enterprise in agriculture, services, and small business and large, semi-private firms having close ties to the state. These industrial groups could participate in the international economy, reaping the benefits of controlled competition, technology transfer, and direct investment that were not available to the USSR.

A variant to this scenario is one in which Russia manages to recreate something like the Soviet Union under the umbrella of the CIS, but without the westernmost edges of the former Soviet Union—that is, those regions that are economically and culturally closest to Western and Central Europe. The leading candidates for exclusion would be the three Baltic states and Moldova, as well as western Ukraine. Depending upon circumstances in Russia and Ukraine, Ukraine could manage to stay independent of a reconstituted union while maintaining its present borders. Alternatively, Ukraine could split, with the east and the Crimea reabsorbed into a Russian sphere and the remainder of the country remaining independent and gravitating toward Poland and the rest of Europe. In yet another variant, Russia's power could be reconstituted in a Slavic/Orthodox Union. In this variant, language, ethnicity, and religion are the dominant factors. Russia manages to reconstitute a large part of the former Soviet Union into a new political entity, but along what might be called cultural or civilizational rather than economic lines. Belarus, Ukraine (or at least those parts of Ukraine that are Orthodox rather than Uniate), and those parts of Kazakhstan and Moldova that are populated by Russians are returned to the Russian fold, while the Central Asian and Transcaucasus countries drift away from Russia and toward Asian and Middle Eastern powers. Such a scenario would most likely occur in a world characterized by a "clash of civilizations" and in which Orthodoxy was regarded and came to regard itself as a separate civilization.

Muddling Along. Another possibility is that Russia will continue to muddle along, more or less as at present. Economic growth would be slow, but not slow enough to trigger upheaval among the population. Some Russian firms and industries would prosper and would carve out growing export markets and even international presences, but this prosperity would occur against a backdrop of extremely uneven overall economic performance. Crime and corruption would be rampant, but would operate in a symbiotic relationship with the legal economy and the political system. Power would devolve to the regions, but without threatening the actual breakup of the country. A number of autonomous regions, Chechnya and Tatarstan, for example, would exercise de facto independence.

Russia might expand its influence in some of the smaller countries of the CIS, notably Belarus and the Caucasus, but two strategically significant trends—consolidation of the independence of Ukraine and the gradual recession of Russian influence in Central Asia—would continue. The Russian military would remain weak, preoccupied with the problems of low budgets, poor living conditions, and sporadic conflicts within Russia itself or on its periphery. Nonetheless, by concentrating its resources in selected areas, the military would remain a viable fighting force, with some ability to threaten both the "near abroad" and the "far abroad." Russia would have prickly but not fundamentally hostile relations with the United States and Western Europe, to which it would continue to look for economic assistance. Overall, Russia would resemble a large developing country before the takeoff stage, neither fully integrated with the West nor hostile to it, and heavily preoccupied with its own internal problems.

Dynamic Russia. The essential feature of this outcome would be a Russian "economic miracle," perhaps analogous to that which occurred in West Germany, Italy, and Japan in the 1950s and 1960s, or such as has occurred in the emerging markets of East Asia in recent years. With a stable political system, free markets, and abundant natural and human resources, Russia might begin an economic "takeoff" in the course of the next several years, and sustain 8–10 percent per annum GDP growth for a decade or more. A dynamic Russia might not have overtly hegemonic aspirations toward the countries on its periphery. Indeed, a focus on improved living standards, consumption, and investment by individuals and firms could direct attention away from international aspirations and could facilitate the normalization of Russia as a nation-state, much the way Japan, France, Turkey, and other countries redefined themselves in the period after empire. Nonetheless, a dynamic Russia inevitably would exercise a high degree of influence on its neighbors through trade and investment, particularly if some of these countries lagged Russia in economic performance.

Sick Man of Eurasia. This outcome represents the opposite of a Dynamic Russia and a sharp deterioration from Muddling Along. Economic and political reform would falter. Governments would be authoritarian but weak. Ethnic and regional secession movements would arise in various parts of the country, and the breakup of the Russian Federation would be threatened or could begin. There would be widespread social unrest and strikes, which in turn would worsen economic conditions. Corruption and crime would expand to epidemic proportions, threatening the very underpinnings of the economic and political systems. Environmental disasters and possible famine conditions in parts of the country would arise with growing frequency. Public health conditions would deteriorate, and there would be growing concern in Russia about a "national demographic disaster." Russia would be a weak power on the international scene, with no ability to project power outside its borders and little influence in international economic and political forums. Countries such as Ukraine, Moldova, and Belarus would define themselves in opposition to Russia, and would gravitate more than ever toward the economic and political sphere of the European

Union. The same trend would be seen in Central Asia and the Transcaucasus, where China, Iran, Turkey, and even Pakistan and India would supplant Russian influence.

The Alternatives

The future strategic order in Europe will be shaped by how each of the key subregions discussed above develops, and how these subregions interact with each other and with the rest of the world. Depending upon these factors, six such alternative strategic worlds could result: (1) Modified Cold War Order; (2) Atlantic Partnership; (3) European Bipolarity; (4) West European Dominance; (5) Rivalry and Fragmentation; and (6) Pan-European Order. The likelihood of each of these alternative orders emerging, over what time periods, and the defense and security implications of these orders for the United States are discussed below.

The present strategic order, it is important to note, is an amalgam of Modified Cold War Order (hence the insistence of the Central and East European countries on joining NATO as a hedge against Russia) and Pan-European Order (hence NATO's efforts to incorporate Russia into European security structures, even while enlarging against Russia's wishes). This amalgam contains inherent contradictions, and it is likely that events will push the strategic order more decisively toward one or the other of these worlds.

Modified Cold War Order. The essential elements of the Modified Cold War Order are, as in the past, a (relatively) weak Western Europe dependent on the United States, and a (relatively) strong Russia that poses a threat to her western neighbors. In such an outcome, Western Europe will have failed to unite to become a self-sufficient power capable of defending itself and its interests, while Russia, alone or in concert with some of the successor states to the USSR, reasserts itself as the strongest power on the continent—a state whose very size and capabilities constitute a threat-in-being to its western neighbors. In such an order, the United States presumably would retain or resume its role as a balance to Russian power in Europe.

Atlantic Partnership. This is a subvariant to the Modified Cold War Order. As in the latter, a militarily weak Western Europe faces a strong and potentially threatening grouping in the East dominated by Russia, which again calls for an American balancing role on the European continent, to deal with both the Russian threat and unstable conditions that are likely to persist in the Balkans and other parts of Central and Eastern Europe if a weak EU fails to integrate or otherwise fashion effective policies toward these regions. In the Atlantic Partnership order, however, the U.S. presence in Western Europe is based on an explicit bargain that takes account of U.S. commitments outside Europe and engages the West European allies in helping to meet these commitments in exchange for continued U.S. commitment to the defense of Europe and to peacekeeping and other missions in Europe.

European Bipolarity. In an alternative to Modified Cold War, Russia/CIS and Western Europe pursue separate and reasonably successful processes of political and economic integration (and develop the accompanying military forces and structures) to establish a rough bipolar balance on the continent. In such an order, the United States might retain a modest or token military presence on the continent, or it could find itself excluded or self-excluded from European affairs for a variety of reasons. The closest historical analogue to such an order would be the 1930s and selected periods in the 19th century, when Russia was one of the strongest continental powers, but was counterbalanced by one or more powers in Western Europe.

West European Dominance. This order would come about if Western Europe managed to create an integrated, presumably supranationally organized Europe, without a countervailing power emerging in Russia and the eastern part of the continent. This order would represent the reverse of the situation that occurred during the Cold War, and would in effect be a (presumably) benign version of the order that took shape in Europe in 1914–1917 and again in 1940–1942. Its essence would be a dynamic European Union or a continental bloc centered around Germany that would be much stronger than Russia.

Rivalry and Fragmentation. Another possible order that could emerge would be one in which Russia/CIS and Western Europe/EU both remain more or less fragmented, and neither is able to fashion itself into a coherent power center capable of providing order on the continent or of playing a decisive role in global strategic affairs. Such an order, which could be seen as an extrapolation of certain trends that are already evident in Europe, would be based upon and in turn could help to perpetuate the kinds of interstate national rivalries that characterized the European order before 1945. Such an order would represent a throwback to 19th century patterns, but with a crucial difference in context—namely, the globalization of international politics, the existence of non-European great powers, and the growing importance of inherently global issues such as immigration, environmental problems, terrorism, and others. Given these factors, intra-European rivalry might be peripheral to world politics rather than central, as was the case in the 19th century.

Pan-European Order. A final order would be a Pan-European one, analogous to the "Europe whole and free" proclaimed by President George Bush. Such an order would be based on a strong, integrated Western Europe, enlarged to include most of Central and Eastern Europe, having good relations with a democratic Russia that was driven chiefly by its own economic dynamism and that was not pursuing policies aimed at preserving or achieving Russian dominance in other countries of the FSU or in regions further afield. This order would come about as a result of a long process of marketization, democratization, and institution-building, the net result of which would be to relativize and negate virtually *all* dividing lines in Europe, including those between Russia and her neighbors.

Probabilities and Time Frames

As noted, the current strategic order in Europe can be characterized as approximating the Modified Cold War Order, albeit with a low level of threat and tendencies toward the Pan-European Order. Movement toward a different strategic order—or several such orders over successive time periods—is likely to occur as the post-Communist transition process is completed, and in response to the secular trends outlined earlier in this chapter.

Rivalry and Fragmentation is perhaps the least likely alternative, although it cannot be ruled out over the very long term—to 2025 and beyond. In the short to medium term, it is difficult to see Western Europe entering an economic and political crisis so acute as to lead to a complete unraveling of the integration process started in the 1950s.

The Pan-European Order is perhaps somewhat more likely to be realized, albeit in the very long run. Certainly much political rhetoric and a number of new and traditional institutions—the Organization for Security and Cooperation in Europe (OSCE), the charter between Russia and an enlarged NATO—give concrete expression to the aspirations to such an order. In the short to medium term, however, effective realization of this order is unlikely because NATO and EU enlargement as well as objective conditions "on the ground" will widen rather than narrow the gulf between Russia (and Ukraine and the other NIS) and much of Central and Eastern Europe.

The most likely medium- and long-term outcomes for Europe are European Bipolarity, West European Dominance, or a continuation of Modified Cold War Order, with Atlantic Partnership a possible variant of the latter. In view of Western Europe's economic preponderance and Russia's deep-seated economic crisis, West European Dominance at first glance would seem to be the most likely outcome. However, Western Europe's own rather halting progress toward unity, the difficulty it is likely to have in fully absorbing the Central and East European states and in implementing EMU, and above all its failure to sustain military spending and to make a real breakthrough toward a common defense and security policy all suggest that a bipolar relationship with a weakened Russia is the more likely outcome. To the extent that U.S. involvement is needed to counter a latent or actual Russian threat to Western Europe, this order could have similarities with the Modified Cold War Order; to the extent that parts of Central, Eastern, or Southeastern Europe remain an unstable gray zone not fully integrated in Western Europe although still free of Russian domination, this order will have elements of Rivalry and Fragmentation.

In addition, the longer the time horizon, the less meaningful it is to talk exclusively of a "European" order or strategic world. Economic globalization, the rise of China, proliferation of advanced weaponry to the Middle East, and the rise of transnational security problems associated with immigration, refugees, crime, drugs, and information warfare all suggest that over the very long term the specific contours of the European order may be less important for U.S. strategic planning than the way in which Europe relates to other parts of the world, notably Asia and the Middle East.

Defense and Security Implications

Each of these alternative strategic worlds has different implications for U.S. defense planning over the long term. These implications can be analyzed along eight dimensions: (1) nuclear deterrence and defense, (2) deterrence and defense against major conventional conflicts, (3) theater ballistic missile defense, (4) Europe as a base for military access to other regions of the world, (5) peacekeeping and related missions, (6) counterproliferation, (7) logistical and other support for allies in major contingencies in which the United States is not directly involved, and (8) the defense industry.

Modified Cold War Order. This alternative strategic world would place high demands on U.S. nuclear deterrence and defense. It is assumed that Russia does not ratify (or, alternatively, ratifies and then later abrogates) START II. U.S. nuclear force levels thus would be higher. Depending upon the nature of the conventional threat to U.S. allies in Europe, U.S. requirements for tactical and theater nuclear forces also could increase.

As in the original Cold War order, the Modified Cold War alternative strategic world would also generate a high demand for conventional deterrence of conventional attacks. Depending upon the process of NATO enlargement and the explicit or implicit security guarantees extended by the United States to other countries, this requirement could be in some respects more demanding than in the original Cold War, because forward defense of such countries as Poland, the Czech Republic, Hungary, Slovakia, and others such as Finland and the Baltics might be demanded. On the other hand, Germany would be united and presumably capable of a large military effort, whereas Poland and other CEE countries would bring substantial forces to an alliance collective defense effort. U.S. access to third areas from and through European bases in the Modified Cold War Order might remain roughly as at present.

The demand for U.S. contributions to humanitarian and rescue missions, peacekeeping tasks, and the use of crisis management—tasks identified by the WEU's 1992 Petersberg Declaration—would be lower than at present. Deep Western involvement in missions in the FSU or in gray zones on the western periphery of a reconstituted Russian power would be less likely because of concerns about provocations and accidental clashes. The return of a measure of Cold War bipolarity might also impose a degree of stability—perhaps artificial and unjust, but stability nonetheless—that might lessen the demands for external involvement.

Atlantic Partnership. This is a variant of the Modified Cold War Order, and the military requirements generated by both strategic worlds are broadly similar. Nuclear deterrence and defense requirements in this alternative world might be even more substantial than in Modified Cold War, as the United States would be under greater pressure and obligation to extend its nuclear umbrella—possibly to include defensive systems—to allies who would be committed to sharing risks with the United States in various global conflict settings. Atlantic Partnership would be the most demanding alternative strategic world for U.S. theater ballistic missile defense requirements, and most likely would be associated with something like a completed MEADS[32] program. For the same reasons, U.S. requirements for counterproliferation capabilities in the Atlantic Partnership would be high, because the United States would have assumed responsibility to deal with potential WMD threats to Western Europe emanating from its southern and southeastern periphery.

U.S. access to third areas through Europe would be high. U.S. requirements to support European allies in Combined Joint Task Force (CJTF)–type operations most likely also would be high, although depending upon how close the Atlantic Partnership was, these requirements could decrease if the United States and its European allies were engaged jointly in virtually all combat operations, obviating any need for "separable" capabilities.

Atlantic Partnership might also be associated with a shift toward cooperation in the defense industry, with the United States and Western Europe sharing the market and jointly developing and procuring systems. Competition with the Russian defense industry would be less of a factor than in some other alternative worlds, if potential buyers in Asia, other parts of the developing world, and Central and Eastern Europe hesitated to buy weapons from a Russia tending back toward self-isolation and competition with the West.

---

[32]Medium Extended Air Defense System.

European Bipolarity.   The requirements of nuclear deterrence and defense drop substantially in European Bipolarity. Western Europe is presumed to be cohesive and strong enough to deter Russian (or other) attacks on its territory, thereby downgrading U.S. extended deterrence to a residual role. The United States might want to remain a player in European nuclear deterrence/defense through the Nuclear Planning Group and some deployments, so as to soften a potential West European-Russian nuclear arms race and to finesse the issue of a German role in a European nuclear deterrent. U.S. requirements in support of conventional deterrence/defense in Europe in major conflict scenarios would decline, although the United States probably would want to retain some ability to intervene in a conflict on the side of allies.

Access to third areas through European territory in European Bipolarity would be uncertain. A Western Europe fully capable of counterbalancing a strong Russia by definition would be cohesive and not beholden to the United States for protection, and thus would be more likely to weigh U.S. requests to use bases in Europe for third-area contingencies against European economic and political interests, which in some circumstances could clash with those of the United States. If European Bipolarity came about as a result of the German Alternative, the United States could come to agreement with Germany on basing and access issues, but the United States might also have additional latitude to work with countries closer to the periphery of the German core, for example, traditional allies such as the UK and Portugal. Under European Bipolarity, occasions might arise under which the United States might cooperate with Russia, Ukraine, or other NIS, rather than with traditional West European allies, on matters of access and third-area contingencies.

Requirements for peacekeeping and other contingency operations, counterproliferation efforts, and logistical and other support for allies all would be low in European Bipolarity. Western Europe on the one side and Russia/NIS on the other both would be strong enough to handle most if not all of these operations. European Bipolarity implies strong competition in the defense industry, with competitors coming both from the EU/Western Europe and Russia/NIS.

West European Dominance. This scenario further downgrades Europe as a determinant of U.S. strategic defense requirements. A weak

Russia and a strong but friendly Western Europe implies low or very low U.S. requirements for nuclear deterrence and defense, for conventional defense, and for assisting European powers with peacekeeping and other contingencies, counterproliferation, and CJTF-type actions. Access to third areas through Europe would be uncertain, and probably would have to be negotiated on a case-by-case basis with a cohesive EU/WEU pursuing a common Europe foreign and defense policy. Competition would be strong in the defense industry, although primarily from the EU rather than from Russia and the EU.

Rivalry and Fragmentation. This scenario would present a complex picture for planning U.S. defense requirements. Nuclear deterrence and defense most likely would require modest capabilities, because the European powers would be preoccupied with each other and unable to pool the resources needed to attain anything approaching the full panoply of strategic nuclear capabilities. On the other hand, rivalry and fragmentation in Europe could take place in a broader context and become part of a breakdown in international arms control and nonproliferation regimes, and could drive the United States to seek more-robust defensive capabilities. For the same reason, counterproliferation requirements for the United States also could be high in this alternative strategic world.

In a fragmented Europe, U.S. requirements for conventional defense/deterrence of a major conflict along the lines envisioned in Modified Cold War and Atlantic Partnership would not exist, but depending upon the level of U.S. interest in Europe, U.S. conventional forces could be engaged in other actual or potential conflict settings on a smaller scale (as is already the case in the Balkans). For the same reason, requirements for peacekeeping and other contingencies would be high. Both competition and cooperation in the defense industry would be low, because a fragmented Europe would not have the resources and organization to pursue leading-edge military technologies. A fragmented Europe probably would pose added problems for the proliferation of medium- and low-technology conventional weaponry, as well as for chemical and biological weapons (CBW) proliferation and possible diversion of nuclear materials to non-nuclear states seeking to acquire nuclear weapons.

Pan-European Order. The defense implications of a Pan-European Order would be highly favorable to the United States, which no longer would need to plan for intra-European conflict contingencies or deter against a possible revived Russian or nuclear threat to other parts of Europe. Peacekeeping requirements would be minimal. Stability would spread throughout Europe, and the major West European states, the EU, and Russia would be capable of handling such peacekeeping tasks that arose.

One potential long-term aspect of the emergence of a Pan-European Order that could have defense implications for the United States would be a growing U.S. and West European stake in bolstering a friendly Russia (and possibly Kazakhstan and other Central Asian states) against a resurgent China. This effort could entail military assistance by the West to Russia, and possibly even the extension of NATO or other security guarantees to Russia (and/or Kazakhstan) at some point in the future.

RADICAL SHIFTS AND BREAKS

We have dealt with projected trends that will shape the security environment in Europe in the 21st century. In some cases, alternative trends or possibilities have been considered, but in all cases these trends can be seen as extensions of patterns that are already apparent. This section shifts the focus to possible radical breaks or changes that cannot be extrapolated from current trends. These radical shifts either could in themselves give rise to conflicts in which the United States might be involved, or they could change the strategic context in which other potential conflicts would unfold and in which the United States might become involved.

Collapse of NATO and/or the European Union

As discussed earlier, Failed Integration and Muddling Along presuppose the continued existence of NATO and the EU, even though both organizations would have ceased to develop and would be weaker than in any of the other West European building blocks of the various alternative strategic worlds. A radical break from these extrapolations of even the most negative trends in European integration would be the breakup of one or both organizations.

Breakup of NATO might be precipitated by an escalating political dispute between the United States and Western Europe over a third area that political leaders were unable to control because of domestic political factors. Breakup of the EU would be an extra-constitutional process that could come about only in the context of severe external shocks—for example, economic depression or war with Russia—that might exacerbate strains among member-states to a breaking point. Either of these contingencies—breakup of NATO or of the EU— would result in a radically different European alternative strategic world (perhaps closest to Rivalry and Fragmentation) for U.S. planners, and would lead either to a U.S. withdrawal from European affairs or, more likely, to a search for new economic and security arrangements that might be based at least initially, on bilateral arrangements with key European states.

Economic Depression

Our analysis of regional trends suggested that economic growth in Western Europe was likely to average just over 2 percent in the next 10 to 15 years, in line with most government and private-sector forecasts. A radical shift from this trend would be a sharp downturn in economic activity, characterized by falling output and prices, as seen in the Great Depression. This downturn would exacerbate social tensions and possibly lead to the growth of political parties on the extreme left or the extreme right. This downturn also would undermine European integration and transatlantic cooperation, and possibly deepen the divide between Western Europe and the rest of the continent.

Breakup of Russia

The analysis of regional trends discussed fissiparous and disintegrative tendencies in Russia that are likely to weaken Russia as an international actor and possibly lead to clashes with neighboring states, although a complete breakdown of central authority in Russia is ruled unlikely. A breakup of Russia into several competing states, possibly led by warlords with conventional and even nuclear forces, would go far beyond this paradigm. A breakup would result in an alternative strategic world of West European dominance by default, but a breakup would also confront other countries with an unstable, chaotic region, parts of which might be allied with or become clients of outside powers such as Iran, China, or Japan.

War Between Russia and China

Regional trends point to the growing importance of China as a global economic power—and the strategic implications for Russia of the geopolitical rise of its eastern neighbor. War between Russia and China would burst the parameters of the alternative strategic worlds outlined above (based on existing regional trends), raising the prospect of an entirely different strategic world coming into being, perhaps built along civilizational lines with Russia allied with the West against China. The position of Japan in such a world would be crucial.

"Clash of Civilizations" Across the Mediterranean

Previous sections have alluded to growing instability in the Mediterranean and to cooperative and competitive efforts by the European states to buffer themselves against threats emanating from the south. Western policy—and the analysis of future alternative strategic worlds on which policy is implicitly or explicitly based—is premised on the assumption that while cultural and religious differences matter, there is *not* a strategically determinative clash of civilizations between (mainly) Christian Europe and the (mainly) Islamic North Africa and the Middle East. A radical break with this assumption would be a clash of civilizations across the Mediterranean, in some ways analogous to the conflict that raged in medieval and early modern Europe. Such a clash would create a radically new alternative strategic world—one that would have to come about as a result of a rapid radicalization of the Middle East, most likely coupled with the appearance of a new leader or possibly even a hegemonic Middle Eastern power capable of organizing the region against Europe and its interests.

Environmental Catastrophe

As was discussed above, environmental experts in Europe see continued deterioration in some areas and progress in others, with long lead times enabling governments and the private sector to adjust to environmental changes. This assessment could turn out to be incorrect if there are environmental effects that are not yet fully understood or predicted, or through a statistically improbable but nonetheless possible concatenation of environmental shocks (e.g., major accidents in several nuclear plants). Major environmental disasters could lead to new conflicts between states, place new demands on the military, or otherwise radically change the economic and social context for defense planning.

Rise of a New Ideology

Conflict in 20th-century Europe has been closely associated with clashes of rival ideologies: Communism, Fascism, Nazism, and, in World War I, theories of imperialism and of the nation that were at least in part ideological. Projections of future political conditions and of possible conflicts in 21st century Europe (including those offered in this chapter) generally assume that ideology as a driver of major conflict in Europe has run its course. They are thus in tacit agreement with the central arguments of Francis Fukuyama in his *The End of History and the Last Man*—namely, that the ideological age has ended and that while history—including wars and other conflicts—will go on, all-embracing theories of history such as Marxism and Nazism have given way to acceptance of the principles of liberal democracy or to various forms of traditional authoritarianism that by their nature are limited to a particular national or regional setting.[33] A radical break with this set of assumptions would be the rise of a new ideology capable of organizing states or nonstate actors for conflict on a large scale. The candidate most often advanced for such an ideology is religion (usually radical Islam), but others might arise as well. Past history suggests that when such an ideology does come into being, it often appears quite suddenly. While unlikely, the appearance of such an ideology could negate assumptions concerning the alternative strategic worlds discussed in this report by creating new cleavages and new sources of conflict, or indeed (depending upon the content of the ideology) calling into

------

[33]See Francis Fukuyama, *The End of History and the Last Man*, New York: The Free Press, 1992.

question the state itself as the fundamental organizing principle of international politics.

REGIONAL CONCLUSIONS AND IMPLICATIONS FOR THE U.S. AIR FORCE

Relative to earlier periods in U.S. history, including during the Cold War, Europe in the coming decades is likely to be less prominent than other regions in driving U.S. defense and aerospace requirements. Nonetheless, it will remain an important area for U.S. interests, and permanent and temporary deployments of U.S. forces to the region almost certainly will be required to defend those interests.

Western Europe has the potential to transform itself into a major political and military power. If it does so, it will change the strategic environment in ways that could lessen U.S. defense burdens but also introduce certain complications in U.S. defense and foreign policy planning. However, even if Western Europe fails to achieve unity, it will remain relatively secure against internal threats or external upheaval. A possible exception is the threat of nuclear or other WMD from outside the region, including Russia and the Middle East.

Russia is going through a long and difficult transition process. It has the potential, particularly toward the end of the relevant time frame (2015–2025), to become a major military threat to Western Europe, especially if the Russian economy takes off and/or Russia manages to reestablish de facto or de jure hegemony over parts of the former Soviet Union. It is less likely to resume its role as a peer competitor to the United States. Indeed, Russia is unlikely ever to exercise the kind of global and European role that it did for 45 years after World War II, especially given German reunification, the loss of influence in Eastern Europe, and the rise of China on its eastern flank.

Large parts of Central and Eastern Europe will be integrated into Western Europe and are likely to share in its stability and prosperity. However, even under the most optimistic assumptions, Western Europe will need decades to integrate and fully stabilize all 15 of the ex-Communist countries that lie between it and the FSU. Thus, even leaving aside the non-Russian NIS—Ukraine, Belarus, and Moldova—there is likely to be a large and potentially unstable "gray area" between Western Europe and Russia.

Although Europe is less unstable and, it could be argued, less complex than Asia (i.e., riven by fewer and less deep "civilizational" cleavages, structured by stronger and more mature international institutions), the range of alternative strategic worlds that in principle could emerge by 2025 is still remarkably open, and thus argues for flexibility and constant review of the strategic situation on the part of U.S. planners. Alternatives range from a highly peaceful and integrated Pan-European Order to Rivalry and Fragmentation reminiscent of the 19th century.

Europe most likely will have a tendency to develop into two opposing groups, one formed by the European Union in the west and center of the continent, the other consisting of Russia and possibly other countries reintegrated into a Russian sphere of influence. But there are major questions surrounding how strong and cohesive these groups are likely to be, and how they will orient themselves toward third powers, including the United States. The possibility of Russia and the United States gravitating toward each other over Asian and Middle Eastern issues while the U.S.-West European alliance lessens in importance cannot be excluded.

There is unlikely to be a West European superpower comparable to the United States today or the USSR in its prime, but the EU is becoming a more cohesive political and economic force, and is striving to develop its defense component. Russia is making progress in reintegrating former Soviet republics into a Commonwealth of Independent States, but there are limits to how far this process is likely to go. Ukraine is managing to consolidate its independence, and Russia appears certain to gradually lose influence in Central Asia. Turkey and Ukraine could emerge as potentially destabilizing elements in a Europe that might otherwise be characterized by stable bipolarity.

The Balkans are characterized by near-term instability, and fighting in the former Yugoslavia could resume in the next several years. Over the longer term, there is a danger that instability in the Balkan region could lead to alignments with rival outside powers with, for example, Bosnia and Albania aligning with Turkey and other Islamic powers; Croatia turning to Western Europe; and Serbia, Montenegro, Bulgaria, Romania, and perhaps even Greece looking to Russia.

In sum, Russia/CIS and Western Europe are both potential "peer competitors" of the United States, but this potential is unlikely to be realized. Western Europe probably will remain allied with the United States and to some extent dependent on it. Russian weakness is likely to persist until well into the next century. Russia is also vulnerable in Asia, and will face a rising and more assertive China. Vulnerability to the south is growing, but slowly; North Africa and the Middle East will not soon replace the Cold War Soviet threat. European states will be affected by nuclear proliferation in other parts of the world, but proliferation in Europe itself is unlikely (although not impossible).

Depending upon what alternative strategic world or worlds come to predominate in Europe, different potential conflict scenarios and requirements for military forces will emerge. Requirements for U.S. military engagement would be highest in the Modified Cold War Order and in Rivalry and Fragmentation, albeit of differing characters. Atlantic Partnership would involve working closely with Western Europe in out-of-area situations, and would enormously complicate U.S. defense planning, even as it ensured the availability of added resources for Persian Gulf and other contingencies.

Specific implications for the U.S. Air Force that would apply to all or most of the alternative strategic worlds include the following:

Diminished peer competitor threats. Although Russia is a potential peer competitor, its military forces have suffered a drastic decline, and it lacks the budgetary resources to revive the kind of extensive R&D and procurement efforts that the Soviet Union mounted during the Cold War. This decline means that the United States and its allies will enjoy a decisive technological superiority over potential adversaries in Europe for the foreseeable future, particularly with respect to air power. This situation could change after 2005–2010, however, and will bear constant watching by U.S. defense planners. Of particular interest will be the evolution of nuclear deterrence and the possible emergence of a system of multipolar nuclear deterrence with China, Russia, the United States, and perhaps other powers wielding major deterrent capabilities.

Continued role of deterrence but in a more complex environment. NATO expansion and the proliferation of situations in which the

United States may have interests without formal commitments (e.g., Bosnia), combined with continued low-level threats and instability, mean that U.S. forces will be needed for their conventional deterrent role. Such forces can be either permanently stationed in Europe or rapidly deployed from the United States. Unlike the Cold War, where there was a well-defined dividing line with a huge network of bases and infrastructure on both sides of the line, the future situation will be more fluid and will call for greater flexibility on the part of U.S. forces. There may be cases in which U.S. forces could be asked to help deter attacks on countries (e.g., Bulgaria) in which the United States and NATO do not have bases or infrastructure.

Importance of cooperation with allies. With the end of the Cold War, U.S. forces in Europe as a share of total forces on the continent have declined. New partners and potential allies (e.g., Poland, the Czech Republic, and even Russia for some purposes) have emerged, while U.S. domestic political requirements place greater emphasis on burden-sharing with allies. Future military operations and planning thus will be heavily influenced by the need to cooperate with allies. These allies, moreover, will be more assertive in pressing for enhanced influence in NATO, even though their actual military capabilities may still be modest for many purposes.

Challenges in the "gray area." Although Europe will tend toward a stable West Europe-Russia bipolarity, for a very long time there will be an unstable "gray area" between the two regions that will be riddled with ethnic and other sources of conflict. This instability will require maintaining U.S. capabilities for peacekeeping and other limited military operations.

Possible counterproliferation roles. As threats from the south emerge, the United States may be increasingly called upon by its allies and by its own defense requirements to develop counterproliferation capabilities and options. Theater missile defense could also be a growing requirement, given the proliferation of missile capabilities in much of the unstable environment to the south and southeast of Europe.

Chapter Six

CONCLUSIONS AND IMPLICATIONS FOR THE U.S. AIR FORCE OF 2025

Zalmay Khalilzad and David Shlapak

In this report, we have tried to illuminate the rough outlines of what the future might hold for the United States and for its armed forces, particularly the Air Force. We have identified key drivers that will shape the future security environment, combined them into alternative strategic worlds, and pointed out some wild cards that could affect the world of 2025.

The analyses in this volume point to three important conclusions.

First, the range of challenges that the nation must prepare for is larger and less predictable than during the Cold War, especially if we want to maintain our position of global leadership. These challenges include not only major regional wars and smaller conflicts but also the possibility of a new global rival and a new Cold War.

Second, protecting the U.S. homeland against a variety of threats such as terrorism, missiles, and information operations is likely to become more prominent in guiding U.S. defense planning. Many traditional distinctions between theaters are eroding because of the spread of missile technologies. More states are likely to acquire the capability to attack the United States with missiles in the next 25 years. Those states that cannot take on the U.S. military directly might use terror as an asymmetric strategy against, among other things, the U.S. homeland. The information revolution and increased international connectivity and networking may well lead to new opportunities and threats. The armed forces might well be instructed to take on new missions as a result of technical changes such as these.

Third, as the world's preeminent power, the United States plays a central role in shaping the future security environment. Our relative position is a key organizing factor in the calculations of many other state and nonstate actors. To maintain our military preeminence in the face of other major trends—such as the diffusion of technology and the change in the relative distribution of power—will be a daunting task.

Assuming continued American global leadership, what kind of Air Force will the nation need to protect and advance its interests through the first years of the next millennium?   In our judgment, four qualities will be critical to that Air Force:[1]

- Global awareness

- Global reach

- Rapid reaction

- Appropriate force.

GLOBAL AWARENESS

The future U.S. Air Force will increasingly find itself in the information business. At the strategic level, the Air Force will be a provider of both collection assets and interpretation expertise, as the intelligence community tracks and evaluates all of the manifold variables that will determine the global security situation. On the operational and tactical planes, the U.S. Air Force will encounter enormous challenges in fulfilling the intelligence support requirements that will be levied by new generations of weapons and new generations of commanders.

---

[1] These qualities seem relatively robust to a reasonable range of variance in the future security context. The threat of NBC weapons, whether or not insurgents actually have access to such weapons, will be sufficiently pervasive across the board that the U.S. Air Force will need the ability to operate in the face of them.

As the primary operator of U.S. military space systems and as the likely operator of the most-capable airborne surveillance platforms (including unmanned aerial vehicles), the U.S. Air Force will be responsible for sustaining the situational awareness not only of its own leaders and operators but also of its sister services and of American allies. Failure to prepare adequately for these missions and execute them will have consequences as disastrous as would shortfalls in other, more traditional "ordnance-on-target" operations. It is a burden the U.S. Air Force must take most seriously.

As an information service, the U.S. Air Force will also need to deal with the increasing "global awareness" of its likely adversaries. With the advent of on-demand commercial remote sensing, for example, the United States will no longer be able to rely on its staple techniques to deny its enemies information about American deployments and intent. Countering enemy information operations and learning to operate in a world of greater overall transparency will be a challenge to the U.S. Air Force.

Finally, the continuing advances in computer technology and the ever-increasing reliance of military organizations on data flows mean that, in the next century, information itself will become a weapon rather than an enabler of weapons, as it is today. The U.S. Air Force may be the most voracious consumer of information in the world, and its appetite—and those of its joint partners and the national leadership—seem certain to grow in the coming years. As the U.S. Air Force works to satisfy those appetites, it must not neglect to protect those information sources and flows from the manifold threats that could confront them. Especially, it must not forget that "defensive information warfare" must deal with both "hard" and "soft" threats; after all, a mortar shell that disables a satellite terminal is just as much an "information weapon" as a computer virus inserted into a network.

GLOBAL REACH

The conflicts of the early 21st century will break out all over the world, and they will provoke varied levels of U.S. military response. It does not seem at all unlikely that the United States could confront several of them at once.[2] The environment will be one in which forward basing and access may be limited in peacetime and after war breaks out as well. Finally, complex operations dependent on networks of staging and transit bases will become increasingly liable to disruption or outright attack by opponents whose NBC and/or unconventional warfare forces have sufficient reach.

In addition to helping protect forward-deployed forces and friendly territory against such threats—by shooting down ballistic and cruise missiles, destroying even deeply buried NBC storage sites and production facilities, enhancing its ability to protect bases from unconventional warfare attacks, and so forth—the U.S. Air Force should also seek to exploit the reach of air power to minimize the numbers of people and machines it must move into the forward area and into the range of enemy offensive capabilities.

Effective response in these cases will demand true multidimensional global reach. One contingency may require that the U.S. military fight a sizable war without extensive forward deployments for fear of presenting an irresistible target for the enemy's nuclear-armed missiles; another may demand the movement and sustainment of thousands of personnel who are responding to a rapidly evolving humanitarian crisis in a distant and primitive area. Both types of contingency could, in fact, present themselves at the same time. Assets capable of striking hard across the globe, or of providing succor at similar ranges, will be at a premium, while "short-legged" platforms, or systems dependent on platforms based in the theater, may find limited use.[3]

A particularly difficult class of contingency may be one that involves supplying humanitarian relief to areas where opposition is expected. Such operations could involve the need to secure airports, maintain clear flight paths into and out of airports, and provide secure refuel-

---

[2]In recent months, the United States has had to support concurrent operations in Haiti, Bosnia, and over Iraq.

[3]Threats to the United States itself will require an increased emphasis on protecting homeland-based installations and facilities critical to power projection regardless of precisely how "global reach" is achieved. Satellite control stations, computer complexes and networks, air bases, and other key infrastructure items will be likely targets for future enemies. For the first time, the U.S. Air Force and its sister services will need to be prepared to counter unconventional warfare operations on American soil.

ing and crew rest facilities. Developing concepts to accomplish these tasks reliably and without the deployment of a large number of U.S. personnel on the ground (and, presumably, in harm's way) will be an important part of achieving the kind of mobility posture that will be needed.

RAPID REACTION

In the future, clear and direct warning—a commodity that planning exercises always assume but that reality rarely provides—will remain elusive. For that reason, force elements configured to respond quickly will remain at a premium, and their value can only grow as forward basing continues to contract.

Air and space power are inherently well-suited for quick response. Assuming bases are available, U.S. Air Force squadrons can rapidly deploy to the remotest corners of the world and begin operations almost immediately. In the absence of extensive prepositioned supplies and infrastructure, however, sustainment must follow close on the heels of the fighters and bombers if the force is to continue operating at an efficient tempo.

One way of increasing the Air Force's ability to react quickly to an emerging crisis is a posture that allows it to take concrete yet easily reversible steps to increase readiness when a situation becomes threatening yet remains too ambiguous to permit highly visible and concrete reactions. Such concepts as the composite wing—a self-contained micro–air force explicitly dedicated to rapid deployment— are valuable in this regard. Other steps could include the following:

- Shifting of responsibilities between the active and reserve components to ensure the instant availability of all critical skills.

- New approaches and systems to allow rapid adaptive planning and to provide flexible command, control, communications, and intelligence (C^3I) capabilities.

- Innovations that reduce the sheer weight and volume of equipment and supplies needed to sustain operations; for example, using advanced explosives to allow the use of much smaller bombs for many targets.

- Development of systems that can provide rapid firepower application at global ranges. Ongoing efforts to enhance the capabilities of the bomber fleet with precision munitions and stand-off weapons are valuable in this regard. Future initiatives could include such systems as the proposed transatmospheric vehicle.

APPROPRIATE FORCE

The Gulf War demonstrated that air power no longer needs to deliver immense explosive power to have a strategic impact on a war's outcome. Although contemporary precision munitions suffer from many limitations, they have greatly enhanced the ability to strike fixed, hard targets and certain classes of mobile targets, such as tanks.

Future scenarios are likely to require attacks not only against massed arrays of armor, industrial facilities, and so forth but also against light infantry units and small, fleeting mobile targets, such as surface-to-surface missile (SSM) launchers. The latter kinds of targets will likely remain difficult to engage even when the next generation of munitions—the Joint Direct Attack Munition (JDAM) family, Joint Stand-off Weapon, Brilliant Anti-Tank, and so forth—comes on line around the turn of the century.

The U.S. Air Force should evaluate whether it can field a surveillance-strike architecture, or family of architectures, capable of supporting operations across the whole gamut of possible contingencies. Just as one does not swat mosquitoes with a sledgehammer, so an enemy's light infantry battalion occupying an oil refinery might not be an appropriate target for one-ton laser-guided bombs. A Joint Surveillance and Tracking Radar System (JSTARS) aircraft—or a JSTARS-like capability on an unmanned aerial vehicle or in earth orbit—may have marvelous capabilities against a column of enemy armor moving down a road, but it may fall short of determining whether three trucks moving along another highway are full of enemy troops or schoolchildren. New concepts for, and improvements in, every aspect of the detect-identify-track-target-and-engage cycle may be needed if the world is as unruly—and messy—as our analyses suggest.

Ongoing evaluation of air-deliverable less-than-lethal weapons should continue; recent interest in developing smaller, highly accurate munitions is also an encouraging sign. Similar improvements in surveillance capabilities against small, mobile targets, including groups of people, are also needed, as is a command and control system designed to facilitate rapid engagement of targets that can disappear as quickly as they pop up.

SUMMING UP

The U.S. Air Force that will operate successfully in defense of the United States will face real challenges and difficult tradeoffs. At first blush, it appears to us that this U.S. Air Force will emphasize quality and agility over quantity and mass.[4] The relative balance between long- and short-range systems will need to be carefully addressed, as will the relative weight given to preparing for the less likely but very stressful contingency of major war versus the day-to-day requirements of peace operations, humanitarian crises, and the other activities that characterize what will pass for peacetime over the next decades. Quick, decisive responses to rapidly changing demands will be the hallmark of a successful 21st century Air Force, and flexible adaptive planning and execution will be the keystones.

To have such an Air Force on the ramp in 2025, the U.S. Air Force leadership must make careful and informed decisions today. We hope that this report and the larger analyses upon which it is based contribute to thought and debate toward that end.

---

[4]Building and maintaining a high-quality force has always been a prime U.S. Air Force objective. However, during the Cold War—and into the current era—tradeoffs between the size of the force and its caliber were often painful; the sheer magnitude of the Soviet armed forces required that the U.S. Air Force maintain a comparatively large force structure. Our point here is that not only is this driver gone, but no other similar power (or coalition of powers) seems likely to emerge in the near future. If this turns out to be the case and the other demands we have outlined here do in fact manifest themselves, the quality-versus-quantity equation should be weighted increasingly in favor of the former.

SELECTED SCENARIOS

David Shlapak

INTRODUCTION

We used scenarios throughout this study, both as analytic organizing constructs and as ways of framing our results. In this appendix, we present a much smaller set of nine future planning scenarios based upon the sum of the three regional analyses.

These nine scenarios do not represent fully the richness and diversity of the larger set used in the regional studies. Neither would we claim that this group spans the entire spectrum of possible—or even plausible—conflicts that the United States could confront over the next decade or two. Finally, they most assuredly do not constitute a best estimate of the most likely future contingencies.

Why, then, bother to produce and present these nine? There are, we believe, at least three reasons to do so:

- First, we found scenarios to be very useful in helping us understand the implications of our analysis. Scenarios are especially powerful for grappling with the "interaction terms" of the future security environment—the way various trends, factors, and events could intertwine to amplify or diminish one another or even to create a radically different situation from that which might be discernible from examining each element independently.

- The sheer number of scenarios developed by the regional studies could deter many readers from perusing them. This smaller set is intended to postulate a wide range of interesting and important problems derived from that work but in a more digestible format.

- Finally, we believe that the nine cases found here, taken together, are a reasonable set to use as a screening tool for force planning. Force postures that appear robust across this set of scenarios will have passed a first test of their ability to cope with the multifaceted security challenges the United States could face in the next 15 to 20 years.[1]

The nine scenarios—which, again, were chosen to represent a cross-section of functional challenges rather than regional balance—describe:

- An opposed evacuation of United States and other Western citizens from a collapsing Egypt,

- The neutralization of nuclear weapons illicitly acquired by a rogue state (Algeria),

- An Iranian attack on Kuwait and Saudi Arabia,

- A clash between Greece and Turkey,

- Internal upheaval in Saudi Arabia,

- Russo-Ukrainian conflict,

- Large-scale humanitarian operations in a combat zone in the wake of an Indo-Pakistani nuclear exchange,

- Conflict between the People's Republic of China (PRC) and Taiwan, and

- Unconventional Iranian aggression against Gulf Arab states.

---

[1]Many other sets of scenarios could serve the same purpose; we make no claim as to the unique value of these nine except insofar as their basis in concrete and in-depth analysis of regional trends and dynamics gives them an especially firm claim to plausibility.

OPPOSED EVACUATION FROM A COLLAPSING EGYPT

Political-Military Context

Egypt is convulsed by internal instability, with the Egyptian government under siege from well-organized and well-financed anti-Western Islamic political groups. The government has not yet fallen, but political control has broken down, and there is a strong likelihood that the government will indeed collapse. There are large numbers of running battles between government forces and the opposition, with the level and frequency of violence steadily escalating.

U.S. citizens are being expressly targeted by the opposition, and many of the 17,000 or so Americans in Egypt—along with other Westerners—have taken refuge in the major urban areas. The Egyptian military has so far proved largely loyal to the government, but some troops—including army, air force, and naval units—have sided with the Islamic opposition, and the allegiances of many other elements are unclear. At least one crack armor brigade has joined the opposition en masse and is operating in the Cairo area. Security at airports and seaports is breaking down, with antigovernment elements in control of some. Opposition leaders have indicated that they will oppose any attempt to evacuate Western citizens with "all available means and the assured assistance of Allah."[2]

U.S. Objectives

Approximately 17,000 to 20,000 U.S., other Western, and friendly Egyptian personnel are now in direct danger as the host government nears collapse. These people are in need of rapid (48–96 hours) evacuation and rescue.

U.S. military objectives are to

- secure necessary aerial and seaports of embarkation to support evacuation operations,

- establish and secure collection points for evacuees,

---

[2]An interesting variant of this scenario might involve a similar situation developing farther from salt water, thus making the use of naval forces somewhat more problematic.

- provide secure air and/or land transportation for evacuees from collection points to points of departure,

- deploy sufficient forces to overcome all plausible resistance, and

- limit damage to relations with existing—and perhaps surviving—government and avoid prematurely prejudicing U.S. relations with a future Egyptian leadership.

Constraints

The evacuees are widely dispersed in heavily populated areas. Strict rules of engagement (fire only when directly threatened) must be maintained to avoid unnecessary conflict with Egyptian forces and minimize casualties to Egyptian civilians. The Egyptian government's operations against the rebels present major uncertainties in determining the friendly or hostile status of host-nation forces at the lowest levels (individual aircraft, ships, air-defense batteries, and ground-force units from platoon size up). The aerial and seaports of debarkation are not secured. Basing access is available only in Israel and Turkey.[3]

NEUTRALIZATION OF NUCLEAR WEAPONS IN ALGERIA

Political-Military Context

Despite the efforts of the Islamabad government and various U.S. national agencies, several (two to five) nuclear weapons were successfully smuggled out of a disintegrating Pakistan. Intelligence reports that approximately 12 hours ago, these weapons were delivered—disassembled—to a remote Algerian air base near the city of Tamanrasset and immediately transferred to a well-defended storage facility in the rugged foothills around Mt. Tahat. It is believed that the weapons could be operational and under control of the radical fundamentalist government in Algiers in five to seven days.

---

[3]A potentially interesting variant would deny access to Turkish bases for anything except transit stops for civil aircraft evacuating civilians from Egypt.

U.S. Objectives

The U.S. National Command Authorities (NCA) have ordered the Joint Chiefs of Staff (JCS) to conduct operations as soon as possible to

- seize and extract all nuclear weapons and/or weapons components from Algeria to friendly territory, and

- defeat Algerian forces as needed to accomplish this goal.

The Algerian air force is expected to contest any violation of national air space. The weapon storage sites are defended by armored units up to brigade size along with advanced radar- and infrared-guided surface-to-air missiles.

Constraints

A high level of operations security must be held until the operation is under way. It is necessary to operate with limited basing and support within the area of responsibility. Operations can be mounted from a carrier battle group in the western Mediterranean and from the United Kingdom.[4] Weapons and components are stored in deep underground hardened facilities. The use of nuclear weapons is not permitted. Operations should be as limited in size and scope as possible to decrease potential adverse political-military responses by other regional powers.

IRAN VERSUS THE GULF COOPERATION COUNCIL, 2010

Political-Military Context

Iran, determined to reassert its role as the dominant power in the region, directs its ongoing military buildup toward achieving a credible power-projection capability against its trans-Gulf neighbors, by restructuring its forces into a smaller, more professional military. By the second decade of the 21st century, these efforts have resulted in a force with considerable amphibious, airborne, and air-mobile ca-

---

[4]A variant would allow access to the United Kingdom and Corsica.

pabilities against the Gulf Arab states. With Russian and Chinese help, Iran also completes development of nuclear weapons and has a small arsenal of warheads, which it can deliver via ballistic missile against virtually any capital in the region.

In 2010, internal upheavals in Saudi Arabia and several smaller Gulf Cooperation Council states present Tehran with the opportunity to exercise its muscle. In a series of rapid moves, Iranian marines attack and secure the Ras Tanura port, and air-mobile forces leap inland to establish an airhead at Dhahran, into which infantry forces begin flowing. Smaller amphibious operations take control of Bahrain and parts of Qatar. Multiple Iranian heavy divisions drive through Shi'ite-controlled territory in the southern part of a divided Iraq and into Kuwait; their objective is to link up with the forces further south in Saudi Arabia.

Iranian submarines and missile boats have sortied into the gulfs of Arabia and Oman, laying mines, patrolling, and essentially taking control of the Strait of Hormuz. Land-based launchers for supersonic, sea-skimming antiship missiles are deployed along the Iranian coast and on several islands near the strait, and long-range strike aircraft, equipped with similar missiles, are reported on alert. Iran also has an inventory of hundreds of advanced naval mines and thousands of older models.

Iran's arsenal of several hundred medium-range ballistic missiles and intermediate-range ballistic missiles (MRBMs and IRBMs)—some dozen of which are equipped with nuclear warheads and many others with chemical payloads—is dispersing or has been deployed into protected caves.

U.S. Objectives

The U.S. NCA have ordered the JCS to conduct operations as soon as possible to

- defend Kuwaiti and Saudi territory,

- halt attacking Iranian forces and eject them from occupied territory, including that of Bahrain and Qatar,

- deter Iranian use of NBC weapons and eliminate Iranian NBC capabilities, including production and development,

- open the Strait of Hormuz,

- evict Iranian forces from Saudi oil facilities and minimize damage to those facilities, and

- help stabilize the friendly Saudi government.

Constraints

U.S. forces face limited access to the region. On the peninsula itself, only a handful of Saudi and Omani bases are considered sufficiently secure for sustained operations. Limited forward basing is available in Kuwait. Diego Garcia is available, and support operations can be undertaken from Egypt.[5]

GREECE AND TURKEY CLASH

Political-Military Context

By the early 21st century, tension between Greece and Turkey will have been a fixture of the strategic environment in the eastern Mediterranean for more than 200 years. Indeed, the revival of regional competition in the Balkans has provided new flash points in the relationship between Athens and Ankara.

In 2003, a crisis arises over the alleged mistreatment of Turks in Greek Thrace. As friction—including several minor border skirmishes that flare when small groups of refugees attempt to flee from Greece to Turkey—increases, the two countries conduct simultaneous and overlapping exercises in the Aegean and begin reinforcing the border regions. Several incidents in and over the Aegean—surface-to-air and surface-to-surface targeting radars locking on to aircraft and ships; a Greek and Turkish frigate suffering a minor colli-

---

[5]An interesting variant would permit combat and support operations out of Israel. For a discussion of the potential value of access to Israeli facilities across a range of Persian Gulf contingencies, please see Zalmay Khalilzad, David Shlapak, and Daniel L. Byman, *The Implications of the Possible End of the Arab-Israeli Conflict for Gulf Security*, Santa Monica, CA: RAND, MR-822-AF, 1997.

sion while playing "chicken"—further increase anxieties and animosities. Finally, a major demonstration by ethnic Turks in Greek Thrace turns into a riot, and Greek paramilitary troops intervene, firing into crowds and killing several dozen Turks.

Denouncing the "genocidal policies of the Greek government," Turkey responds by launching a sudden but limited thrust across the border into Thrace aimed at seizing key centers in which the Turkish population resides—in essence establishing a protected safe haven. Greek forces try to hold this invasion at the border, and Athens declares a 12-mile territorial-waters zone in the Aegean, effectively closing Turkish access to the Aegean. The Greek air force attacks Izmir and other Turkish cities, and the two countries also clash in and over the Aegean.

Objectives

The U.S. NCA have ordered the JCS to conduct operations as soon as possible to

- protect U.S. forces in the region from attack by either combatant,

- protect the lives of U.S. citizens in the two countries,

- limit escalation in the immediate term, and

- terminate the conflict and restore the prewar territorial status quo in Thrace and the Aegean.

Constraints

Basing for U.S. forces is obviously not available in either Greece or Turkey. Indeed, forces already in the region—at Incirlik and on Crete, for example—may need to be withdrawn or protected. Basing is available in Italy, Israel, and Egypt. Nonlethal or minimally destructive means of neutralizing military facilities and systems will be especially useful.

INTERNAL UPHEAVAL IN SAUDI ARABIA

Political-Military Context

In 2005, the central leadership of the Al Saud is being wracked by a host of internal challenges to their rule over the Kingdom. A series of rapid successions to the throne (three kings in the decade following the death of Fahd), each accompanied by internal power struggles and positioning, has substantially weakened family solidarity and, with it, the effectiveness of rule over the Kingdom.

This weakening contributed to the propagation of a number of fissures within Saudi Arabia. First and perhaps foremost, the slipping grip of the Al Saud permitted the survival and expansion of a younger generation of extremely conservative religious leaders who have come to reject openly and forcefully the traditional alliance of the religious authorities with the Al Saud, citing the royal family's corruption, mismanagement of the kingdom's affairs, and subservience to the United States. Through an extensive internal network built up through local mosques, they use popular pressure in an effort to compel the older religious establishment 'Ulema to break with the Al Saud, delegitimizing the monarchy's principal basis for rule. Other strata of Saudi society, including much of the business and academic communities, are equally frustrated with the growing ineffectiveness of the Al Saud in running the country.

The minority Shi'a population, concentrated in the oil-rich Eastern Province around Qatif, is increasingly restive as well. The Shi'a see opportunities to pressure for greater local authority and rights as the Al Saud struggles, but also fear the consequences to themselves of a conservative Sunni-Wahhabi success against the Al Saud. Their response to these twin threats is to organize and coordinate their political activities while expanding contacts with outside patrons, an activity that is far more possible now in the wake of a growing breakdown in Saudi internal security.

Events escalate as the opposition religious figures stage large demonstrations, often coordinated at several locations throughout the Kingdom. Efforts by internal security forces to quell the demonstrations prove ineffective. The National Guard is called in, resulting in a mix of poor crowd control and high civilian casualties. The Shi'a sectors of the Eastern Province are especially hard hit by the Guard in a preemptive effort to suppress any "subversive" activity there, resulting in hundreds of deaths. Elsewhere, several mosques used by demonstrators for refuge are attacked. These attacks are widely publicized by the opposition, along with reports that U.S. military advisors are now directing Guard activities.

Rioting breaks out in several additional cities spanning over half a dozen Saudi provinces. Well-known businesses and residences of Saudi royals are targeted, along with American commercial interests. The establishment 'Ulema, breaking with their traditional support for the Al Saud, issue a public decree demanding that the king cease all violence against his subjects. National Guard forces now appear fragmented and paralyzed as reports of civil violence mount, word of the 'Ulema decree spreads among its ranks, and instructions from Riyadh become confused and contradictory.

The Shi'a take this opening to organize against any further attack and position themselves in the turbulent political environment. Breaking out arms caches, including stockpiles of Iranian origin, they begin to seize control of key oil installations from Western and Saudi management personnel in an effort to, in effect, hold them hostage. The Shi'a also move to gain control of key port and other facilities at Ad Dammam. Many non-Western expatriate laborers, resentful of past Saudi treatment, cooperate actively and passively in these efforts. Western Aramco personnel are encouraged by Shi'a leaders to leave or "face the consequences of supporting the corrupt and criminal regime." Street executions of Saudi management personnel are reported.

The Saudi Arabian Land Forces, Royal Saudi Air Force, Air Defense Force, and Royal Navy are still abiding by previous orders from their commanders to remain in a stand-down posture. However, the royals of the officer corps are becoming increasingly fearful of events and are pressuring Riyadh to take decisive military action. The attitudes of the rank and file are far less clear. Splits are apparently emerging from within the ruling elite over how best to restore order, resulting in further paralysis of decisionmaking in Riyadh.

Senior members of the Saudi General Staff have been in contact with their American military counterparts. The Saudis have expressed grave concerns that the situation is getting dangerously close to chaos and that the military must move now to restore order. They are prepared to act but confide that they will not be able to restore order throughout the entire country quickly. They request both U.S. political support in the undertaking and U.S. military assistance in the oil sectors of the Eastern Province, in recognition of their own limited capability to restore order there without risking severe damage to the facilities and high casualties to the remaining foreign workers. The Saudis also express concern that Iraq and Iran may well seek to take advantage of the current situation and argue that a U.S. presence in the north would deter this until the Saudi military restores order.

U.S. intelligence reports that Iran appears to be redeploying some air and missile forces, and increased Iranian naval activity is reported in the Gulf. Tehran, meanwhile, is warning that it would view any "outside interference" in Saudi affairs as a "grave provocation to the Islamic Republic" and has threatened Riyadh with "grave consequences" if it escalates its use of military force against the Shi'a.

U.S. Objectives

The U.S. NCA have ordered the JCS to conduct operations as soon as possible to

- protect the lives and property of U.S. citizens in Saudi Arabia,

- deter or defeat any outside intervention in Saudi Arabia,

- assist Saudi authorities in protecting key economic and military installations, including oil facilities, ports, and air bases.

Constraints

Basing in Saudi Arabia is obviously highly problematic at this time. Bahrain, Qatar, the United Arab Emirates, and Oman have all concluded that any direct military cooperation with the United States under these circumstances would be impossible for them politically, as have Egypt and Jordan. Turkey is willing to host only support forces, not combat units. European leaders are adopting a "wait-and-see" attitude and will not support military action at this time.

Only Kuwait has come forward to offer full access to its bases and facilities.

Israel concludes that its strategic relations with neighboring Arab leaders would be directly jeopardized by visible military cooperation with the United States, although it is not opposed to U.S. military efforts to stabilize the situation in Saudi. Israel also expresses its concern over the disposition of Saudi high-performance fighters and the Saudi stockpile of long-range missiles and informs Washington that it cannot rule out strikes against these offensive threats to Israel in the event the Al Saud appears ready to collapse and be replaced by a more hostile regime.

WAR BETWEEN RUSSIA AND UKRAINE

Political-Military Context

Russia has evolved toward its own variant of semiauthoritarian rule based on a strong president and market capitalism dominated by huge quasi-monopolist firms in key sectors. Fears of encirclement by hostile powers—aggravated by NATO's expansion to include Poland, the Czech Republic, Hungary, and Slovakia in 1999 and continued talk in the West about admitting the Baltic states and Ukraine to the alliance—are a growing source of pressure in Moscow's decisionmaking.

By 2005, Ukraine has made substantial progress toward building a bona fide state and a viable national economy, but the country remains poor by European standards and critically vulnerable to Russian pressure from a variety of sources, including critical dependence on Russian energy supplies, extensive Russian ownership in key economic sectors, penetration of Ukrainian offices by Russian intelligence, and dependence on Russian suppliers for arms and spare parts.

NATO has been weakened by the effects of enlargement and disputes among its members on a variety of issues, including containing Chinese expansion in Asia and deterring Iranian adventurism in the Gulf. Western Europe has established an energy community with Russia, from which it obtains an increasing share of its oil and natural gas.

Partly in response to rising unemployment linked to a worldwide recession and what is seen as a worsening international climate, an anti-Western nationalist candidate is elected Russian president in 2005. In Ukraine, the cyclical effects of the recession and the longer-term structural shifts in the economy are placing increasing strains on national unity. Western Ukraine remains strongly anti-Russian, a trend that has been reinforced by the increasing movement of labor back and forth across the borders with Poland, Hungary, and Slovakia and the development of low-wage but profitable factories in western Ukraine that subcontract to German-owned firms across the border. The eastern parts of the country, meanwhile, have stronger cultural and economic ties to Russia, and many there feel that they are being left behind as the western parts of the country exploit their European connections to grow relatively wealthier.

These strains increase to the point where regional authorities and groups in eastern Ukraine and the Crimea call for secession and union with Russia. These pro-Russian elements are small but both vocal and violence prone, and their calls are picked up by nationalists in Russia. The status of Crimea and Russian access to the naval base at Sebastopol become particularly emotional issues, given rising tension between Russia and Turkey and growing fear in Moscow of an alleged alignment between Ukraine and Turkey against Russia.

Within Ukraine, response to the secessionists is confused. Some favor permitting or even encouraging a split, which would enable the rump Ukraine to join its destiny to Western Europe more fully; others take a harder line on retaining unity. The result is policy paralysis and the sending of confused signals to Russia and the outside world. It is reported that Russia is providing support to secessionist terror groups, which have attacked a number of Ukrainian military and economic targets.

Ukrainian demonstrations—both for and against secession—quickly turn violent. Using loyal troops mainly from the western part of the country, Kiev attempts a major crackdown on secessionist forces in the east. Hundreds of pro-Russian demonstrators are killed and the conflict appears on the verge of escalating into a civil war.

Reaction from Moscow is swift: The nationalist Russian government announces that it has no choice but to occupy eastern areas of

Ukraine and the Crimea to restore order, protect the lives and property of ethnic Russians, and stop attacks on Russian-owned pipelines and other economic assets. When rioting and violence continue, Russia moves into Ukraine with its Immediate Reaction Forces—some half-dozen well-trained, highly mobile divisions. Russian air strikes neutralize much of the Ukrainian air force on the ground and begin attacking key Ukrainian military targets, although Kiev is spared in the initial onslaught.

Ukraine formally appeals to NATO, the United States, and the EU for help. U.S. intelligence indicates that, in addition to the Immediate Reaction Forces, Russia has deployed an additional 12 to 15 divisions, which could be in action within 10 to 14 days. Several hundred combat aircraft are forward deploying from around Moscow to reinforce the units already in the western sectors of the country.

U.S. Objectives

The U.S. NCA order the JCS to prepare to execute operations aimed at

- deterring further Russian aggression,

- restoring the territorial status quo, and

- having accomplished this, preventing the outbreak of a major civil war in Ukraine.

Constraints

EU and NATO response to the crisis has been tepid at best. The German government blames Ukraine for setting off the confrontation; privately, it regards partition of Ukraine as essentially a fait accompli that the West must accept and manage. The remainder of Western Europe appears inclined to follow Germany's lead. Within pre-1999 NATO, only the United States, Great Britain, and Turkey are urging a forceful military response.

Poland, the Czech Republic, and Hungary have also called for a strong Western response to defend Ukraine against Russian aggression. However, Warsaw in particular makes clear that its support is contingent upon broad alliance support involving Germany and other European allies, as well as the United States; Poland does not want to stand alone as a forward U.S. base in a Russo-American war. There is a possibility, however, that a strong and forceful U.S. response could rally Poland.

LARGE-SCALE HUMANITARIAN OPERATIONS IN A NUCLEAR COMBAT ZONE IN SOUTH ASIA

Political-Military Context

By 2005, the insurgency in Indian Kashmir has become unmanageable. Despite the best efforts of the Indian government, the insurgency has begun to spread into Punjab. Recognizing that it has been left behind in its conventional military competition with India, Pakistan sees these revolts as an indirect way of weakening its great rival and increases its material and diplomatic support, including training and sanctuary, to both insurgencies.

By early the following year, Pakistan's involvement—never precisely subtle to begin with—becomes highly visible when two Pakistani soldiers, acting as trainers for Kashmiri insurgents, are captured in an Indian commando raid on a rebel-controlled village. India warns Pakistan to desist from supporting the insurgencies and threatens dire consequences. Pakistan initiates diplomatic efforts to isolate India while increasing levels of covert support to the insurgents.

In the spring of 2006, India dramatically increases its counterinsurgency operations in both Kashmir and Punjab, and the rebels are pushed into precipitate retreat. Pakistan responds by infiltrating a number of special-forces teams, which attack military installations supporting the Indian operations. India mobilizes for war and launches major attacks all along the international border, accompanied by an intense air campaign. The Indian Army makes significant penetrations in the desert sector and achieves a more limited advance in Punjab, capturing Lahore and heading north toward Rawalpindi and Islamabad. A supporting attack from Kashmir is poised to go at the proper moment. Conventional missile and air strikes have done extensive damage to Pakistani military infrastructure, while India's air bases, in particular, have been hard hit by the Pakistanis.

The Pakistani military is not fully prepared for the magnitude and ferocity of the Indian offensive and suffers major setbacks. The air force is mauled in its initial engagements with the Indians, and the army's Strike Corps and the Headquarters Reserve are under extreme pressure on the desert front. Fearful that the Indians will use their emerging air superiority to locate and destroy the Pakistani nuclear arsenal and perceiving their military situation as desperate, Islamabad demands that India cease all offensive operations and withdraw from occupied Pakistani territory "or face utter destruction." India presses its conventional attacks while announcing that while it would not "initiate the escalation of the conflict," it would "surely respond in an appropriate and devastating manner" to any Pakistani gambit.

As Indian forces continue to press forward, Pakistan detonates a small fission bomb on an Indian armored formation in an unpopulated area of the desert border region; it is unclear whether the weapon was intended to go off over Pakistani or Indian territory. India responds by destroying a Pakistani air base with a two-weapon nuclear attack. Condemning the "escalation" to homeland attacks, Pakistan attacks the Indian city of Jodhpur with a 20-kiloton (kt) weapon and demands cessation of hostilities. India strikes Hyderabad with a weapon assessed to be 200 kt and threatens "ten times" more destruction if any more nuclear weapons are used. Pakistan offers a cease-fire in place.

Meanwhile, pictures and descriptions of the devastation in Jodhpur and Hyderabad are broadcast worldwide, and Internet jockeys—playing the role ham radio operators often have in other disasters—transmit horrifying descriptions of the suffering of the civilian victims on both sides. The United Nations immediately endorses a massive relief effort, which only the United States—with its airlift fleet and rapidly deployable logistics capability—can lead.

Within 48 hours—after the cease-fire has been accepted by India but before it is firmly in place—the advance echelons of multinational, but predominantly American, relief forces begin arriving in India and Pakistan. Several Islamicist groups in Pakistan announce their opposition to the "Western imperial occupation" and warn of unspecified actions to drive them out of the country.

U.S. Objectives

The U.S. NCA have instructed the JCS to conduct operations to

- support the urgent provision of all necessary humanitarian relief to civilians in Jodhpur and Hyderabad,

- evacuate all U.S. civilians from both India and Pakistan,[6] and

- ensure that relief forces are protected in the event of any resumption of hostilities.

Constraints

The war has rendered many air bases in both India and Pakistan only marginally usable for airlift operations. U.S. citizens are scattered throughout both countries, and the host governments' attitudes toward their evacuation are not known. The cease-fire must be assumed as likely to collapse at any moment. The U.S. president has assured the nation in a broadcast address that only the "smallest practical number" of troops will be deployed on the ground in either India or Pakistan.

CONFLICT BETWEEN THE PEOPLES REPUBLIC OF CHINA AND TAIWAN

Political-Military Context

Mainland China's military power continues to grow through the first decade of the 21st century. By 2010, Beijing deploys forces that are considerably smaller, but much more modern, than those it fielded in the 1990s. China's navy was a particular beneficiary of budgetary largesse, with its amphibious capability being enhanced in particular. Other power-projection forces—including airborne and airmobile army units, longer-range air forces, and ballistic and cruise missiles—also saw great improvements at the expense of traditional army divisions. China established itself as a global leader in developing and introducing directed-energy weapons.

---

[6]This could degenerate into a variation of the first scenario above, the opposed evacuation from Egypt.

During this period, meanwhile, Taiwan's domestic political process has generated steadily increasing pressures for greater international recognition and a clearer domestic expression of de facto independence from Beijing. Taiwan's highly popular president, leading a largely pro-independence political coalition, continues to chip away at the legal fiction of "one China" in a variety of ways, without actually declaring independence.

Beijing reacts predictably, conducting "saber-rattling" exercises and hurling threats at the Taipei government and its "American puppeteers." In the face of ever-growing pro-independence sentiments on Taiwan and growing ties between the Taipei regime and the outside world—including what many commentators view as "virtual recognition" of Taiwan by Washington—Beijing decides in 2010 that it can tolerate the situation no longer. The Chinese military is instructed to compel Taiwan's acceptance of Beijing's terms for reunification, if necessary by invading the island outright.

The scenario begins as China deploys large naval forces into the Taiwan Strait and announces a total air and sea "quarantine" of the island to "prevent the introduction of nuclear-weapon components" that Beijing claims to have evidence are en route. Amphibious and airborne forces are used to seize, in *coup de main* fashion, several off-shore islands in the strait. The Chinese and Taiwanese air forces clash over the strait, and several aircraft are lost on both sides.

U.S. intelligence reports that large amphibious forces are loading in several ports in Fujian province, and elements of the 15th Airborne Army are prepared to go into action within 24 hours. Several dozen fighter and fighter-bomber regiments, including many of China's most modern aircraft, either have forward-deployed into Zhejiang, Fujian, and Guangdong provinces or are preparing to move.

Taiwan announces full mobilization and asks the United States for direct assistance in repelling "Communist aggression." China warns Taiwan to stand down and declares its intent to resist "with all possible means" any "outside intervention in internal Chinese affairs."

U.S. OBJECTIVES

The U.S. NCA have ordered the JCS to

- deter or defeat any Chinese aggression against Taiwan,

- protect the lives of U.S. citizens in Taiwan, and

- prevent the use of nuclear, biological, or chemical weapons by any party to the conflict.

Constraints

Tokyo has informed the U.S. government that it will allow no combat operations against Chinese territory or against Chinese forces in international waters or airspace to be mounted from its territory. The Philippines will permit only noncombat operations.

UNCONVENTIONAL IRANIAN AGGRESSION AGAINST GULF ARAB STATES

Political-Military Context

Iran's internal political divisions continue between the ideologically driven religious authorities and the more pragmatic "realists," leading to an increasingly weakened Iranian state. Internally its economy continues to decline, with its ability to draw in foreign Western capital and expertise extremely limited. On the foreign-policy front, Iran continues to advocate many ideologically driven policies that are anti-U.S. and/or anti-Western in their orientation. Within the Gulf, Iran continues to have frictions with its neighbors, predominantly over their continued close cooperation with the United States and the consequences for Iran.

Russian and Chinese attitudes toward the Islamic Republic have been mixed. Neither has adopted the hard line of the United States—both have sold weaponry to Iran—but they have not cultivated a close relationship.

The decade-long uninterrupted flow of relatively inexpensive oil from the region has further weakened Iran's position, both in terms of revenue generated and its seeming inability or unwillingness to directly challenge this situation. From Tehran's perspective, the Arabian peninsula states of the upper Gulf (most notably Kuwait, Saudi Arabia, and the United Arab Emirates) have been conducting economic and political warfare against Iran underneath the umbrella of U.S. military power. The United States has in turn used its regional military power and security guarantees to ensure that the oil-producing states of the Arab Gulf adopt political and pricing policies designed ultimately to cripple Iran. Iraq, victim to the same strategy, has for the last several years been forced to comply with the pricing policies of the lower Gulf states, given its weakened condition and need for further rehabilitation.

While Iraq thus poses little immediate military threat to Iran, Tehran finds itself in an increasingly desperate internal and external situation that propels it to take extreme risks to alter these realities. It therefore decides to induce shock into the existing system by destroying or damaging as many commercial oil and gas facilities, shipping, and other high-value assets as it can inside the Gulf in an extremely intense but brief surprise strike.

This strike would be waged principally by aircraft, short-range surface-to-surface missiles, cruise missiles, and naval raiding parties. The strike would also include use of Iran's small submarine force against surface shipping. Military targets and engagements are avoided as much as possible in an effort to minimize initial losses when striking commercial assets. Extensive clandestine reconnaissance is conducted in advance to determine the disposition of American and other Western naval and land-based air forces inside and near the Gulf (and to time the campaign so that no carriers are in the Gulf or on station nearby) and to establish the precise locations of all anticipated commercial targets. Actual military preparations will be designed to mimic normal "background" as much as possible in the run-up to the strike and will take place against the general political backdrop of long-term tensions. The strike campaign is designed for a duration of 24 to 36 hours—long enough to inflict substantial damage but short enough to be completed before major U.S. defensive and offensive force can be brought to bear. The strike will be launched from the Iranian homeland and from a number of missile sites located on the islands of Abu Musa, Qeshm, Forur, and Sirri. In an effort to further concentrate its efforts (and perhaps sow division within the Gulf Cooperation Council), all Omani territory and offshore facilities are excluded from attack.

Following the strike campaign, all aircraft will be dispersed throughout Iran, fixed missile sites used for strikes abandoned, and naval forces dispersed as much as possible, including to inland waterways, where feasible. Ground and civil defense forces will be put on alert to defend against anticipated air attack and to ensure effective crowd control in major population areas.

Iran's relatively large inventory of medium-range ballistic missiles will not be used in the initial strike but will be widely dispersed aboard land transports. The Iranian operational plan is to use these weapons only if necessary to wage a "war of the cities," targeting capitals and other major metropolitan areas throughout the peninsula. Like the strike in the Gulf, the attacks, if launched, would be massed and concentrated in time to maximize destruction and minimize the U.S. ability to interdict or defend against them.

Iran has a known chemical and biological weapon capability, including known tests of ballistic missile delivery. Tehran's nuclear arsenal is small, if it exists at all.

The scenario begins in 2005 when U.S. intelligence detects the final preparations for the shock campaign about 12 to 24 hours before it begins.

U.S. Objectives

U.S. NCA direct the JCS to

- defend against impending attack to minimize damage to commercial assets,

- protect heavily populated areas on the peninsula against the mobile ballistic missile threat, and

- develop options to eliminate remaining Iranian offensive capabilities.

APR 1 4 1998

Constraints

The primary constraint in this crisis is, obviously, time. Additionally, all European countries, including Turkey, deny transit during the brief crisis phase; Egypt, Israel, Jordan, and Kuwait grant full access. Saudi Arabia grants U.S. airspace access for transit of U.S. forces to "exercise" in Kuwait, but no combat deployments are allowed into the kingdom for fear of provoking an attack that Riyadh is desperately trying to avoid.

APR 1 4 1998